RADICALIZATION IN INDIA

An Exploration

RADICALIZATION IN INDIA

An Exploration

Abhinav Pandya

Vivekananda International Foundation
New Delhi

PENTAGON PRESS LLP

Radicalization in India: An Exploration

By Abhinav Pandya

ISBN 978-81-941634-6-6

First Published in 2019

Published by
PENTAGON PRESS LLP
206, Peacock Lane, Shahpur Jat,
New Delhi-110049
Phones: 011-64706243, 26491568
Telefax: 011-26490600
email: rajan@pentagonpress.in
website: www.pentagonpress.in

Printed at Aegean Offset Printers, Greater Noida, U.P.

CONTENTS

DIRECTOR'S FOREWORD

The Vivekananda International Foundation is happy to present to the public Mr. Abhinav Pandya's book *Radicalization in India: an Exploration.*

The systematic study of radicalization and its link with terrorism is an under-researched subject in India. This is partly due to the absence of empirical research and partly owing to a desire to be politically correct. However, the rising trend of terror attacks in South Asia, inspired by extreme radical ideologies, cannot be ignored. The need for preventing radicalization of the young minds and adopting effective counter-terrorism strategies and practices based on a deeper understanding of the divert factors which encourage radicalization is paramount.

Mr. Abhinav Pandya's book fills that gap. The author has done extensive literature survey on radicalisation and terrorism and carried out case studies of radicalization trends in Kerala, Udaipur, and Kashmir. Based on his research, he has suggested strategies and measures for countering radicalization and developing a de-radicalization programme for India.

I hope that the book will be useful for the student of terrorism as well as for practitioners of counter-terrorism.

New Delhi
23 May 2019

Dr Arvind Gupta
Director
The Vivekananda International Foundation

FOREWORD

by HE Shri Satya Pal Malik,
Governor of Jammu and Kashmir

Violent extremism has emerged as one of the most paramount challenges in today's globalized world. On the one hand, we see the human race exploring the new terrains of artificial intelligence and colonizing planets in the exterior space; at the same time, on the other hand, we are witnessing quite contrary and atavistic tendencies of violence arising from political ideologies and the misinterpretation of religious doctrines.

Role of religious radicalization as a causal factor in today's violent Islamist movements – the subject matter of Abhinav Pandya's book – has remained an uncomfortable and largely unchartered territory for academicians and policy wonks. I have observed an acute dearth of systematic and evidenced-based research on the subject and hence, it remains a dark underbelly – perhaps deliberately and conveniently ignored, but always making the menace of terrorism more and more complex and dangerous.

The author has in his book done a remarkable job in first outlining the main theories, academic debates and discourses in the intelligence world on radicalization as a significant cause of terrorist violence perpetrated by jihadi outfits across the world. The chapters tracing the history of Wahhabism, Barelwi and Deobandi schools of thought are highly enlightening. Author's analysis of the history of communalism in India in a balanced and objective manner turns out to be extremely useful in charting the right future course to address the challenge of jihadi extremism in India. Abhinav's approach in the case studies on Kerala, Islamic Sate of Iraq and Syria (ISIS), or just Islamic State (IS), and Al Qaeda is unique in the fact that there is a robust attempt to make a threat assessment for the future and come out with efficient and reasonable solutions.

Furthermore, the case study on Kashmir is profoundly insightful, comprehensive and, to an extent, even alarming. The author conducted his field study in Kashmir last year for this book and has also recently published a report on the state of militancy in Kashmir. Interestingly, his findings and predictions about the growth of the caliphate sentiment and ISIS-like suicide bombing are very prophetic in nature. The analysis of radicalization in Kashmir, made last year, when seen in the light of the recent tragedy of Pulwama, appears highly accurate. His assessment can be immensely helpful in understanding the future trajectory of the intense wave of jihadi radicalization, fast eroding the spiritual foundations of Kashmiriyat.

Abhinav has shown immense courage to translate his research efforts into the difficult area of suggesting ways to address the challenges of Jihadi radicalization in an innovative and comprehensive manner. His reiteration of the idea of developing the concept of National Radicalization Index can be a powerful tool in the hands of the policymakers and the national security apparatus.

Overall, the suggestions on the important aspects of counter-radicalization and de-radicalization measures reflect an unbiased, objective and comprehensive approach – a rather difficult feat while addressing a sensitive issue like jihadi radicalization. Also, at a young age, he has exhibited a deep understanding of human psychology, sociological, economic and emotional aspects of terrorism and the role of spirituality in transforming one's mind. One needs to be clear in mind that while dealing with radicalization and outfits like Jamaat-e-Islami, the battle is against an idea and not any specific entity. Hence, any attempt to take a purely security-centric approach is bound to fail. Developing an India-specific counter-narrative, to counter the challenges posed by forces of global radicalization, is essential; the sooner, the better. The author's approach at developing a counter-narrative is holistic, reflecting an in-depth understanding of the strategy and the nature of violent and non-violent jihadi outfits and the Kashmir conflict.

Ever since the beginning of my political journey, I have been a keen observer of the militancy and the separatist movement in Kashmir. Call it destiny or a quirk of fate, at this stage of my political career, I got the opportunity to serve the country as Governor of the state of Jammu and Kashmir and my journey in understanding the complexities involving various facets of the problems facing the state began with lengthy discussions on Kashmir issue with the author. I have since read many articles of Abhinav on international relations and security affairs written for various national and international publications.

As a fellow and a student council leader at Cornell University, his efforts resulted in the setting up of a foundation of International Affairs Forum at the university that has played an important role in dispelling the false and negative propaganda done by Pakistan in western academic campuses.

Over the last eight months of my stay in Jammu and Kashmir, I have had several interactions with the author and have immensely benefitted from his insights. I have no hesitation in commending his book on radicalization to young researchers in the field of terrorism, young recruits to the India's civil services, police services and the intelligence professionals working in counter-terrorism.

I wish him continuing success in the difficult and challenging journey ahead.

PREFACE

Terrorism has emerged as one of the gravest security threats faced by humankind. Unlike in the case of conventional war, the security forces, intelligence agencies, law enforcement machinery and the society, in general, find it extremely challenging to deal with terror due to its elusive, hybrid and diffused nature.

To this date, there is no global consensus even on the definition of terrorism. The discourse on terrorism is still haunted by the old dictum of 'one man's terrorist being another man's freedom fighter'. A range of scholars, practitioners, and counter-terrorism policymakers have attempted to explain terrorism and its causal factors. Overall, the trend has been to view terrorist violence as a multi-causal event – a result of several factors such as poverty, civil wars, ungoverned territories, unemployment, perceived marginalization, human rights abuses, deprivation and an acute sense of injustices accompanied by a range of facilitating conditions that result in terrorist violence. However, after 9/11, Radicalization, i.e. the belief in an extremist political or religious ideology has attracted the attention of counter-terrorism community across the world as one of the necessary causal factors of terrorism.

Though radicalization-based approaches have a significant presence in the current discourse on terrorism, there is also a tendency to knowingly avoid its exploration and elucidation, either out of the fear of wading into politically dangerous waters or due to lack of awareness and insight. However, it is increasingly being realized by the counter-terrorism community that the war on terrorism cannot be confined to the traditional domains of law-enforcement, security and terror financing.

With the rise of Al Queda (AQ) and now ISIS, Jihadi Terrorism has emerged as a phenomenon having strong roots in the theological discourse which is used to radicalize a potential terrorist either online or through in-person contact. Therefore, the war on terror or rather the engagement has to be multipronged, focusing on the role of theology and the psychological states which respond to such religious indoctrination. The efforts need to focus on preventing individuals from becoming terrorists. For that, one needs to begin with the study of the phenomenon of radicalization caused by extremist religious discourse. The dominant trend in discourse on radicalization-based approaches has been to argue that the phenomenon of radicalization is a result of deprivation, poverty, corruption, ungoverned places, civil wars, and repression at the hands of state authorities, discrimination, marginalization, human rights abuses, perceived sense of injustices, personal crises and the yearning for identity and a sense of belonging. The mainstream narrative downplays the role of the extremist Islamist ideologies such as Wahhabism, Salafism, and Deobandism in jihadi radicalization and terrorism.

In the 21st century, the Zeitgeist of liberal democracy and multiculturalism, where protection and respect for the religious and cultural rights is a gold standard, the idea of religious ideology, being a significant causal factor of terrorism, has poor acceptability in the academic discourse and is considered politically incorrect in the policymaking world.The other reasons for such an attitude are electoral compulsions, the fear of losing face as free community respecting human rights and diversity, and the fear of being exterminated from the mainstream intellectual, academic and journalistic discourse. However, the increasing number of incidents and accompanying human casualties in terrorist violence across the world have injected a sense of realization that this hitherto unexplored domain cannot be left untouched anymore merely for political convenience.

Empirical evidence also suggests that radicalization has played a substantial role in preparing a socio-cultural milieu providing a certain degree of social legitimacy to terrorist violence. Furthermore, it makes the logistics comfortable by providing a ready supply of recruits, public sympathy, political patronage or at least an attitude of tacit acceptance, and the finance for terrorist operations. Kosovo, which greeted NATO forces as the harbingers of liberal democracy in 1996, has sent more per capita foreign fighters[1] than any western European country, to ISIS. Over the last two decades, Kosovo went through an intense wave of Wahhabi radicalization.[2] Similarly, in Catalonia[3]

in Spain, it was found that over the last 20 years, rigorous Wahhabi radicalization work was in progress. The other western countries that sent a sizable number of foreign fighters to ISIS also witnessed mosque-level, in-prison and online radicalization in some form or the other.

This book attempts to explore the phenomenon of radicalization in India where counter-terrorism approach has primarily focused on military and law-enforcement measures. The study of Islamic radicalization has by far remained on the sidelines. While it is highly encouraging that even with world's third largest Muslim population, merely 104 youngsters have attempted to join ISIS from India, yet this may be a mere tip of the proverbial iceberg. Most of the research work of the Indian scholars and policy specialists is focused on those individuals who got radicalized through online channels and attempted to join ISIS. However, India and the other South Asian nations are going through a different kind of radicalization that happens in the remote rural and urban areas of India through Tablighi activity and Wahhabi missionaries. Purportedly, these do not seek to destabilize the country or support terrorism, but in a very subtle manner nurture extremism and separatist and exclusivist mindset. There is a strong need to study the contours of the above-mentioned ongoing radicalization in India.

In several quarters, it is argued that there is no concrete evidence for direct linkages between Islamic radicalization and terrorist violence. However, I would like to suggest that even if the idea of radicalization is de-hyphenated from the central debate on terrorism, the menace still needs to be studied and tackled in its own right, because even if one discounts the possibility of it leading to major terrorist violence, one cannot deny the fact that it generates a separatist, exclusivist, orthodox, rigid and a hateful mindset which is highly detrimental to the communal harmony and peace in India. In a multicultural and multi-religious country like India, a vast mass of population getting under the sway of an extremist ideology can be extremely dangerous.

In India, there is an acute dearth of serious and well-researched literature on the subject. In the leading universities of India engaged in the studies of International Relations, any attempt to initiate a sincere investigation of the said phenomenon is perceived as a case of 'majoritarianism' and 'sectoral extremism'. One even comes across the outright denial of the existence of the phenomenon of radicalization even in the upper echelons of academia, the intelligence set-up, and the policymakers. Whatever little work concerning data collection and analysis is being done is mostly by the intelligence agencies. The access to such data is, naturally, almost impossible due to the secretive nature of their inquiries.

It is therefore proposed in this study, to address the knowledge gap in the field, as mentioned above. The idea is to generate awareness among the policymakers, academicians, practitioners (police, military, para-military community) and the counter-terrorism policymakers regarding the issue and to equip them with the mediate-level knowledge of the essential concepts of Islamic radicalization. Such exposure is expected to lead and generate innovative thinking to find solutions to the problem of radicalization professionally, without any fears and biases.Some of the important questions sought to be addressed in the course of this research would naturally revolve around linkages between radicalization, extremism and fanaticism and terrorist violence; what leads a radicalized individual towards terrorist violence; role of religious doctrines like Takfiri and Jihad in radicalization; current situation of Islamic extremist radicalization in India at the grassroots level and developing an effective counter-radicalization policy and possibility of developing a tool to measure radicalization, i.e. a National Radicalization Index?

The established norms for research of this nature include *Quantitative/ Qualitative data collection from Primary/Secondary Sources; Interviews with experts; field work etc.* In consultation with my guide/supervisors, the strategy for this research was mostly qualitative since obviously the basic theme of the research defies tested and dependable mode of quantification. Therefore, in compiling this work, I have mostly depended on interviews with experts and field groups (structured, unstructured and semi-structured), Document Review, Literature Review, Participant Observations and Ethnographic Studies. The interviewees came from a range of diverse backgrounds, including radicalized individuals, those who are in the process of being radicalized and the ones who abandoned either both, i.e. terrorist violence and the belief in jihadi ideology, or one of them. Additionally, the interviewees included lay followers of Islam, Madarasa students, Maulvis teaching them and the community leaders. The interviewees also included national and international counter-terrorism experts (both practitioners and academicians), NGO workers, district-level and senior intelligence officials, members of the police services and judicial fraternity, military personnel, civil servants and some international diplomats engaged in countering violent extremism, journalists, religious leaders and as required.Literature review included online scholarly papers, articles, briefs and long-form commentaries published by global and domestic magazines and newspapers, and the books.

In India, one comes across a lack of advanced and sophisticated research work on radicalization. Hence, I had to draw extensively from the scholarly work done by the established think tanks in the West, and then critically analyze their adaptability and utility of such models for India.Document Review included review and analysis of the websites of NIA, Union Home Ministry, UN Counter-Terrorism Committee and the official documents, policy papers of national and multilateral bodies and the foreign countries. Analyzing the financial and other records of terrorist organizations was helpful in exploring the magnitude of the focus of terrorist organizations on radicalization.

The project included a field research in Kashmir valley to study the dynamics of radicalization in those areas. The idea was to examine the patterns of radicalization and the measures taken by law enforcement machinery to address the issue and to prepare a template of best practices that can be implemented in other areas or even at a national level to deal with radicalization.As a qualifier, I would like to mention that this research intends to explore the reality at the grassroots and come out with a rigorous analysis and a sensible policy guideline to address the challenge of radicalization. Hence, one had to venture beyond the conventional methodological tools of qualitative analysis or improvise them to meet the needs of my research project.

The research work had to be necessarily undertaken in a dangerous conflict zone where I and the individuals who volunteered to meet me could even face threat to their lives. As a result, as a researcher I did not have the privilege of conducting a research work that satisfies all the rigorous academic standards and criteria of an academic research paper. However, I have tried to provide the best output within these constraints. Also, as the author I vouch that the study reflects the sentiments and the developments that exists at the ground level, in the real world. Besides, the interactions with the real-life terrorists, recruiters and counter-terrorism experts associated with India's external and internal security agencies helped me immensely in generating a realistic output. Furthermore, due to security reasons, it has not been possible to provide the names of all the people interviewed and details of the surveys conducted for this study.

It is my earnest hope that this study will be beneficial in providing substantial insights into the radicalization scenario in India and that it would be useful for the further academic research on the subject. The objective is to strengthen the understanding of a complex phenomenon like radicalization having multiple aspects such as social, geopolitical, religious and political, of the senior- and junior-level police officers, intelligence officers, civil society groups and civil servants, in a highly simplified manner.Furthermore, the outputs of this study will be immensely useful in developing an effective counter-radicalization and de-radicalization policy which is within the context and relevant to the specific needs of India. The current global scenario in Jihadi terrorism strengthened in its capacity to influence young minds through social media and mass media has the potential to radicalize a large segment of our youth population. And, this can generate social unrest and be highly detrimental to economic growth and the democratic ethos of India. It is the right time to monitor, track and detect radicalization activities and neutralize their potential for disruption through an effective counter-radicalization strategy.

It is hoped that the case studies will help in knowing the psychology of a terrorist's mind, involved pathways, and underlying networks both local and transnational, the influencing factors such as the social milieu, political and economic conditions and the role of the coordinators involved in the process. The study will also be beneficial to the legal fraternity in developing a robust legal apparatus to address the challenges of radicalization and terrorism.

Before I end, I would like to record my immense gratitude to my supervisor Mr. CD Sahay.

Abhinav Pandya

NOTES

1 Nadaff, NJ, "Kosovo, home to many ISIS recruits, is struggling to stamp out its homegrown terrorism problem," *Washington Post*, August 24, 2018, https://www.washingtonpost.com/world/2018/08/24/kosovo-home-many-isis-recruits-is-struggling-stamp-out-its-homegrown-terrorism-problem/?noredirect=on&utm_term=.32f16e63ae6f

2 Gall, Carlotta, "How Kosovo was turned into fertile ground for ISIS?" *New York Times*, May 21, 2016., Accessed October 4, 2018, https://www.nytimes.com/2016/05/22/world/europe/how-the-saudis-turned-kosovo-into-fertile-ground-for-isis.html

3 Vidino, Lorenzo, "The roots of the Barcelona attack," *Foreign Affairs*, August 25, 2017. Accessed October 4, 2018, https://www.foreignaffairs.com/articles/spain/2017-08-25/roots-barcelona-attack

ACKNOWLEDGEMENTS

Writing this book has been a great journey. It is not just about the field trips to remote conflict areas of Kashmir and the cold deserts of Ladakh, but also about the enlightening mental journey of discovering myself as a human being, researcher, writer, philosopher, spiritualist and a peace-maker. I want to express my sincere gratitude to all those who helped me in writing this book and became a part of this journey.

To begin with, I would like to express my heartfelt gratitude to my Sadgurudev Param Pujya Gulvani Maharajji and Gurudev Param Pujya Prabhu Baa. Without their blessings and spiritual guidance, it would have been impossible to complete this massive project which involved working in life-threatening situations. Besides, all my experience, academic knowledge, and formal research training in the subject, I believe that the perception and intuition that I could develop by the daily-meditation I practiced under Gurudev's divine blessings, was instrumental in developing my understanding of the subject and helping me in achieving the clarity of thoughts, acutely needed for an effective policy-formulation.

I want to thank my supervisor Mr. CD Sahay (Former RAW Chief), who, as Distinguished Fellow at the Vivekananda International Foundation, New Delhi, right from the inception helped me on various occasions in crafting the research strategy, fieldwork and drafting the final book. His profound insights into the intelligence affairs condensed in his "subtle-and-succinct-one-liners" often reminded me of India's ancient Sanskrit-based knowledge traditions where great masters like Patanjali and Panini showered wisdom in short aphorisms viz. "sutras."

Further, I would like to thank my parents, my brother and my sister who encouraged me and remained the source of my strength in this journey. My earliest exposure to the challenges of radicalization and pan-Islamism was during my father's posting as Additional SP, CID Zone, Udaipur Range of Rajasthan. I saw him working with various stakeholders at the ground level, analyzing and finding innovative solutions rooted in the regions cultural and religious traditions. Those observations enlightened me in many ways apart from motivating to pursue my interests and career in the field of counter terrorism. I express my heartfelt thanks to Dr. Anita Jain, my colleague at Vidya Bhawan Rural Institute and an expert taxonomist of Mewar, for her support and help. I also thank Dr. Jain for providing me her calm and serene office for the writing work. A taxonomist's questions were helpful in injecting a humanitarian flavor to a text devoted on a security and intelligence- focused subject of terrorism. I also want to thank my friends Mr. Kailash Ratnoo, IRS, Mr. Jyoti Pande (Retired IFS), Mr. Pankaj Kumar, IRS, Mr, Suveer Mishra, IRS, Mr. Siddharth Ratnoo, RAS and Mr. Ajay Bhargava from the "Mard-e-Momin" whatsapp group. The discussions on Islamism and West Asian politics added tremendously to my knowledge of the subject.

I would also like to thank Mr. Syed Asif Ibrahim (Former DIB), Mr. Sultan Shaheen (Islamic Scholar), Maulana Madni Sahab (General-Secretary, Jamait Ulema-i-Hind) and Dr. Adil Rashid (Fellow, IDSA) for enhancing my understanding of Islamic theology and the political and religious history of Islam in West-Asia and India. In particular, I would like to convey my special thanks to Mr. Asif Ibrahim Sahab whose insights were immensely helpful in developing my note on the counter-narrative. I also express my sincere thanks to Mr. AS Dulat (Former, RAW Chief), Mr. SM Sahay (IPS), Mr. Arun Kumar (Akhil Bhartiya Prachar Pramukh, RSS), Dr. Sudhir Bloeria, IAS, (Former Chief Secretary, J&K), Mr. Bharat Bhushan Vyas (Former Adviser to J&K Governor), Jammu and Kashmir Study Center (Delhi), Mr. Tejendra Khanna (former Lt. Governor of Delhi), Lt. Gen. (Retired) Rameshwar Roy, Mr. Sadanand Date (IPS), Mrs. Humra Qureishi, Mr. SP Pani (IPS) and Mr. KM Singh (Former DG, CISF) for helping me with their insights on the dynamics of conflict in Kashmir. My special thanks to Mr. Vicky Nanjappa for enlightening me about the radicalization scenario in Kerala.

Besides, I would also like to express my sincere gratitude to Mr. Zafar Manhas (MLC, J&K), Waheed Para (Kashmiri Politician), Safina Beigh (Kashmiri Politician), Amanjeet Singh (President, Sikh Youth Forum, Kashmir), Mr. Hashim Qureishi (Political & Social activist, Kashmir), Maulvi Hanif, Srinagar, Prof. Abdul Gani Butt (Hurriyat Conference) for rendering their valuable insights on the current political, social, cultural and radicalization trends of Kashmir.

Without Nadir Ali Sahab (Director, Center for Peace and Justice), and his team, my field research would have been impossible. Majid Hyadri Sahab and Dr. Ishrat Naved Khan Sahab's help in my field research in Central Kashmir and North Kashmir was extremely helpful in studying the activities of Jamaat-i-Islami and Ahle Hadith in the region. I also express my sincere thanks to Mr. Ashiq Hussain, Mr. Mubashir and Mr. Majid for exposing me to the dynamics of radicalization in the young generation of Kashmir.

The journey of writing this book also churned me from within as an author and a human being. When I was driving back to Srinagar from Budgam, Shopian and Pulwama on the chilly, still and eerie nights after the intense and hectic day of field research, I got the first-hand experience of life in a conflict zone. On every corner, when one warns you of a possible ambush or a military cordon, the brutal fear of living in terror stares in your face. When I was advised to take off my amulets and other religious symbols before traveling into some interior areas, I realized what extremism could do to a free society. In this discovery and learning, I was helped my several young men and women of Kashmir. Unfortunately, I am not in the position to thank them by their names due to security reasons. However, I express my heartfelt thanks and best wishes for the future of Kashmir to them.

Finally, I extend my sincere thanks to DR. Arvind Gupta, Director, Vivekananda Foundation for giving me this opportunity to write a book on an extremely important subject of contemporary national and global relevance. I do hope that this effort will make a small contribution in India's war against terror and radicalisation and contribute to world peace.

1

Introduction and Concepts: Radicalism, Extremism and Terrorism

Etymologically, the word Radicalism originates from the Latin word "radix" that can be translated as "root", which aligns well with some to the connotative meanings of radicalism such as fundamental, thorough, drastic and rigorous.[1] The dominant narrative in 18th and 19th centuries identified radicalism with anti-establishment socio-political doctrines that were largely emancipatory and ushered in progressive socio-political changes like the voting rights for women, the abolition of slavery and regulations to bring better working conditions for labor. Modern radicalism transformed the liberating ideas mentioned above into an essential element of the mainstream narrative of the western democracies. Radicalism aimed to bring fundamental and far-reaching changes without completely overthrowing the existing socio-political order. Intellectually, radicalism has no inherent commitment to the use of violence to achieve the desired objectives, though some radicals did advocate it. Hence, "radicals" may have different opinions from the mainstream, but as far as they are committed to the fundamental democratic socio-political order, their presence is desirable for healthy functioning and evolution of any society.

Extremism, however, is a way of thinking that brooks no compromise, rules out the possibility of any middle ground and warrants no limitations on its objectives and the means to achieve them. Schmid[2] aptly summarizes extremism: "while radicals might be violent or not, might be democrats or not, extremists are never democrats. Their state of mind tolerates no diversity. They are also positively in favor of the use of force to obtain and maintain political power.... Extremists generally tend to have inflexible 'closed minds', adhering to a simplified mono-causal interpretation of the world where you are either with them or against them, part of the problem or part of the solution." Extremism is more closely tied to a belief in the efficacy of violence to achieve the desired objective; hence, it is a more appropriate term to describe a mental state/conviction that finds terrorism as justified and necessary. However, the relation between extremism and terrorism is not of a necessary causality. Not all ideological extremists become terrorists. At best, radicalism and terrorism can be defined as "different points on the scale that reflects the degree to which violence is seen as legitimate and necessary to achieve far-reaching changes." Thus, radicals may see violence as a legitimate option under certain conditions while the extremists will always favor the use of violence.

Radicalism and extremism influence one's behavior and they may lead to the next stage of terrorism. There is still no universally accepted definition of terrorism. The questions that arise are "can one man's terrorist be another man's freedom fighter?," secondly, "is terrorism a tactic or a kind of war?", thirdly, "are only the non-state actors committing terrorist violence?" According to the Alex Schmidt 2011 Academic Consensus Definition, "Terrorism refers on the one hand to a doctrine about the presumed effectiveness of a special form or tactic of fear-generating, coercive political violence and, on the other hand, to a conspiratorial practice of calculated, demonstrative, direct violent action without legal or moral restraints, targeting mainly civilians and non-combatants, performed for its propagandistic and psychological effects on various audiences and conflict parties."

From the definition mentioned above, it follows that terrorism is not solely a domain of non-state actors. It is a kind of warfare that can be resorted to by both state and non-state actors if it is deemed fit to serve the interests of the perpetrator groups and individuals. Furthermore, it is a tactic that advocates the use of brutal force and it may emanate from extremist ideological beliefs or the reasons of expediency. For example, WWII bombing campaigns targeting civilian populations were aimed to terrorize them to the point that they would force their government to request for peace. They were purely out of pragmatic considerations rather than out of any extremist ideological position. Hence, it is irrational to conflate radical or extreme beliefs with involvement in terrorist violence. Not all extremists become terrorists, and not all terrorists are ideological extremists.[3]

Radicalization

Over the past decade, the general trend among counter-terrorism experts, both scholars and security professionals, is to see radicalization more broadly as a process that ultimately leads to involvement in terrorism. According to John Horgan,[4] "violent radicalization" includes the phases of (a) becoming involved with a terrorist group, and (b) remaining involved and engaging in terrorist activity." McCauley and Moskalenko view radicalization as "development of beliefs, feelings, and actions in support of any group or cause in a conflict" or "increased preparation for and commitment to intergroup conflict." Several relatively complex models explaining involvement in terrorism such as Moghaddam's "staircase" and McCauley and Moskalenko's "pyramid models fit this interpretation of radicalization", even though some of their authors never used this terminology.[5] For Kruglanski et al., radicalization is "a movement in the direction of *supporting* or *enacting* radical behavior."[6] Neumann argues that at the most basic level radicalization can be defined as "what goes on before the bomb goes off," i.e. a process whereby people become extremists. In the current context, radicalization can be defined as a road to terrorism, a slide into fundamentalism, extremism and a journey towards justifying violence and finally, personally engaging in it. Thus, I view radicalization as a process, generally a gradual one, the final result of which is a person involving in a violent movement to effect a social change. There are two stages of radicalization: endorsing beliefs and acting upon them. There is no steadfast temporal sequence and an element of necessity in the two stages mentioned above. One could even act without holding radical beliefs or one might not act upon his radical beliefs.[7]

The Government Circles

The German Federal Police (BKA) defines radicalization as "increasing adoption among individuals and groups of an extremist way of thinking, an action and the growing willingness to support and/or use illegitimate means, including the use of force, to achieve their objectives." For European Commission, violent radicalization means people embracing opinions, views and ideas which could lead to the acts of terrorism.

Along with the broader conceptualization of radicalization as a process of becoming involved in terrorism, there are several explanations about its potential drivers. Koehler identifies four such approaches.

Firstly, **Sociological Perspectives Theory** emphasizes the influence of the environmental conditions.

Secondly, **Social Movement Theory**, propounded in the 1940s, states that the radical social movements rise from strained socio-political conditions which fester in a mass sentiment of discontent. This theory emphasizes the role of radical milieus, small-group dynamics and antagonistic competition with the state as driving forces. People join such movements as they passively succumb to overwhelming social forces. Quintan Wiktorowicz has explained the phenomenon of Islamic radicalization, with this theoretical framework, through his four-component development model for radicalization.

The **Socio-psychological Approach** delves into the social and psychological factors. The focus is on the mind of a terrorist. The theory believes that there are "people with particular personality traits and tendencies drawn disproportionately towards terrorist careers."[8] The focus is on factors such as deprivation, altruism, identification with the victims of perceived injustice and several emotional, social and cognitive benefits of a group membership to account for involvement in terrorism. Among psychological factors, experience of personal crises acts as the potential "spark" that may explain why only some individuals adopt extremist beliefs and violent ways of behavior in spite of the fact that many others are exposed to similar circumstances. In the Kashmir valley, in several cases an individual became a militant because of the death of his family member in police firing or a security operation. In fact, the families of the dead militants have become a major source of recruitment.

By studying the thinking and the acting of the individuals and smaller groups, the scholars want to find out the characteristics which make one vulnerable to radicalization. Besides, this approach also investigates the group processes, the influence of the peer groups and like-minded people in radicalization and leading a peace-abiding individual towards a violent extremism. Jerold M Post and Clark McCauley have been the strong proponents of this theory.

French scholar Olivier Roy[9] opines that most of the Islamic State of Iraq and Syria (ISIS) foreign fighters have hardly any religious motivations. They have been into homosexuality, drugs, and relationships. They are second-generation Muslim migrants who joined terrorism out of frustration, deprivation, alienation, stigmatization, and rejection, feelings of revenge, discrimination and difficulties in integration with the host society. Their problems emanate from the confused identity. Hence, the solution lies in psychological investigations.

In the **Conversion Theory**, radicalization is explored through focusing on the ideological changes one undergoes after converting to a religion or an extremist school of that religion. Given the fact that extremist religious ideologies play a very strong role in radicalizing a person, Lewis Rambo has developed a seven-stage model for studying the impacts of conversion.[10]

Besides the pathways mentioned above, there are factors promoting radicalization which emanate from an overall radical social milieu and the larger forces like national politics, governance issues, strained majority-minority relations, geopolitical factors like civil wars, and the wars over religious ideologies.

Graeme Wood, in his long essay "What ISIS Really Wants?"[11] has outlined the religious motivations of ISIS in details. Unlike Olivier Roy, Graeme Wood and others, like Giles Sepel, do not believe in the undermining the role of religious motivations in radicalization, whereas counter-terrorism analysts, like Ali Soufan, focus more on economic deprivation, poverty, civil wars, unemployment and deprivation in explaining the radicalization pathways.

Asta Maskalunaite[12] has presented a comprehensive assessment of the main theories dominant in the radicalization studies. Psychological traits theory states that persons engaging in terrorism have some abnormal psychological traits. However, such theories have been proven false and denied on various occasions. Research on violent leftists of 1970s and the later studies confirmed that the terrorists were not notably different from the non-violent political activists, in psychological traits. Nevertheless, the attempts to find common traits among the terrorists have not ceased and receive a special focus in the law-enforcement world to locate the potential terrorist. The profiling has taken place on three lines: racial-physical, psycho-pathological and socio-economic characteristics. A former NYPD[13] report on radicalization identifies such individuals as "particularly vulnerable" to step on the ladder that leads to terrorist attacks: "fifteen to thirty-five year-old male Muslims living in male-dominated societies" especially as part of Muslim diaspora in the West and particularly if they belong to middle-class families and/or are students. Such attempts have led to the profiling of terrorists and have faced criticism on the grounds that in such initiatives, specific communities get targeted for the crime of a few, leading to the alienation of the other members of that community.

The psycho-pathological[14] or simply psychological approach (discussed above in the socio-psychological approaches) argues that some people with particular personality traits are disproportionately drawn towards terrorism (J Post's theory). Identity theory emphasizes that ideologies assist identify and joining a terrorist group is a strong "identity stabilizer," giving the recruits a sense of worth, meaning and purpose in life. Finally, the cognitive theory links cognitive capacity and violence, and explores the relation between "cognitive style and individual's disposition to join a terrorist group".[15] However, psychological approaches have not been successful and in various cases, terrorists have been found to be normal people.

Coercion/Motivation theories analyze the external actors: charismatic leaders, firebrand preachers, radical clerics or intellectual gurus, and assess their role in recruiting new members for terrorist organizations. An article by Trujillo et al.[16] recognizes two kinds of recruitment to terrorism: first is self-recruitment where a group of friends get radicalized through internet, and the second type of recruitment is an outcome of "the process of systematic directed and conscious psychological manipulation, very similar to that produced by sectarian or totalitarian groups." These theories are very popular in law-enforcement circles as they are helpful in identifying the select preachers, ideologues and charismatic leaders. These theories are used to advocate "targeted killings." Besides the importance of a leader or a preacher, there are two more types of pressures: (1) peer pressure exercised in the tightly knit groups of close friends that join the cause together as is often examined in the social networks approach. (2) McCauley and Moskalenko's "Slippery Slope" radicalization where a person reluctantly moves from legal activism to radical forms, ultimately engaging even in violent acts. These two paths exemplify the phenomenon of "involvement without radicalization."

Grievance-based explanations usually focus on structural level flaws and the way these encourage individuals to engage in political action and its extreme forms. Perceived injustice has been observed as one of the strongest motivator to join social movements and terrorist organizations. The structural conditions that generate a sense of grievance include civil wars or deep-rooted conflicts, invasion and occupation by foreign military forces, economic under-development, bad governance and corruption penetrating the state at all levels, rapid modernization or technological developments like the rise of internet and social media. The lack of political opportunities along with the social exclusion, disaffection of a religious-ethnic minority and wrongful foreign policy also constitute such structural flaws. Furthermore, personal and group grievances, both contribute to individuals joining a terrorist organization. However, the theory fails to explain a situation where the structural flaws spread across the social spectrum in a region or a community but only a few, join militancy. Moreover, according to this theory lack of political opportunities must lead to grievances and terrorism, but there are many dictatorships which do not face terrorism whereas many democracies face the menace of terrorism.

Rational Choice theory[17] appears to be the most promising one to explain radicalization. It sees the radicalization as a product of rational choices and decisions, i.e. involvement in terrorism is a result of a cost-benefit analysis that one does for any other serious activity. Martha Crenshaw is a strong proponent of this theory. Ronald Wintrobe, in the framework of this theory explains in his article, "Can Suicide Bombers be Rational?" that suicide bombers are also perfectly rational individuals and that suicide bombings can be seen as a kind of rational activity that is "an extreme example of a general class of behavior in which all of us engage." Hence, rational choice theorists are more interested in behavior than the psychological traits. The basic assumption is that individuals make rational decisions based on costs-and-benefit analysis. Daniela Pisiou[18] uses this framework to analyse Islamist radicalization in Europe and states that transforming into an engaged Islamic radical is "occupational change process." Individuals decide to pursue a "career in terrorism" as they choose any other career, evaluating its downsides, and also the "reward, standing and recognition." A sense of heroism and elitism also gets linked to this factor. Rational choice theory also has links to social network theory. The ultimate engagement and involvement in terrorism depends on the social networks that support and promote such activity. Such supporting social networks maintain a focus on action and make it difficult to leave the group. The primary motivation for the continued engagement becomes the loyalty to the organization or the commander rather than belief in any organization.

The rational choice theory also does not provide all the answers. A number of issues still remain: e.g., (1) the specificity problem, why actually only some people choose to become terrorists, (2) are there any personal characteristics that induce some and not others to choose such an occupation?

Social networks theory does provide and answer to this but then questions are about the rationality of the choice. If two out of the five friends become jihadis just to follow the suit or out of peer pressure, then the question arises, "Is than choice rational?" The answer is that may be it is rational for them to choose a path chosen by their friends or even commanded by a preacher. The rationality, if it is defined as a typical cost-benefit assessment may have different meanings and different decision outcomes for different people.

If one analyses the phenomenon of individuals joining terrorism in Kashmir, one comes across a combination of all the factors mentioned above. However, the most dominant ones in the combination are social network, followed by madrasa-cum-online radicalization (motivation) and the grievances. (The case study on Kashmir, later in the book, will discuss all of them in detail.)

In the recent trends, scholars like Bart Schuurman and Max Taylor[19] have discussed that the concept of "radicalization" is not enough to account for individuals engaging in terrorist violence. They state that in the radicalization-based approaches, there is a tendency to overemphasize the role of extremist beliefs in motivating one's involvement in terrorism. There is a trend of "conflating ideas with behavior." However, this is not only conceptually problematic but empirically poorly supported as well. The vast majority of radicals never become terrorists and not all terrorists are primarily motivated by their beliefs. After this critique, they offer the concept of "fanaticism' which explains the conditions under which a radicalized individual will turn to the acts of violence.

Fanaticism offers a behaviorally oriented perspective on if and when extremist beliefs can lead to the involvement of an individual in terrorist violence. This element of conditionality sets "fanaticism" apart from radicalization.

Fanaticism can be defined as a behavior that displays excessive enthusiasm for certain religious or political beliefs. According to Schuurman and Taylor, fanatical convictions can influence behavior because they essentially prescribe a variety of rules that link an individual's current action to distant outcomes. For instance, religious belief can motivate specific behaviors by connecting distant outcomes such as salvation in an afterlife to one's routine practices such as prayers and observance of the religious rules in social conduct. For a fanatic, the influence of ideology is so strong that it completely nullifies or majorly diminishes the other social, political and personal forces that might be expected to control and influence behavior. It appears that fanaticism is an extraordinarily emotionally charged state which leaves no space for one's rational faculties.

Fanatical behavior includes 10 qualities:[20]

1) An excessive focusing on issues of concern to the fanatic
2) A worldview that is solely based on ideological convictions
3) An insensitivity to others and to "normal" social pressures
4) A loss of critical judgment: the fanatic is apt to pursue ends and utilize means that seem to run contrary to his or her personal interests
5) A surprising tolerance for inconsistency and incompatibility in the beliefs held

   People engaged in fanatical behavior are further apt to display
6) Great certainty in the appropriateness of the actions taken
7) A simplified view of the world
8) High resistance to facts or interpretations that undermine their convictions
9) Disdain for the victims of the fanatic's behavior
10) Construction of a social environment that makes it easier to sustain fanatical views.

The concept of fanaticism is a great addition to the current threat assessment procedures. It allows scholars and security professionals to identify those individuals who are more likely to act on their extremist beliefs. It can also be seen from the 10 qualities mentioned above that fanatics try to create a congenial social environment where their beliefs find confirmation and legitimacy. This quality aligns well with the fact that the vast majority of terrorist violence is perpetrated by groups.

Furthermore, the possibility of fanatical convictions leading to violent behavior is conditioned on three contextual factors:[21]

1) Millenarianism: The belief that the world is facing an impending and apocalyptic disaster or change. Some ideologies support violent action to hasten the advent of a new world.
2) Totality of the ideological control: It rules out any debate or challenge to the fanatic's belief system, and the control of the ideology over every aspect of the adherent increases over time.

3) Militancy of the ideological beliefs, i.e. the degree to which it provides, or can be construed to provide, motivations or justifications for the use of terror.

In the case of India, it may be mentioned that in spite of its lacunae, the concept of radicalization is very useful in the national security discourse. The concept of fanaticism is an excellent tool for threat assessment. It can also be called the highest degree of the influence of the beliefs over behavior. However, in a multicultural society like India, even radicalization of the religious communities *en masse* presents a grave threat to the communal harmony of the society. Moreover, this does not advocate the study of radicalization only from the narrow prism of terrorism. Agreed that very few individuals ultimately resort to terrorist violence and such violence needs a much advanced infrastructure, however, there is an even bigger threat to security in India which comes from communal riots. Despite the co-existence of more than 1000 years and the flourishing of communal harmony and syncretic Hindu-Muslim culture, there is a history of violent and brutal communal riots[22] between the Hindus and Muslims. This leads to the belief that more direct impact of radicalization of Muslims will be in the form of communal riots and the radicalization of Hindus in reaction.

Furthermore, in India, Muslims are the largest minority and they are spread over the entire country. In almost every village, one can find Muslim residents. With such a widespread presence across the country, the communal fault-lines are also very active. Hence, in such a scenario, radicalization of Muslims and Hindus will be devastating. Radicalization of the Muslim community will lead to the development of extremist sentiments and exclusivism. Social discourse with other communities will be disrupted. In such case, more communal riots are likely to happen and the dialogue-based channels for conflict resolution will shrink. Furthermore, radicalization of one community will lead to the radicalization of the other one too, i.e. Hindus, and more riots. In India, the recent changes in religiosity of Muslims with the advent of Wahabbism and expansion of Deobandi missionaries, coupled with global Islamism and cross-border terrorism, have led to suspicions in the Hindu community. Hindu community's threat perceptions have magnified and these days, one can witness high levels of radicalization sweeping Hindu community also. Hinduism is undergoing a transformation of which the major determinants are globalization, ICT revolution, rise of populism and Islamic extremism. Islamic extremism and global Islamism have emerged as the most powerful influencers in this transformation of Hinduism. Attempts are being made to erect the doctrines of political Hinduism parallel to political Islam.

Furthermore, communal riots generate a strong sense of insecurity and victimhood. In such scenario, religious fundamentalism and radicalization find a smooth acceptance in the Muslim societies. Terrorist organizations harness the fertile grounds generated by victimhood and insecurity. They play upon the fears of Muslims and recruit cadres which in turn lead to further radicalization of Hindus and it becomes a vicious circle.

Hence, the concept of radicalization is more important in India's case. In India, the state is functional, tolerant and liberal; the judicial system is fair and democracy is representative. Minority rights and privileges are guaranteed by the constitution. Moreover, there is a robust legacy communal harmony, and the family system is still strong. In such a scenario, the non-religious/non-ideological factors have a very minor role in radicalization whereas the religious and ideological factors have a very dominant role in radicalization. Later in the monograph, the readers will learn that among those who joined ISIS from India or showed pro-ISIS leanings, religion was the strongest motivation. Islamic extremist organizations like Popular Front of India and Jamaat-e-Islami prepared the ground for radicalization for decades. Given the limitations of India's security and intelligence establishment and sheer size and diversity of the country, a radicalized mind cannot be allowed to become fanatic. Radicalization is likely to be the appropriate stage where right kinds of interventions are needed: preemptive and corrective both (will be discussed later in the monograph). If there is a choice in allocating resources for the policy intervention in India's case, the author would like to recommend more allocation for counter-radicalization programs. Moreover, Schuurman and Taylor[23] clearly state that the concept of fanaticism is not a replacement for radicalization-based thinking but an addition to the debate about how and why participation in terrorist groups and terrorist violence can occur.

Wahhabism

In popular perception across the world, Wahhabism is regarded as synonymous with extremism and the main driver of jihadi terrorism across the world. In 2013, the European Parliament at Strasbourg identified Wahhabism as the main source of global terrorism.

History

Wahhabism was founded by Ibn Abd al-Wahhab (1703-92). He addressed it as an innovative and reformist movement in Islam. He emphasized that there was no need for any intercession between the Allah and the devotee. He even rejected the intercession of Muhammad between the devotee and the Allah. He denounced pilgrimages to saints' tombs and even supported the idea of destroying the tombs and domes of saints. Wahhabism believes in the literal interpretation of Quran and Hadith. Wahhabism advocates the return of Islam to the purity of its golden age—the age of the Prophet and the first four caliphs, i.e. the age of Salaf or Sahaba (companions of the Prophet). His ideas were deeply influenced by the teachings of Ibn Taymiyah (1263-1328), for whom the state was an adjunct of religion. He rejected discursive theology.[24] Taymiyah declared war on Shi'ism, Sufism and Greek philosophy. He was strictly against visiting the grave of the prophet and the celebration of his birthday and declared that all such behaviors represented mere imitation of the Christian worship of Jesus as God (i.e. idolatry). Abd al-Wahhab assimilated all this earlier teaching, stating that "any doubt or hesitation" on the part of a believer in respect to his or her acknowledging this particular interpretation of Islam should "deprive a man of immunity of his property and his life."[25] Like Taymiyah before him, Abd al-Wahhab advocated that the era of the Prophet Muhammad's stay in Medina was the golden age of Muslim society (the "best of times"), which all Muslims should aspire to emulate (this, essentially, is Salafism).

In the 18th century, when Abd-al-Wahab began preaching his revivalist Islam to the Bedouins of Najd (Central Arabia), his teachings were rejected as too simplistic and heretical by most of the clergy at the prominent centers of Islamic learning like Al Azhar. Wahhab argued that decline of Muslim world[26] was due to foreign influences (European modernism) and also various elements of traditional Islam.[27] He called all such practices as shirk (apostasy) and wanted to take Islam back to its form that prevailed in seventh-century Arabia. The main emphasis was on *tawhid* (monotheism and absolute sovereignty of God), condemning many traditional Muslim practices as shirk (polytheism). There was an unusual focus on jihad in his teachings. The Wahhabis called themselves Muwahideen (monotheists)—to call themselves Wahhabis was considered shirk. Wahhabism was adopted by the family of Al Saud in 1744.

Abd al-Wahhab began his teachings in Huraymila town in 1740. His father was a Hanbali Islamic jurist. Wahhab's ideas were rooted in Hanbali School of Islamic law but the Hanbali officials of Huraymila and Uyahnah rejected and expelled him. In 1744, he arrived at Al-Dir'iyyah where his ideas received the patronage of the Emir Muhammad Ibn Saud.

From then on, the political fortunes of the Wahhabi movement were closely allied to those of the Saudi dynasty. By the end of the 18th century, they had brought all of Najd under their control, attacked Karbala, Iraq, a holy city of the Shi'ite branch of Islam, and occupied Mecca and Medina in western Arabia. The Ottoman sultan brought an end to the first Wahhabi Empire in 1818, but the sect revived under the leadership of the Saudi Faysal I. The empire was then somewhat restored until once again destroyed, at the end of the 19th century by the Rashidiyyah of northern Arabia. The activities of Ibn Saud in the 20th century eventually led to the creation of the Kingdom of Saudi Arabia in 1932 and assured Wahhabi religious and political dominance on the Arabian Peninsula.

The Al Saud—in this 20th-century renaissance—were led by the politically astute Abd al-Aziz. He unified the fractious Bedouin tribes and launched the Saudi "Ikhwan" in the spirit of Abd al-Wahhab's and Ibn Saud's earlier fighting proselytizers.

The Ikhwan was a reincarnation of the early, fierce, semi-independent vanguard movement of committed armed Wahhabist "moralists" who almost had succeeded in seizing Arabia by the early 1800s. In the same manner as earlier, the Ikhwan again occupied Mecca, Medina and Jeddah between 1914 and 1926. Abd al-Aziz, however, began to feel that his larger interests were being threatened by the revolutionary "Jacobinism" exhibited by the Ikhwan. The Ikhwan revolted and that led to a civil war that lasted until the 1930s, when the King finally curbed them ruthlessly.

For this king (Abd al-Aziz), the times were changing. Oil was being discovered in the peninsula. Britain and America were courting Abd al-Aziz, but still were inclined to support Sharif Husain as the only legitimate ruler of Arabia. The Saudis needed to develop a more sophisticated diplomatic posture. King Abd al-Aziz made a subsequent shift towards statehood in 1920s and 30s, to foster diplomatic relations with nation-states like Britain and America. A compromise was reached with the Wahhabi clergy who supported the Saudi king in all political matters in lieu of the state support for the religious ideology.

So, Wahhabism was forcefully transformed from a movement of

revolutionary jihad and theological takfiri purification, to a movement of conservative social, political, theological, and religious da'wa (Islamic call). The transition was accompanied by its emergence as the staunch guard of the Saudi royal family and the King's absolute power.

In 1925, though Wahhabis had seized Mecca, the state continued to allow pilgrims of all Muslim traditions to observe their rites during the hajj. In the late 20th and 21st centuries, the preeminence of the Wahhabi religious establishment has ensured that the Kingdom of Saudi Arabia remains significantly more conservative than other states in the region. The powerful religious police enforces strict codes of public behavior—including, for example, mandatory observance of Islamic rituals and gender segregation.

The Interior Ministry runs the religious police which is extremely harsh against illegal alcohol and ensures that the shops are shut during mosque time. Wahhabists enforce public attendance at prayers, forbid shaving and the smoking of tobacco. Their mosques are plain.

Because Wahhabism prohibits the veneration of shrines, tombs, and sacred objects, many sites associated with the early history of Islam, such as the homes and graves of companions of Muhammad, were demolished under Saudi rule. Preservationists have estimated that as many as 95 per cent of the historic sites around Mecca and Medina have been razed.

With the advent of oil wealth, Saudi Arabia's ambitions were to spread Wahhabism globally. After the Yom Kippur war in October 1973, the petroleum exports ballooned and the oil prices quadrupled. As a result, billions of dollars began to be spent by Wahhabis to spread Islam at the global level. The diversities and the local variants of Islam were sought to be gradually marginalized. The motivation behind exporting a standard version of Islam was to strengthen Saudi Arabia as the leader of the Muslim world. Wahhabism became the pillar of Saudi Arabia's soft power. During the reign of King Fahd[28] (1985-2005), over $75 billion was spent in efforts to spread Wahhabi Islam. The money was used to establish 200 Islamic colleges, 210 Islamic centers, 1,500 mosques, and 2,000 schools for Muslim children in Muslim and non-Muslim majority countries. The schools were "fundamentalist" in outlook and formed a network from Sudan to northern Pakistan. Saudi Arabia funds a number of international organizations to spread fundamentalist Islam, including the Muslim World League, the World Assembly of Muslim Youth, the International Islamic Relief Organization, and various royal charities.

The Saudi ambitions of managing Sunni Islam across the world suited the geo-political interests of the western world, in particular Americans to counter the Soviet influence. Earlier, in 1920s and 30s, the British had supported the jihad of Wahhabis against the Sharif Hussain family and Ottomans, and in 1980s, interestingly the USA, the political successor of Britain in world affairs after the WWII, encouraged Saudis in their export of the puritanical version of Islam across the world. In particular, the jihad against Godless communists of Soviet Russia in Afghanistan required a much needed oxygen of religious passion and jihadi fervor for which Wahhabi ideology was the perfect choice.

Westerners were also deluded with the rapid modernization of the Saudi kingdom and thought that Saudi control of the global Sunnism through the export of Wahhabism will serve America's geo-political interests. They wrongly assumed that it will not get out of control and believed that ultimately the logic of modernization will supplant the spirit of jihadism (earlier wielded by the religiously passionate Ikhwani fighters). However, they were mistaken. The Saudi Ikhwani approach to Islam did not finish in 1930s. It retreated and maintained its control over the parts of the system. It returned in 1970s when the hardline Islamist clergy felt that Saudi regime had not remained pious enough and was corrupted by the oil wealth. The signs of increasing liberalization—women appearing on TV without headscarves—widened the rift between the Wahhabi clergy and the royal family. They agitated for ousting the Saudi royal family. The radical Islamists laid siege to Mecca mosque in 1979[29] under the leadership of the conservative ideologue Juhayman-al-Otaibi. Otaibi and his followers were executed. The rebels who survived their sentences went on to join Al Qaeda (AQ). Finally, Saudis managed to neutralize the terrorists inside the mosque with the help of French counter-terrorism squad.

The siege of Mecca marks a breakthrough in the history of modern global jihadi movement. After the siege, the Saudis withdrew from social reform and unleashed conservatism in social and political matters to keep the Wahhabi clergy happy. They began investing heavily in the export of Wahhabi ideology across the world. Furthermore, as Trofimov[30] notes, "the Saudi government strove to expunge the siege from the public memory and to channel the energies of its more hostile citizens to crises afflicting the Islamic world, beyond its borders, such as the war in Afghanistan." In addition to the siege of Mecca, the Shia revolution in Iran and the Soviet invasion of Afghanistan in 1979, gave a strong fillip to global jihadism. With the Shia revolution began the famous Saudi-Iranian or rather Sunni-Shia rivalry for the leadership of the Muslim world. Afghan invasion by Soviet Russia ultimately led to the mobilization of the mujahidin fighters from across the world and strengthening of the narrative of global jihad. The stateless and ungoverned mountainous terrains of Afghanistan emerged as the center of global jihadism, with terrorist organizations like Al Qaeda and Taliban strongly entrenched there. Afghanistan has not been able to recover yet and lately has emerged as stronghold of Islamic State in Khorasan Province (ISKP).

The emergence of Al Qaeda and ISIS is the manifestation of the old Saudi Ikhwani spirit. The Saudi duality in its approach towards ISIS is the result of this Ikhwani spirit. It is still dominant in certain sections of clerics and sheikhs who believe that the state of Saudi is not the rightful heir of Islam because of the royal family's hobnobbing with the apostate western world. ISIS is deeply Wahhabist but it rejects Saudi State. It is ultra-radical and could be seen essentially as a corrective movement to contemporary Wahhabism or rather a revival of the Ikhwani approach to Islam. Hence, in many quarters the phenomenon of ISIS challenging Saudi legitimacy is seen as the revival of the original Saudi-Wahhabi project.

Takfiri[31]

The main tenet of Abd al-Wahhab's doctrine was the key idea of *takfir.* Under the takfiri doctrine, Abd al-Wahhab and his followers could declare fellow Muslims infidels should they engage in activities that in any way could be said to encroach on the sovereignty of the absolute Authority (i.e. the King). Abd al-Wahhab denounced all Muslims who honored the dead, saints, or angels. He held that such sentiments detracted from the complete subservience one must feel towards God, and only God. Today, Takfiri is one of the central pillars of the ideology of ISIS.

Furthermore, Wahhab also demanded conformity—a conformity that was to be exercised in physical and tangible ways. He argued that all Muslims must individually pledge their allegiance to a single Muslim leader (a Caliph, if there were one). Those who would not conform to this view should be killed, their wives and daughters violated, and their possessions confiscated, he wrote. The list of apostates deserving death included the Shiite, Sufis and other Muslim denominations, whom Abd al-Wahhab did not consider to be Muslim at all.

Wahhabism is not a monolith. It must be noted that there are minor doctrinal differences between Saudi Wahhabism, moderate opposition to Saudi state, Salafism (Egypt) and Ahle Hadith but all of them are normally bracketed in one category as they represent an ideology which favors a literalist and a fundamentalist interpretation of Islam.

On one hand, the state of Saudi Arabia is officially a Wahhabi state and on the other, terrorist organizations like ISIS, Al Qaeda and Lashkar-e-Taiba follow Wahhabism. The question that perplexes one's mind is that then why ISIS is a threat to Saudi Arabia.

Ideologically and in the interpretation of religion, there is no difference but ISIS does not believe in institutionalization of the Abd al-Wahhab's doctrine of "one ruler, one authority, one mosque" which taken together, refers to Saudi King, the absolute authority of official Wahhabism. It is this denial of ISIS which made it a grave threat to Saudi Arabia.

However, interactions with the Wahhabi clerics discovered that there has been a tremendous amount of distortion of the Wahhabi teachings; hence, categorizing all the Wahhabis as terrorist may not be a rational approach. According to an experienced Salafi cleric of Srinagar, their views are counter to the ones propagated by transnational terrorist organizations as listed below:

1) Kitaab-al-Imarah maintains that Muslims cannot revolt against the Islamic government. Even if the government is oppressive, a true Muslim has to exercise patience as all accounts will be settled on the Day of Judgment. Al Quran (chapter 4, verse 59) says that obey Allah, Rasool Sallalahe Wasallam (prophet) and your king.
2) For the Caliph (Imam/Rahnuma/Badshah), three things are needed— a legitimate state with geographical territory, military power and knowledge. Further, the Caliph has to be the one elected by Ummat.
3) In the case of Muslims not having power and a leader, they cannot bring sharia rule by force. If they are living in a country ruled by non-Muslim government, they have to obey the government of that country. Even if the infidel government suppresses their religious rights, they can only request and send a note of advice but not revolt.
4) Quran says that choose a small harm over the larger harm. It implies that without adequate military power if one non-state actor begins an illegitimate jihad against an oppressive and a powerful government, it will result in chaos and anarchy. Hence, such jihad is not allowed.

By this definition, the jihad in Syria or by terrorist organizations, like Al Qaeda, ISIS, LeT and Boko Haram, is not sanctioned by Quran.

5) Furthermore, he said that if a Muslim lives in a non-Muslim state and a society that allows alcohol and other sacrilegious practices, he will not be accused of shirk.
6) In India, the Muslims have all the religious, social, cultural and political rights and opportunities. The state is just and fair, so any jihad in India against the government has no place or justification in Quran. All those who claim to launch jihad in Kashmir are sinful because they are doing it to acquire political power, land or to seek revenge. Jihad is for furthering the cause of Allah and not for personal gains.
7) Wahhabism does not advocate violence as a modus operandi for achieving its goal of return to the original Islam. Jihadism, its violent offshoot, does. However, modern jihadism is a political concept and does not have any grounding in Quran and Hadith.[32]

Nevertheless, empirically, the fact remains that the spread of Wahhabism has led to the universalization of Islam, rise in fundamentalism, exclusivism and extremism which in turn has led to radicalization of Muslims and prepared a fertile ground for the spread of jihadi terrorist organizations across the world.

Deobandi School of Islam[33]

Deoband is a revivalist movement within Sunni (primarily Hanafi) Islam. It is centered in India, Pakistan, Afghanistan, and Bangladesh. It has also spread to the United Kingdom and has a presence in South Africa.

The movement derives its name from Deoband, India, where the school Darul Uloom Deoband is situated. The movement was inspired by scholar Shah Waliullah Dehlawi (1703–1762), and was founded in 1867 in the wake of the failed revolt of 1857 in north India. The Disband movement developed as a reaction to the British colonialism which was seen by a group of Indian scholars—consisting of Rashid Ahmad Gangohi, Muhammad Yaqub Nanautai, Shah Rafi al-Din, Syed Muhammad Abid, Zulfiqar Ali, Fadhl al-Rahman Usmani and Muhammad Qasim Nanotwi—to be corrupting Islam. The group founded an Islamic seminary known as Darul Uloom, Deoband, where the Islamic revivalist and anti-imperialist ideology of the Deobandis began to develop. In time, the Darul Uloom Deoband became the second most significant center of Islamic teaching and research after the Al Azhar University,

Cairo. Through the organizations such as Jamiat Ulema-e-Hind and Tablighi Jamaat, the Disband ideology began to spread.

During India's independence movement, the Deobandis advocated a notion of composite nationalism by which Hindus and Muslims were seen as one nation who were asked to be united in the struggle against the British. In 1919, a large group of Deobandi scholars formed their political party, Jamiat Ulema-e-Hind. Later, they opposed the Pakistan Movement. A minority group joined Muhammad Ali Jinnah's Muslim League, forming the Jamiat Ulema-e-Islam in 1945.

Deobandi school of thought is generally regarded as South Asian cousin of Wahhabism. Like Wahhabism, Deobandi school of thought is also against the worship of shrines and tombs and the celebration of the Prophet's birthday. Their attitude towards Shias and infidels is closer to that of Wahhabis. In social and religious domains, they are very conservative. Though they opposed partition of India, the reasons were not entirely secular.

Their missionary arm Tablighi Jamaat (TJ) engages in religious proselytization. In many quarters, it is believed that TJ plays an indirect role in jihadi radicalization (discussed in detail in the next chapter). But the Deobandi School unlike Wahhabis believes in Taqleed and follows the Hanafi School of Islamic jurisprudence.

Taliban and Jaish-e-Muhammad subscribe to the Deobandi school of thought. However, it must be highlighted that the Deobandis in India have shunned jihadi violence and given strong fatwas against terrorism.[34]

Deobandi clerics in India have maintained strong nationalist demeanor. They constitute 20 per cent of India's Muslim population and are often at odds with the majority Barelwis school of thought. Furthermore, they also oppose Wahhabis on ideological grounds.

Barelwis[35]

Barelwism, with over 200 million followers in South Asia, is a movement following the Sunni Hanafi School of jurisprudence. Like the Deobandis, the name Barelwi also derives from the north Indian town of Bareilly, the hometown of its founder leader Ahmed Raza Khan (1856–1921). Although Barelwi is a commonly used term in the media and academia, the followers of the movement often prefer to be known by the title of *Ahle Sunnatwa Jama'at*, or as *Sunnis*, a reference to their perception as forming an international majority movement.

The movement emphasizes personal devotion to the Prophet and a synthesis of Sharia with Sufi practices such as veneration of saints. Because of this, they are often addressed as Sufi Muslims and constitute the overwhelming majority of the Muslims in India and South Asia. It is regarded as the Islam of the ordinary and poor Muslim masses. They are also regarded as the liberal and tolerant face of Islam. However, it must be highlighted that Barelvis supported the movement for separate Pakistan during India's independence struggle. They are also not immune to extremism and agree with the theology of consensus in Islam (basic tenet of the primacy of Quran and hadith, i.e. the dominant discourse of Islam). Their frictions with Hindus often manifest in violent communal riots. Their attitudes on religious and social issues like the status of women are conservative. The practice of Halala is present among Barelwi Muslims.

The Sachar Committee findings showed that the indicators in lower, higher and technical education are poorest for the Muslim community. Similarly, the economic indicators are also very poor. Among Muslims, the Barelwis constitute an overwhelming majority; hence, the pitiable economic and educational indicators of Barelwis hardly need any further detailed analysis for this brief overview section. With their meager financial resources, they are facing stiff competition from foreign extremist ideologies (Wahhabi/Salafis) which have strong petro-dollar funding. Their domestic competitors, i.e. Deobandis also have a much better organizational cadre strength, structure, financial resources and political clout.

Self-employment in petty businesses such as cycle and bike repair shops, electronics, and auto-rickshaw is very common among the poorer Barelwis. Going further down the ladder of social-economic status among Barelwis, one can also find active participation in crime (in the lower income Barelwi Muslims). But the traditions of multiculturalism and syncretic Hindu-Muslim culture are most vibrant in the Barelwi community's belief system, culture and lifestyle. Since the Barelwis are economically and educationally modest, they live with non-Muslims in a symbiotic existence so the exigencies of pragmatism make them the most accommodative, tolerant and liberal ones. Centuries of co-existence with shared political, cultural and social experiences enabled the flourishing of the common Hindu-Muslim culture, which, in the common parlance, is known as "Ganga-Jamuni Tahzeeb." This imparted Barelwi Islam with a very distinct Indian flavor. For instance, it is very common to find Barelwi Muslims observing Hindu worshipping rituals (Devi pujan) in Rajasthan. One can even spot Barelwi Muslims with a Tilak their forehead praying in Nakoda Jain temple (Rajasthan). Such examples are many and spread across the country.

However, because of this accommodative attitude resulting in the co-opting of many Hindu customs, traditions and rituals (this mutual harmony, respect for each other's belief systems and healthy exchange was the soul of India's communal harmony and the essence of India's secularism), they have also become the targets of the extremist Sunni ideology that completely disregards local culture, promotes a monochromic Islam and accuses Barelwis of shirk (apostasy). Further, the Barelwi Imams are not as well educated as compared to the Deobandi and Wahhabi Imams. Barelwi practices focus on the internal and spiritual aspects of religion rather than ritualistic aspects—an idea very similar to the Bhakti way of Hinduism (focuses on faith rather than logical reasoning).

However, lately, Sufi shrine worship system has witnessed huge corruption and superstitions which has disappointed the young generation. Hence, Barelwi's mystic and faith-based worship system hardly appeals to the new generation of young and educated Muslim middle and upper classes. The youngsters in middle and upper class are the ones majorly drifting towards extremist Sunni ideologies. This young generation rejects their parents' Sufi Islam. The best examples of this phenomenon can be witnessed in Kashmir and Kerala (case studies discussed in subsequent chapters).

However, they also perceive a strong threat from the Hindu radicalization which has also intensified lately. Barelwi Muslims constitute the common masses among the Muslim community, so whenever there is a communal riot, they are first in the line of fire. Such horrifying experiences of communal riots in the past have made them highly skeptical and wary of Hindu radicalization.

Having perceptions (partly real and partly imagined) of existential threats from Hindu radicalization and the competition from the foreign extremist ideologies, the Barelwis have also started asserting themselves to protect their identity. In this quest for survival, some of them are becoming more extremist, abandoning Sufi message of inner journey to purify one's inner self, and syncretic Hindu-Muslim rituals and practices. In the competition to sound more Islamic, one can witness the phenomenon of extremism rising among Barelwis. The tendency to emulate extremist ideologies is also becoming stronger among the Barelwis. But, yes the names are still different keeping the bitter sectarian tensions alive, sometimes turning violent also.

Barelwis, these days are identifying their Islamic identity more with the West Asia, rather than India. One can witness the fact that Barelwis are developing more interest in global Islamic movements and their emotional and other affiliations with global Islam are getting stronger. In many cases, the heroes of young Barelwi Muslims were Osama Bin Laden, Erdogan and Al Baghdadi. With this increasing outreach of global Islamism, the participation of Barelwis on the issues concerning the Muslims worldwide is becoming stronger. For instance, Barelwi Muslims of a laid-back town like Udaipur staged a big protest rally requesting the government of India to provide shelter to Rohingyas. In Kashmir, even in the rural areas with Barelwi majorities, there is a strong awareness of global conflicts involving Muslims such as the war in Yemen, Rohingya crisis in Myanmar and events in Middle East. However, their awareness on such issues is highly one-sided presenting only the religious and extremely fanatic version of the issues underlined above. Here, one would like to highlight that those Barelwis who are not adopting Wahhbism and Deobandism are also coming under the grips of global Islamism. This is happening through social media and WhatsApp messaging. They may be ideologically at cross-roads with Salafism and global Islam, but their affiliation has more to do with the global Islamic identity, i.e. the brotherhood of Ummah. This is strengthening the psychological bond with global Islamism. Furthermore, the said phenomenon is dissociating them from local socio-cultural, religious and historical roots and encouraging fundamentalism and extremism among them.

For the future, it appears that Barelwi Muslims will not be able to give a strong counter to the foreign extremist ideologies and they are likely to weaken into the more standard and austere versions of Islam, later or sooner. This is also because of the fact that their counter strategy against them is fallacious. Rather than harnessing the strengths of communal harmony between Hindus and Muslims, which has evolved and matured over almost last 700 years, they appear to have chosen the extremist and fundamentalist way. To prove themselves as purer Muslims, they are basically adopting the ways and attitudes of puritanical/extremist schools in question, but without changing the name. This will alienate them from Indian socio-cultural ethos and produce more fault-lines between Hindus and Muslims.

A Dive into the Hindu and the Muslim Mind in India

Discussions in this section are largely based on the author's observations and analysis, and inputs derived from MJ Akbar's "Tinderbox: The Past and Future of Pakistan", Satish Chandra's "History of Medieval India", Vipin Chandra's "Modern India", Sumit Sircar's "Modern India", Anand Rangnathan's "Dismantling Sainthood: Ambedkar on Gandhi" and "Ambedkar on Islam: The Story That Must Not Be Told". Therefore, the issues discussed herein need further research and exploration. The objective here is to provide a brief overview of Hindu-Muslim relations and the communal dynamics that will be immensely helpful in a nuanced understanding of the story of radicalization in India.

Islam arrived in India from the land and the sea. Its arrival in the southern state of Kerala has been discussed in the case study on Kerala. This section basically gives a brief overview of the evolution of Islam in the plains of North India. In Northern India, Islam arrived with the Arab invaders who conquered Sind in 712 AD. After that, they were mostly confined to the Sind region for about 300 years. The Gurjar-Pratiharas gave a stable rule to North India. King Nagbhatta gave a crushing defeat to Arabs. In the north, the Lalliyashahis of Kabul and Zabul could stop the Islamic invaders for about two centuries.

Ghaznavid attacks on India were the next major event in the political history of India. His plundering raids left a deep impact on the Hindu subconscious in India (990 AD to 1025 AD). This narrative of Afghan invaders as plunderers goes back a 1000 years, and its perhaps most iconic reference point is the figure of Mahmud Ghaznavi, an 11th-century ruler who conquered his way through modern-day Afghanistan, eastern Iran and north-western India. In Hindu memory, two aspects of Ghaznavi's actions stand out: his determination to spread Islam and to punish "idolators" (later invaders took the titles of *butshikan* (iconoclast) and *ghazi* (religious warrior) to indicate their similar fervor.[36]

The left-wing historians' counter-argument that the Muslim Sultans killed an equal number of fellow Muslims they considered heretics, and that the overriding motivation for all these historical figures was economic, not religious, has little impact. In the words of the eminent politician-scholar of India, KM Munshi, "For a thousand years Mahmud's destruction of the iconic Somnath shrine has been burnt into the Hindu collective sub-conscious as an unforgettable national disaster."

Regarding the state system during the Muslim rule in India, it can be stated that the tussle between the theologians and the political rulers existed since the rule of the sultanate kings in India. From the discourse between the Qazi Mughis-ud-din of Bayana (he regarded Hindus as enemies of the state) and Sultan Allaudin Khilji, the conflict between the clergy and king is explicitly clear. The said discourse also makes it clear that the Sultanate king never supported the idea of a theocratic state in India.[37] The Islam in India had arrived after 400 years of its exposure to non-Muslim societies on the way to India. The Sultans had realized the futility of the literalist and extremist interpretations of the faith (the ones that prevailed in Arab region) in multicultural societies. Hence, for reasons of political expediency, they strove to create space for non-Muslim majorities, and their recourse to religion in political and social sphere was mostly out of political motivations or to appease the Islamic clerics barring few cases of the rulers themselves being religious fanatics.

In the state-system, the king was called Zill-e-Ilahi, i.e. the shadow of God. The concept of Zill-e-Ilahi accorded superior and divine status to the king vis-à-vis the clergy. In the social sphere, the spread of Sufism presented the soft and moderate face of Islam. Sufi and Bhakti movements led to the birth of syncretic Hindu-Muslim culture in India, known as Ganga-Jamuni tahzeeb in popular perception. Many Hindus converted to Islam under the influence of Sufism. Sufi saints were venerated by both Hindus and Muslims. Mughal emperor Akbar abolished Jizyah (religious tax levied on non-Muslims), participated in Hindu festivals and promoted the culture of communal harmony. In the state-system, he integrated Rajputs as junior partners.

However, along with the trends mentioned above, there were episodes of temple destructions, Jauhar, forced religious conversions, execution of people because of their non-Muslim religious identity and the levying of Jizyah. Buddhist universities such as Nalanda and Vikramshila were ravaged by Bakhtiyaruddin Khiljhi, the general of Muhammad Gauri. Jizyah continued to be levied on Hindus until Akbar banned it. It was again resumed by Aurangzeb in 1704 to garner the support of Muslim clergy. As late as the reign of Aurangzeb, the temples continued to be destroyed. Sheikh Ahmad Sirhindi, the Mujaddid, advocated strict sharia and harsh treatment with Hindus during the reign of Jehangir (1605-27). Belgian Historian Konrad Elst and Dr. KS Laal have given vivid accounts of the mass conversions and execution of non-Muslims. Laal, in his book, "Growth of Muslim Population in India", writes that Hindu population declined by 80 million between 1000 AD and 1525 AD. Dr. Elst in his article, "Was There an Islamic Genocide of Hindus?", quoting Ferishta, the Muslim historian of India, says that Bahmani sultans alone (1347-1528) killed more than 100,000 Hindus, and it was a second-grade provincial dynasty.

In Aurangzeb's reign, the nature of state changed. Personally also, he was a devout religious man and projected himself as "shahidarvesh". Dara Shikoh, Aurangzeb's brother and the ideological successor of Akbar's moderate Islam, was executed. Jizyah was levied and once again an era of forced conversions and temple destructions began. Historians argue that his motivations were non-religious as he wanted to garner Muslim support by appeasing the clergy with his Islamic behavior, against the Rajput uprisings and Maratha revolt. However, no amount of justification can deny the fact that Aurangzeb's reign represents an anti-thesis to the centuries of communal harmony that existed between Hindus and Muslims, as a result of Sufi and Bhakti movements and the state created by the tolerant kings like Akbar.

The real problem begins after the decline of Mughal Empire. After the decline of the Mughal Empire, the Muslim mind in India came to be gripped with the fear of the future and pride of the past. The fear began as anguish set in among the Muslim elite during the long decline of Mughals in the 18th century. It began hesitatingly, in the shadow of the decline in 1750s, when the collapse of Mughals and the gradual disintegration of the so-called Muslim rule in India could no longer be hidden by explanations, theories and the hope of revival. However, for long it was in an embryonic stage.

The first phase began with the defeat of Mughals by Nadir Shah in 1739. He plundered Delhi and massacred Hindus and Muslims for three days in Delhi. An estimated 20,000 were killed, women raped and the capital was plundered of the private and public wealth.

Shah Waliullah, the Sunni theologian and the leading intellectual of his age, read several meanings in the disaster. The security that Muslims had enjoyed for centuries was shattered. Hindu dynasties had emerged as powerful contenders of the throne. Delhi was plundered by Nadir Shah who belonged to the "deviant sect" of Shias who were regarded even worse than infidels. Shah Waliullah proposed the theory of distance and protection of "Islamic purity" as his prescription for the community that was facing an imminent threat from the cultural power and the military might of the infidels.

He feared that, in the absence of strong religious leadership protected by the political power, there might be a relapse of Hindu practices among the Muslim population, the majority of which was constituted by the converts. Hence, he argued that Islam could be preserved in India by keeping a physical, ideological and emotional distance from Hindus.

In 1757, the battle of Plassey ended the Mughal rule in Bengal, one of the richest provinces of the empire. But Shah Waliullah's followers refused to accept the defeat. One of them, Syed Ahmad Barelwi, inspired the long jihad against the British that began in 1825 and continued even after his death in 1831, on the battlefield at Balakote (Pakistan).

The doctrines of Jihad inspired the Muslims even in the revolt of 1857. The British felt an existential threat to their empire in India from the jihadi ideology of Muslims. Even the revolt of 1857 was categorized as Muslim revolt in many British policy circles of the time. As a result, after 1857, Muslim aristocracy was severely persecuted and was marginalized. Prominent Muslim clerics fled to West Asia. Muslim elites felt squeezed from both sides—the fellow Indians and the foreign British. The Hindus had the advantage of numbers and the British had the advantage of power. After the failed revolt of 1857, the British feared the revival of Mughal Empire because symbolically the Mughal king could still unite Indians of diverse faiths and traditions. They characterized Muslims as the followers of a war-like ideology of Jihad and preferred the Hindu elites in jobs. As a result of this, mistrust of Hindus, the basic tenet of Waliullah's distance theory, became fundamental to Muslim politics later when it tried to find its political space in the British Raj.

Meanwhile, in the age of overall decline, the Muslim clergy energized the despondent Muslims across the country from 1825 through 1870, i.e. the age of people's war. Waliullah's son Shah Abdul Aziz (1745-1824) issued an influential fatwa in 1803 that declared India a "house of war" and his son Syed Ahmad Barelwi (1786-1831) launched Jihad in 1825. He mobilized subaltern forces. Donations came from the poor Muslim homes and were carried by the network of clerics. When peasants in Bihar and Bengal ate a meal, they set aside a handful of uncooked rice for the jihadi fighters of Barelwi. This long war further confirmed in the British mind that Islam was a faith that inspired permanent war. For two decades after the revolt of 1857, the Muslims continued to be marginalized by the British.

In 1870, William Hunter, a British civil servant, wrote a seminal work,

"Indian Musalmaan" which advocated that the British should co-opt Muslims within the mainstream and the state system to counter the growing influence of Hindu elites who by then had started showing early manifestations of demands of the civil and political rights. Before that, Lord Canning, the last Governor General, had already written to Vernon Smith, the President of the Board of Control, in 1857, "As we must rule 150 million of people by a handful of Englishmen, let us do it in a manner best calculated to leave them divided (as in religion and national feeling they already are) and to inspire them with the greatest possible awe of our power and with the least possible suspicion of our motives".

British divide and rule policy used several options: competition for jobs, the lure of advancement through preferences in language, education and the economy. Administrative measures such as the partition of Bengal (1908) were also aimed to stoke the communal rivalry between the Hindus and Muslims. Another provocation for the discord was history. Both Hindus and Muslims sought refuge in an imagined past. Muslim intellectuals glorified invaders like Ghazni and Ghori as the icons of Islam in India and they encouraged Muslims to think that they were superior to Hindus. They denigrated Hindus as cowards. In contrast, Hindu intellectuals sought glory in the ancient history of India and the more recent Maratha warriors. They projected Muslim rulers as rapacious barbarians against non-violent and civilized Hindus. The upper-caste Hindu resurgence of the 19th century had a strong element of anti-Muslim bias, in which Muslims had to be punished for their real or imagined sins from the past. British historians presented ancient period as the Hindu period, the medieval period as the era of Muslim rule and persecution of Hindus and the modern period as the British rule, as an era of redemption.

The 19th-century nationalist movement leaders such as Bankim Chandra Chatterjee had overt sentiments of Hindu grudges against the Muslim invaders. The Shivaji and Ganesh festivals of Tilak galvanized Hindus. The other Maratha figures like Chapekar brothers and Veer Savarkar had overt sentiments of Hindu nationalism.

The alchemy of the rise of Hindu nationalism, the sense of loss after the Mughal decline and the persecution after 1857 fed the narrative of past superiority and the fears of future insecurity among the Muslims. The modernist Aligarh movement of Sir Syed Ahmad Khan that intended to integrate modern science with the traditional theology of Islam, and encouraged

Muslims to learn English and Western education, very soon, adopted separatist and exclusivist overtones. By 1888, Ahmad Khan had already become a separatist.

Muslim separatism nourished the foundation of Muslim League by the landed Muslim elites and the mercantile elites in 1909. It was supported by the British Viceroy Lord Minto to fracture the unity of Indian national movement gradually maturing under the leadership of Indian National Congress. The league demanded separate electorates for Muslims. Minority-appeasing concessions were given in the reform acts of 1909, 1919 and 1935. There was a systematic attempt by the British to inject the idea of the political domination and suppression of Muslim minority under the Hindu rule.

The fault-lines already existed and were becoming more prominent with the onset of representative social and political movements under the British Raj. British simply added fuel to the fire.

Gandhi attempted to unite Hindus and Muslims with the launch of Khilafat movement in 1919. He protested against the abolition of the Ottoman Caliphate by the British after the First World War. It was the first non-violent struggle launched for the restoration of the caliphate and his suzerainty over the holy cities of Mecca and Madina. The period saw flourishing of the Hindu-Muslim unity. Hindu leaders like Swami Shraddhanand were invited to address the Muslim crowds from the pulpit of Jama Masjid. The traditional and orthodox Islamic clergies including the Ali brothers of Punjab supported Gandhi in the khilafat movement. The caliph was the last symbol of the Muslim might against the sweeping onslaught of British and European imperialism, which is where it intersected with Gandhi's needs. Gandhi saw a great opportunity in this movement of uniting Hindus and Muslims and once unity was achieved, he promised Swaraj within one year. Only Jinnah, the founder of Pakistan, warned Gandhi about the dangers of mixing religion with politics.

However, Gandhi could not control the violence that was bursting in pockets across the country and he unilaterally withdrew the Khilafat movement in February 1922, to the utter shock of his Muslim supporters. The impact of failure was so deep that Muslims never really returned to Gandhi's Congress.

Perhaps, Gandhi's strategy was more of appeasing the traditional and orthodox Muslim clergy to achieve a unity that was ephemeral and superficial. In 1921, violent communal riots broke out in Kerala in which the Moplah Muslim peasants under the leader of Kun Muhammad Haji massacred the

Hindu landlords. Though Marxist historians opine that Moplah riots were a peasant revolt against Hindu landlords, the rebellion had very strong religious and communal overtones. Gandhi's silence over the Moplah atrocities against Hindus was questionable and smacked of political motivations. Later, violent communal riots broke in several parts of the country. The Hindu-Muslim rift was becoming more pronounced.

Arya Samaj's shuddhi movement of reconverting Muslims to Hinduism further communalized the environment and bitterness increased. Muslims had almost drifted away from the mainstream national movement. The civil disobedience movement of 1930 had very little Muslim League cadre participation. Swami Shraddhanand was killed by an extremist and the publisher of Rajkamal Prakashan (who published an objectionable book on prophet titled "rangeela rasool") was killed by Ilmuddin. Ilmuddin was hailed as a Shaheed and was given huge respect by the Muslim community across the country. Gandhi's controversial silence on the matters of increasing Islamic extremism might have appeared like an escape from the realities and planted seeds of distrust and insecurity among the Hindu majority also, about the motivations and the political honesty of their so-called secular Hindu leaders.

Later, Muslim separatism further developed into the demand for the separate nation of Pakistan in the Lahore session of Muslim League in 1940. The course of history, later, hardly needs any elaboration. India witnessed most horrifying communal riots in the wake of partition. The riots that accompanied partition, when it finally happened in 1947, led to more than a million deaths and saw savage sexual violence in which 75,000 women were raped.[38] The Independent India also witnessed horrifying communal riots—be it Gujarat (1969) or Bhagalpur (1986) or Assam (Nellie massacre) or Gujarat (2001) or the most recent Muzaffarnagar riots (2013).

Simultaneously, with the development of Pakistan movement, the Hindu nationalism had also perfected itself and emerged in an organized manner through organizations like RSS and Hindu Mahasabha. After India's independence, the differences on the issue of secularism were reflected on several occasions. Congress leader KM Munshi demanded that the government of free India should take the responsibility of constructing the temple of Somnath. Many others including Jawaharlal Nehru were against the idea and found it sacrilegious to the spirit of secularism. President Rajendra Prasad was in the favor of the reconstruction of Somnath temple. Finally, the temple project was financed by individual donations and a grant of five lakhs by the Government of Saurashtra (KM Munshi was the premier). President Rajendra Prasad, much to the chagrin of PM Nehru, attended the inauguration of the temple.

Conclusion

It appears that in practice, the concept of secularism in India is detached from its roots in India's culture, history, and civilizational ethos. In popular perception, it is perceived as a lofty ideal abused by political parties to condone extremism for electoral gains and also to shield their incompetence and corrupt practices. In the academic circles also, the Nehruvian model of secularism emerged as a dominant narrative, over the last 60 years, allegedly with the support of the establishment. Over the years, strong feeling among Hindus, centrist and the right-wing organizations have developed that the Marxist historians whitewashed the history of the persecution of non-Muslims especially Sikhs and Hindus, for their religious beliefs during the medieval period.

In politics also, the narrative of downplaying minority extremism suited well for the reason of vote-bank politics. Furthermore, the majority community's grievances also include that the Indian state follows appeasement policy and tolerates archaic and inhuman religious practices and social laws of the minorities through special constitutional privileges for minorities.

Such narratives fueled the growth of Hindu nationalist organizations which made an appeal to a large segment of Hindu society, in the absence of a rational, sensible and robust narrative of the "state" on the issue of secularism. Shah Bano case (1987) further exposed the weakness of the mainstream political parties on the subject of secularism.

Ram temple movement and Babri mosque demolition was another breakthrough in the history of Hindus and Muslims in India. After the episode of destruction, the radicalization of both the communities has increased resulting in more sensitive situations facilitating communal riots and the emergence of home-grown terrorist organizations. Terrorist organizations have used the incident of Babri mosque demolition to incite fears among the Muslim community and hatred against the Hindus.

Furthermore, country's so-called liberal-intellectual class has also not played an objective, impartial and fair role in the analysis and opinion building on the issue of Babri mosque. The comparisons of Hindu nationalist organizations with Taliban, ISIS[39] and the Fascist forces of yester years' Europe over sporadic incidents of communal riots, lynching and the demolition of Babri mosque are not only fallacious and display lack of intellectual depth but also smack of sleazy political motives and encouragement by foreign actors willing to pounce upon every opportunity to stoke communal fires in India and threaten India's security.

There is indeed a substantial amount of truth in the allegations against the Marxist historians and the Nehruvian discourse on secularism. There is something inherently wrong with the "discourse" of secularism in India. It appears highly biased. The roots of the idea of "secularism" as defined and practiced in our public intellectual, social and political space need to be entrenched in the civilizational ethos of India. Even today, the attitude of denial of extremism or conversion issues is prevalent. The recent ruling[40] of Kerala high court, that supporting ISIS ideology is not waging war against the nation, in a way encourages jihadi extremism or facilitates a defense which makes the possibility of secular counter-narrative very difficult.

In the post-independence India, the Muslim community has integrated well into the state system, social and economic mainstream. Their participation in politics, police, judiciary, and lower and higher civil service cadres has been impressive. The history of syncretic Sufi culture and Hindu-Muslim coexistence still has a deep imprint on the minds of Hindus and Muslims which is evident in the fact that Al Qaeda and ISIS have more or less failed in India. It is highly encouraging that India's multiculturalism and democracy have strengthened. The overall political and intellectual narrative is against extremism but not against the idea of communal harmony and minorities being an inalienable part of India's culture and history.

NOTES

1 Schuurman, Bart and Taylor, Max, "Reconsidering Radicalization: Fanaticism and the Link Between Ideas and Violence," *Perspectives on Terrorism,* February 12, 2018, Accessed October 5, 2018, http://www.terrorismanalysts.com/pt/index.php/pot/article/view/675/1347

2 Schmid, Alex.P, "Radicalization, De-Radicalization, Counter-Radicalization: A Conceptual Discussion and Literature Review," in ICCT Research Paper (The Hague: International Centre for Counter-Terrorism, 2013), March 2013, Accessed October 5, 2018, https://www.icct.nl/download/file/ICCT-Schmid-Radicalisation-De-Radicalisation-Counter-Radicalisation-March-2013.pdf

3 Schuurman and Taylor, op. cit

4 Horgan, John, "Walking Away from Terrorism: Accounts of Disengagement from Radical and Extremist Movements," Routledge, 2009

5 Schuurman and Taylor, op. cit., p. 7

6 ibid

7 Maskalunaite, Asta, "Exploring the Theories of Radicalization," *Interdisciplinary Political and Cultural Journal*, Vol. 17, No. 1/2015, Accessed October 5, 2018, file:///C:/Users/Owner/Downloads/Exploring_the_Theories_of_Radicalization.pdf

8 ibid

9 Roy, Olivier, "Who Are the New Jihadis?" *The Guardian*, April 13, 2017, Accessed October 5, 2018, https://www.theguardian.com/news/2017/apr/13/who-are-the-new-jihadis

10 Rambo, Lewis, "Theories of Conversion: Understanding and Interpreting Religious Change," *Social Compass*, 1999, Vol. 46., pp. 259-271. https://doi.org/10.1177/003776899046003003.

11 Wood, Graeme, "What ISIS Really Wants?" *The Atlantic,* March 2015, Accessed October 5, 2018, https://www.theatlantic.com/magazine/archive/2015/03/what-isis-really-wants/384980/

12 Maskalunaite, op. cit

13 ibid

14 ibid

15 Dalgaard-Nielsen, "Studying violent radicalization in Europe. Part II: The potential contribution of socio-psychological and psychological approaches", 2008, Accessed October 5, 2018

16 Maskalunaite, op. cit

17 Maskalunaite, op. cit

18 Maskalunaite, op. cit

19 Schuurman and Taylor, op. cit

20 ibid, p. 13

21 ibid

22 Pandya, Abhinav, "India and Pakistan Are Still Haunted by Partition and Its Bloodshed. Is That Fate Now Facing Israel and Palestine?" July 22, 2018, Accessed October 6, 2018, https://www.haaretz.com/middle-east-news/.premium-the-politics-of-partition-from-india-and-pakistan-to-israel-palestine-1.6291891

23 Schuurman and Taylor, op. cit

24 "What is Wahabbism? The Reactionary Branch of Islam from Saudi Arabia 'Said to be the Main Source of Global Terrorism,'" *The Telegraph*, May 19, 2017, Accessed October 6, 2018, https://www.telegraph.co.uk/news/2016/03/29/what-is-wahhabism-the-reactionary-branch-of-islam-said-to-be-the/

25 Crooke, Alastair, "You can't Understand ISIS if You Don't Know the History of Wahhabism in Saudi Arabia," *Huffpost*, August 2014, Accessed October 7, 2018, https://www.huffington post.com/alastair-crooke/isis-wahhabism-saudi-arabia_b_5717157.html

26 Teitelbaum, Joshua, Oschenwald, L, William, "Sauda Arabia," *Encyclopedia Britannica, inc.,* June 1, 2019 Accessed October 7,2018 https://www.britannica.com/place/Saudi-Arabia/The-Wahhabi-movement

27 Stanley, Trevor, "Understanding the Origins of Wahabbism and Salafism," *Terrorism Monitor*, July 15, 2005, Accessed October 6, 2018, https://jamestown.org/program/

understanding-the-origins-of-wahhabism-and-salafism/

28 "International Propagation of Salafism and Wahhbism," *Wikipedia*, https://en.wikipedia.org/wiki/International_propagation_of_Salafism_and_Wahhabism

29 Rakowski, Stephen, "How the 1979 Siege of Mecca Haunts the House of Saud?," *STRATFOR*, July, 2017, Accessed October 7, 2018

30 Trofimov, Yaroslav, "The Siege of Mecca," 2007, Accessed October 7, 2018

31 Crooke, op. cit

32 "Many Faces of Wahhabism," *STRATFOR*, July 2003, Accessed October 7, 2018

33 Wikipedia

34 "Indian Muslims Condemn Terrorism," *BBC News*, November 10, 2008, Accessed: October 7, 2018, http://news.bbc.co.uk/2/hi/7719059.stm

35 *Wikipedia*, Accessed October 7, 2018 https://en.wikipedia.org/wiki/Barelvi

36 Pandya, op. cit

37 Chandra, Satish, "History of Medieval India," 2007, Orient BlackSwan

38 Pandya, op. cit

39 *Asian Age*, November 2, 2015, http://www.asianage.com/india/historian-irfan-habib-likens-rss-isis-149

40 *India Times*, October 5, 2018, https://www.indiatimes.com/news/india/supporting-islamic-state-ideology-is-not-waging-war-against-the-nation-rules-kerala-high-court-354274.html

2

IS WAHHABI RADICALIZATION FINDING ROOTS IN INDIA?

A 360-degree View of Radicalization in India

Lately, changes even in the hinterlands of India are hard to miss. Sleepy and laid-back towns like Udaipur (Rajasthan) have witnessed huge protests and agitation in favor of Myanmar's Rohingya Refugees, not out of rational and enlightened concerns of internationalism but out of the feeling of being an inalienable part of the Ummah, the global Islamic brotherhood. The Persian "Khuda Hafiz" and the holy "Ramzaan" are gradually giving way to Arabic "Allah Hafiz" and "Ramadaan"[1] as a wave of Wahhabi proselytization sweeps across the country.

Islamic State of Iraq and Syria (ISIS) recruiters have been caught in cities like Jaipur and Ajmer, and several youngsters from relatively prosperous states like Kerala, Karnataka and metro cities like Hyderabad[2] have travelled to Syria to join ISIS (caliphate). In small cities like Udaipur, there have been violent clashes between the Deobandi and Barelvi-Sunni Muslims. In one of such incident,[3] a Deobandi Muslim's dead body was exhumed from the Barelwi graveyard and sent back to his relatives. In the border areas of Rajasthan, several new foreign-funded mosques have sprung up and the hardline Deobandi preachers can be seen engaged in intense proselytization.

The above-mentioned events are merely the symptoms of the malaise of radicalization that is much larger in magnitude and deep-rooted in nature. India is at the crossroads. Its Muslim community that has so far remained resilient to the global spread of Jihadi ideology is now showing signs of coming under its sway. Extremism is eating away at the roots of the South Asia's Barelvi school of Islam which is relatively liberal and based on Sufi traditions. It has 200 million[4] followers in South Asia. Named after the north Indian town of Bareilly where it was founded by Ahmad Raza Khan (1856-1921 AD), the Barelvis believe in personal devotion[5] to Prophet Muhammad through intermediaries called dervishes (saints).

The South Asia's Islam, despite a history of communal violence, has a unique and distinct nature that has evolved over centuries of interaction with other faiths in a multicultural society of South Asia. But, of late, India's version of Islam is facing an existential threat from the extremist ideologies like Wahhabism, Salafism and Deobandism—all are extremist and literalist schools of Islam. Such ideologies are both domestic and foreign. For example, Wahhabi School originated in Saudi Arabia and the Deobandis originated in India. The Deobandi school of Islam[6] is named after the small town of Deoband in North India where a Madrasa (religious school) was established in 1867. But the Deobandi tradition is much older than the above-mentioned madrasa. It was inspired by the teachings of orthodox Indian Sunni cleric Shah Walliullah of the 18th century.[7] Its founders were Qasim Nanotwi and Abdul Rashid Gangohi.[8] Deobandis are influenced by the Wahhabi practices and are often at cross with Barelvis for their Sufi practices. Deobandis believe that Muslim societies have fallen because they have come under the influence of the amoral culture of the western world. Deobandis (20 per cent of India's Sunni Muslims[9]) do not believe in the concept of nation states and they maintain that a Muslim's first loyalty is towards Islam. They follow an austere and fanatical version of Islam.

The general perception among the intellectuals and intelligence community in India is that the real threat lies in the challenge from Wahhabi radicalization financed and propped by Saudi money.[10] Most of the relevant stakeholders that include India's academic experts in geopolitics and security studies tend to ignore the role played by the domestic Islamic extremist groups like the Deobandis and their affiliate Tableeghi Jamaat. Recently, during a lecture on terror financing at a premier research institute of strategic studies in India, one was confronted by objections to the idea of grouping of Deobandi and Wahhabi ideology in one category. Academics in attendance were found to be lacking sufficient understanding of the indicators of radicalization, like the changes in dress patterns, social behavioral attitudes and the establishment of the large number of Wahhabi mosques with foreign funding. In fact, the level of awareness about these issues is so minimal that very senior police, foreign-service and administrative officials do not even know the basic differences between Deobandis and Barelvis. The intelligence officials at the district level are mostly unaware of the pan-Islamic forces spreading jihadi ideology.

Evidence-based quality research on the missionary activities of Deobandis and Wahhabis is hard to come by. Except for a few brief and superficial articles by Brookings,[11] Carnegie[12] and *The Hindu*,[13] an in-depth study on radicalization in India seems largely lacking. Few right-leaning online magazines do publish articles on the subject, but the veracity of the facts is in doubt, and the authors lack academic expertise and advanced research skills in the field of terrorism and counterterrorism.

At the Mumbai airport, in a casual conversation a senior Anti-Terrorist Squad (ATS) official mentioned about the rampant radicalization at the ground level going on unchecked in the name of protecting religious and cultural freedom of minorities. According to the official, any concrete action in such matters gets mired in politics, and ultimately the responsible police officer has to bear the brunt of opportunistic politicians and compromising superiors in the department. Furthermore, he informed that the state police do not have the requisite skills and infrastructure to detect such trends and take effective action against them.

Later, when the matter was raised with senior intelligence officials in Delhi, many of them agreed about the gravity of the problem. They said that because of the politically sensitive nature of the problem and in the absence of any national-level strategy and program to address radicalization, most of the time it is left to the state police to deal with such matters in a way that they deem fit, politically and pragmatically.

Understanding Radicalization

Before one begins to think of effective strategies to address the challenges from extremist ideologies, it is imperative to understand the true meanings and the implications of their teachings. Just like other religions, Islam has undergone several waves of reformist movements, such as Wahhabism and Deobandism. But unlike other religions, the reform movements in Islam have generally been anti-evolutionary in that their objective was to bring back the puritan and orthodox form of Islam. Wahhabism and, in essence, Deobandism too, aimed to bring back the Islam which prevailed in the seventh-century Arabia during the time of Prophet Mohammed and the reign of the first four caliphs, often referred to as the Golden Age of Islam.

Just like terrorism, there is a huge debate on the definition of radicalization. Getting into the complicated and abstract academic debates on the definition of radicalization is beyond the scope of this study. However, to create a degree of general awareness of the dominant academic trends on the subject under study, a brief overview of the concepts of radicalism, radicalization, extremism and fanaticism has been discussed in the first chapter of this book. For the purposes and interests of policymaking in the world of security and intelligence, it could be understood as a process where a text like the Quran is interpreted in a literal sense resulting in an exclusivist, hateful and intolerant mindset toward non-Muslims and those Muslims who do not subscribe to the literal interpretation of the text. Radicalization is a phenomenon which has a strong likelihood of transforming into violent extremism or jihadi terrorism. And, radicalization prepares a fertile ground for producing extremists.

For the purpose of this discussion, Wahhabism and Deobandism are being explored as ideologies and missionary projects whose end result is radicalization and preparing an extremist, exclusivist and intolerant mindset. Thus, any prudent counter-terrorism strategy would want the menace of radicalisation, to be nipped in the bud. And to do that, it will have to target those nurseries where radicalization takes place and the "software," i.e. the "ideological nukes" of terrorism.

The counter-terrorism strategy being advised is not against the lay Wahhabi Muslims or Deobandi followers. A majority of them and their religious institutions formally condemn the acts of terror. In fact, the first clue of Ahmedabad serial blasts of 2008[14] was provided to the police by a Wahhabi. But, the fact that they emphasize the literal interpretations of the Quran and especially those scriptural injunctions on jihad, which, if interpreted literally, have all the potential to fire the engine of terrorism merits serious attention. Furthermore, they condemn the syncretic and liberal Islamic strains like Sufism as apostasy and un-Islamic behavior that draws the Barelvi Sufi followers into their fold of rigid and austere Islam and results in eroding the secular base of our social existence.

What's in a Name?

Primarily, it must be clear that Wahhabis, Salafis, Ahle Hadith and Deobandis are simply different names for what is essentially the same message. The differences are minor, but the trajectory is the same. Those who think that because Deobandis do not explicitly incite any anti-national sentiments and have adopted a nationalist stand by opposing partition of India in 1947,[15] they must be dealt in a sympathetic manner, are either highly mistaken or engage in wishful thinking. Perhaps they do not understand the Deobandi ideology.

The main objection of the Deobandis to the creation of Pakistan was not on nationalistic but rather on religious grounds. Maulana Hussain Ahmad Madni, Jamaat-ul-Ulema-i-Hind chief, argued at a conference in Delhi in 1945[16] that confining Muslims and Islam-based governance in a small area is basically shrinking the space for the expansion of Islam and eroding the demographic base for missionary and conversion activities. Deobandis argued that in undivided India, they will have the opportunity to make entire country Dar-ul-Islam, whereas carving out a small Pakistan will restrict activities to a small geographical area, depriving them of the major chunk of the landmass and population base for their missionary activities.

STRATFOR's Fred Burton and Scott Stewart[17] inform that 14 Islamic radicals (12 Pakistanis, 1 Indian and 1 Bangladeshi) were arrested in Barcelona for planning to bomb targets in the city belonged to Tablighi Jamaat (TJ). They write that the TJ's name had figured earlier in connection with terrorism plots like October 2002 Portland Seven, September 2002 Lackwanna Six cases in the US, August 2006 plot to bomb airliners en route from London to the US, July 7, 2005, London Underground bombings (suspects Shahzaad Tanveer and Muhammad Khan[18]) and July 2007 (suspect Kafeel Ahmad) attempted bombings in London and Glasgow, Scotland.

All the apologists of Deobandis need to know that TJ, literally meaning "group for preaching," was established in Mewat, India, in 1927, and it stems from the Deobandi brand of Hanafi School of Islamic jurisprudence. It is the largest global Muslim network with its activities in 150 countries and about 70 to 80 million followers.[19] Its annual congregations held in Pakistan, India, and Bangladesh attract largest numbers of Muslim devotees after the Hajj. TJ has a very strong presence in the UK and lately, as confirmed by FBI, its presence in the US is also increasing at a rapid pace with about 50,000 people associated with TJ missions and their mosques operating in Texas, California and New York.

At face value, TJ is an apolitical, peaceful and egalitarian movement[20] that works at the grassroots level aiming to bring wayward Muslims to puritanical and orthodox practices of Islam. It asks its followers to engage first in internal jihad for spiritual purity rather than seeking political power to establish an Islamic state and imposing Sharia. However, STRATFOR briefs confirm that there are strong pieces of evidence of indirect connections between TJ and global/wider nexus of Deobandi extremist organizations like the Taliban, anti-Shiite groups and Kashmiri militants in Afghanistan, Pakistan and India respectively.

Through such links, the TJ cadres disgruntled with its apolitical stance get a chance to join jihadist organizations. Members of TJ's military offshoot, Jihad-bi-Al Saif, were accused of plotting to kill Pakistan's former PM Benazir Bhutto in 1995. When TJ cadres travel to Pakistan for training and religious congregations, they are lured by terrorist organizations like Al Qaeda (AQ), Harkat-ul-Mujahiddin, the Taliban and Lashkar-e-Taiba to join them. Superficially, TJ's message may be peaceful and benign, but ultimately it espouses the same conservative Islamic values that are adhered to by the above-mentioned militant organizations. Hence, TJ acts as a de facto conduit for terrorist organizations for recruitment. Besides, TJ is also used by terrorist organizations as a cover for travel and recruitment.

History of Wahhabism and Salafism in India[21]

Charles Allen in his paper, "The Hidden Roots of Wahabbism in British India,"[22] defines Wahhabism as the reformist theology first expounded by Muhammad Ibn Abd al-Wahhab in the 1740s in Najd and espoused by the local chieftain Muhammad Ibd Saud. Later, it was applied by the royal houses of Al Saud and Aal-as-Sheikh (descendants of Abd al-Wahhab) in an interdependent alliance that lasted into the 1920s, when Wahhabism became the established religion of the state. The unique selling point of Wahhabism is its literalism and the seriousness with which it reads and follows religious texts. This made it the most authentic throwback to the Islamic world of the seventh century, providing strong theological justifications that are difficult to counter as the ideological narrative, it presents to the Muslims.

The roots of Wahhabi history in India can be traced back to the days of British Raj. Charles Allen, in his paper, further states that the man credited with importing Wahhabism into India is Syed Ahmad of Rai Bareli (1786-1831) who returned from Mecca in 1824 to wage a jihad against Sikhs and return the political power to Muslims. Further, in 1871, Lord Mayo, the British Viceroy was assassinated by Sher Ali Afridi, a Wahhabi, for personal reasons (though still a matter of debate) in the Andaman Islands.

Syed Ahmad was born in Bareli in Awadh in the present-day UP, in 1786. He left home at the age of 13. In Delhi, he offered *bai'at,* the oath of allegiance to Shah Aziz. In 1812, while searching for ways to confront British, he joined the army of Nawab Amir Khan of Tonk. Amir Khan later settled issues with the British and avoided confrontation. Syed Ahmad had warned Amir Khan that British were treacherous and his prophecy came out to be true when most of Amir Khan's army was disbanded and he was reduced to a petty chieftain without power. Syed Ahmad returned to Delhi in 1818, where he was joined by Shah Ismail and Shah Abdul Hayy, his companions in Jihad against the British. They compiled a manifesto, the *Siratul Mustaqim,* or the Straight Path, in 1818. Its main theme was that contamination had affected Indian Islam, not only from Hindu practices but also from Sufism. The manifesto stated that Sufi superstitions and evil practices of Niyaaz and Nadhar (offerings of prayers and eatables in the names of dead) had polluted the Islam of its pristine purity. It also criticized large-scale wedding ceremonies, singing and dancing in weddings and celebrating birthdays of saints (Urs) and Prophet Muhammad. He compared Jihad to the heavenly rain which will bring salvation for Muslims and inspire non-Muslims towards Islam. He was true disciple of the hardline master Shah Walliullah. His fame was spreading in the plains of North India and he commenced his mission of building a Muhammadi order. Sir William Hinter, a British Civil Servant submitted a seminal report in 1871 on the Wahhabi revolt (the report later influenced British policy towards Muslims): "He (barelwi) appealed with an almost inspired confidence to the religious instinct, long dormant in the souls of the countrymen, and overgrown with superstitious accretions, which centuries of contact with Hinduism had almost stifled Islam." In 1821, Barelwi established an office in Patna from where they regulated and spread his network of missionaries in rural India. The Patna establishment was modeled on the lines of Islamic Caliphate: four vice-regents and a Shaikh-ul-Islam, equivalent to a state's head priest. He was presenting himself as Caliph to lead the Jihad. Several Muslims joined him in his Haj pilgrimage which he wanted to undertake before the Jihad. On his way to Calcutta to board the ship to Mecca, he preached his Islamic doctrines to large crowds of Muslim. He reached Mecca in 1822. In Mecca, Barelwi realized that the key elements of Wahhabi doctrine aligned well with his plans for the Indian Muslims. The key points of absolute consensus were unwavering faith in the Tawheed (indivisibility of God as a counterpoint to the Christian view which divided divinity into father and son), rejection of any intercession between Allah and his devotes by saints or Sufi mystics, rejection of the clergy that owed its loyalties to government than to God, hatred towards rituals that had become a corrosive overlay on faith, complete surrender to Imam who will guide the faithful in Jihad, and jihad against foreign infidels who had conquered Muslim lands. When he returned to India in April 1824, in the words of the veteran scholar MJ Akbar, "he brought back embers of a desert fire that had been doused but not extinguished."

On his return, he was given an Imam's welcome and was proclaimed Mahdi, promised by the Prophet. For two years, after his return, he propagated the message *Hindustan ... ast ke aktharash darin ayyam daru'lharb gardida* (India has become a house of war). Barelvi tried to cultivate good relations with Hindu chieftains like Hindu Rao, the Maratha chieftain and brother-in-law of Maharaja Daulat Rao Scindia. He sent a missive promising that after the British were ousted, the traditional rajas will get back their territorial possessions including the Hindu kings. He branded foreigners, i.e. the British, as the enemy number one who had come as traders and occupied India. His aim was to get the support of local Hindu rajas in the jihad against the British. He chose to fight the British at Balakote near Peshawar in North West Frontier Region. He even declared his journey from Barelvi to Balakote as Hijrat (Prophet's march from Mecca to Madina). On his journey to Balakote, he was greeted with donations by Hindu Rao at Gwalior and his former master Amir Khan at Tonk. But the Muslim kingdoms like Pir of Pagara, ruler of Baluchistan, within the vicinity of the Sikh kingdom avoided him. Most of them were waiting for him to set up a base in Balakote and then respond. However, the Durrani chiefs of Afghanistan saw a threat in him. They did not join his forces against the Sikhs. Barelvi was routed by the Sikh army of 10,000 led by General Budh Singh. The jihadis of Barelvi were hardly motivated by religion. Their main aim was plunder which ultimately led to their defeat.

In 1827, to generate more jihadi fervor, Barelvi declared himself Imam and demanded absolute loyalty in the name of Islam. Coins were struck in his name describing him as "Ahmad, the just, defender of the faith, the glitter of whose sword scatters destruction among the infidels." His ghazis called him "Amir-ul-Momineen" (commander of the faithful) and he became famous as Sayyid Badshah in the region. He described himself as caliph. From this newly acquired position of Caliph, he asked the rulers of Kashmir, Chitral and Bukhara to join him in the jihad. But once again religious fervor could not be of much help. Durranis made a deal with the Sikhs and stood out of the fighting in which 80,000 Jihadis of Barelvi were routed by Budh Singh's disciplined 30,000 Sikh soldiers. Earlier, Sikhs had tried to buy out Barelvi by offering him land worth the revenue of Rs. 900,000 but he was incorruptible. His Ghazis were, however, induced by the lure of money, not the religion.

After losing the battle, Barelvi borrowed Rs. 35,000 from Hindu moneylenders of Manara (Hund) at an exorbitantly high interest rate. He tried to collect taxes and impose Sharia rule in his territory which was bitterly resented by the local Muslim chiefs. The chiefs also did not approve of the political order in which the Ulema dominated the power circles. The chiefs preferred the Sikh rule better than the Sharia regime and Barelvi's jihad turned into a war between him and the Muslim chiefs. He was much weakened because of the internal strife. In his last battle in 1831, the Pathans once again deserted him and he was surprised by the Sikh army led by Sher Singh. Barelvi chose martyrdom. His burial is shrouded in mystery. There are stories of Sher Singh giving him an honorable burial, but some stories show that Sikhs interred his body, next day. The mysterious circumstances prevailing around his burial has given rise to the theories of his disappearance.

His martyrdom made him a symbol of jihad. Today, the shrines of Barelvi and his associate Shah Ismail in Balakote have become centers of pilgrimage. His death led to minor insurrections across India and generated a huge wave of sympathy for his cause. Barelvi perished but the seed of Islamic nizam or rule had been sown in the region, which is today a hotbed of activities of Taliban, AQ and Tahreek-i-Taliban Pakistan.

Earlier, during his visit to Mecca, Barelvi had met a Bengali from Chanpur, Nisar Ali, popularly known as Titu Miyan. After his return, Titu Miyan mobilized Muslim peasants against the oppressive Hindu landlords and set up a parallel government in the districts of 24 Parganas, Nadia and Faridpur.

Finally, British army defeated his determined troops in November 1831, killing Titu Miyan. Even after the deaths of Barelvi and Titu Miyan, Wahhabi activities continued across the country.

The problems for the British were not yet over. After defeating the Sikhs in 1848, the British took direct control of the North West region. They feared a revival of Muslim rule in Multan-Peshawar which had already become a stronghold of Barelvi-Wahhabis. Lord Hardinge, Governor General (1844-48), noted that Wahhabis had made a comeback in Multan and Peshawar in the vacuum created by the weakening of Sikh authority. He further noted that Wahhabi success in Punjab could revive the hopes of Muslims all over India, and therefore, Wahhabi threat needed to be eliminated at any cost. Even in eastern India, Wahhabis were instigating people against the British in Rajashahi district of Bengal.

Barelvi's jihadi successors were the brothers: Wilayat Ali and Enayat Ali, known as Patna Khalifas. In 1850, Wailayat Ali left Patna and reached Delhi with his 250 followers. He was gaining in popularity among local Muslims. His charisma had taken even the royal court under its grips. The then emperor Bahadur Shah was very impressed by the philosophical and spiritual insight of Wilayat Ali. British got suspicious. Wilayat Ali, sensing danger, left for Ludhiana before he could be arrested. In 1851, both the brothers were instigating people for treason on the Punjab frontier. In 1852, they tried to spark a revolt in 4th Native Infantry posted in Rawalpindi. During the revolt of 1857, Enayat Ali was active in Mardan Mountains in Peshawar. The sepoys of 55th Native Infantry revolted and joined the Wahhabis. Between 1850 and 1857, the British sent 16 expeditions involving 33,000 troops to suppress the revolt. Finally, after four more expeditions, Wahhabis were defeated in 1863 AD.

Even though real fighting took place in North-West Frontiers, the mood of jihad was prevalent among the Muslims across the country. TE Ravenshaw, the magistrate of Patna reported to Bengal government in 1865 that as long as Wahhabis continued their activities in the North West, the minds of Muslims in Bengal will remain disturbed. Further, he noted that all the groups like Fairazis, Hidaytees and Muhammadiyas wanted to restore Muslim power. The "*Risala-Jihad*" Wahhabi war song extolled the rewards of martyrdom and urged every Muslims to surrender his loyalties to the Imam and Islam. Wahhabi maulvis Niyamatullah and Karam Ali were active in the Gangetic plains. They disseminated teachings on Koranic prophecies about Mahdi and predicted the happening of the holy war under another Mahdi soon. *Jama Tafseer*, a Delhi newspaper (1867), opined that Indian Muslims had only two options after the failure of 1857—either Jihad or emigration out of the British Empire. It condemned those who wanted accommodation with the British as Munafiqeen (hypocrites). The newspaper urged all Muslims to join the jihad against the British. Wahhabi missionary network extended from the frontier region to Bengal in the east and Hyderabad in the South. They were successful in establishing contacts with the units of company's army and incited conspiracies and revolts in many cantonments from Punjab to Calcutta. Wahhabism had spread to small towns and villages. As pointed out by a British civil servant in 1865, "They (Wahhabis) have under the very nose and protection of the government authorities, openly preached sedition in every village of our most populous districts, unsettling the minds of the Mussalman population and obtaining an influence for evil as extraordinary as it is certain."[23]

Thus, it can be seen that Wahhabism had established a very strong base in India by late 1800s. It had captured the imagination of Muslim minds all over the country. The caliph/Imam had always been a very powerful emotional institution to mobilize people. That sentiment continued. It has already been discussed in the previous chapter how Gandhi's Khilafat movement (1919) in favor of Caliphate galvanized Muslims with determination and passion across the country.[8]

Quietist Salafis

Similarly, the "quietist Salafis"[24] (term popularized by Greame Wood in his article on ISIS, published by *The Atlantic* magazine; the question debated is that whether quietist salafis offer an alternative to violent salafis like ISIS) offer an extremist alternative to the violent Salafis like Islamic State (ISIS), but they are just as uncompromising as ISIS in their ideology. They are committed to expanding Dar-ul-Islam (land of Islam) with the implementation of brutal practices like amputation of limbs and slavery—but at some point in future. Their first priority is of self-purification and religious observance. They believe that Salafis must stay away from politics and must not disrupt governments as chaos creates hurdles in the goals of self-purification. Just like TJ, the conservative Islamic values they propagate nourish the fertile ground for ISIS-like extremist organizations, hell-bent on the literal interpretation of the text and restoring each and every single thing of the socio-political and religious system that prevailed in seventh-century Arabia.

Similarly, Deobandi cadres in India are strictly against worshipping *pirs* (saints) and tombs, and favour strict implement of the Sharia law in the matters of dress, worship and hygiene. These ideologies may not be violent in themselves, but they fire the forces of radicalization in a vigorous manner that helps in creating foot soldiers for the jihad, including lone-wolf attackers.

In India, hundreds of Wahhabi and Deobandi mosques are mushrooming across the length and breadth of the country, loaded with foreign money. Deobandi and Wahhabi preachers[25] have penetrated the remote areas of the country—a phenomenon that has largely gone unnoticed. There are visible changes in the dress patterns with an increasingly large number of women wearing the burka or the hijab. In the state of Kerala, one finds a process of Arabization that is reflected in language, eating habits, belief systems and dress code.

Christopher Jefferlot, in his article "The Saudi Connection,"[26] observes that Salafis are gaining a stronghold in Kerala. He notes that "According to a Saudi embassy cable in Delhi, millions of riyals have been reserved for the Islamic Mission Trust of Malappuram (Kerala), the Islamic Welfare Trust and the Mujahideen Arabic College in Palakkad. Two Islamic organizations have benefited from Saudi financial support: The Popular Front of India and the Social Democratic Party of India. Their names do not reflect their religious overtone, but they are propagating a Salafi version of Islam. He further opines that pan-Islamism is more pronounced among the local reform movements like Kerala Nadvathul Mujahideen which, though founded in India in 1950, developed through its connections with the Arab world.

It is also quite surprising that the appeal of Salafi and Wahhabi ideologies is higher among the educated classes, so much so that the Sufi practices are regarded as ignorant and superstitious beliefs of rural Mapilla Muslims. The southern states like Kerala, Karnataka and cities like Hyderabad have Muslims[27] comparatively better off politically, educationally and economically, and yet, have supplied the majority of ISIS recruits from India. This is not just a mere coincidence but the result of the long history of their connections with the Arab world through the vast Indian Muslim diaspora working in the Gulf that comes from these southern states.

Wiki cables suggested[28] that Saudi Arabia is uncomfortable with the rising Shia influence in India and Tehran's overtures. So in order to counter it, the Saudis are pumping in money to promote Wahhabism in India. According to a report attributed to the Intelligence Bureau (IB),[29] from 2011 through 2013, 25,000 Wahhabis visited India, conducted seminars in several states of the country. For these activities, USD 17 billion were spent.

According to journalist Vicky Nanjappa's[30] report dated August 1, 2014, there are 1.8 million Wahhabi followers in India. Nanjappa wrote, quoting an IB report about Saudi funding that USD 124 million was earmarked for setting up four Wahhabi universities, USD 62 million for building 40 mosques, USD 46.5 million for madrasas and USD 15.5 million for the upkeep of existing mosques. Tufail Ahmad,[31] an expert voice on radicalization, also quoting Nanjappa's report wrote in "The Muslim Times," "The radical Jamiat Ahl-e-Hadith, which first set up base in Kashmir, is spearheading Wahhabi operations across India." He further informs that after persuading around 400 mosques in Kashmir to follow its ideology, the Wahhabis have now zeroed in on Maharashtra and Kerala. Maharashtra government seems to be unaware about the rise of Wahhabism in the state but Wahhabis control over 40 mosques in Maharashtra. In Kerala alone, Wahhabis have taken over around 75 mosques.[32]

Graeme Wood describes ideologies like Wahhabism or Salafism the "pre-terrorists"[33] among us. It is evident from the long process of radicalization that went unnoticed in places like Kosovo, Catalonia and Pakistan. Today, Kosovo has become a major supplier of foreign fighters to the Islamic State. Since 2000, Kosovo has witnessed vigorous Wahhabi radicalization sponsored by petro-dollars.[34] Similarly, the recent Barcelona attack came on the back of Wahhabi radicalization in Catalonia,[35] and the outcomes of the decades of radicalization started by Zia-ul-Haq's regime in Pakistan need little elaboration. Today, in Pakistan the foot soldiers of Lashkar-e-Taiba and Jaish-e-Muhammad are joining ISIS[36] in large numbers, impacting the fortunes of the pro-establishment sub-contractors of jihad like Hafiz Saed.[37]

Discourse on Radicalization in India

In India's mainstream academic, public intellectual and media discourse on the issue of radicalization, one can witness strong political overtones. Even the statements of some historians and public intellectuals with high credibility tend to provide a protective cover to the ongoing phenomenon of radicalization.

Eminent historian Irfan Habib has drawn strong parallels between the Hindu nationalist organization Rashtriya Swayamsevak Sangh (RSS) and ISIS.[38] There were serious attempts by the civil rights activists of India to annul the death sentence of Yakub Memon, one of the main plotters of the Mumbai serial blasts of 1993. The issue was made into a political controversy after the suicide of Rohit Vemula who was protesting against the death sentence of Yakub Memon. His death sentence was projected as an agenda of right-wing nationalists. Some of the electronic media channels went to the extreme of portraying Yakub Memon as a non-violent believer of Mahatma Gandhi. Eminent public intellectual and historian Ram Chandra Guha tweeted, "Masood Azhar may never have turned his attention to India... were it not for the demolition of Babri Masjid."[39]

The examples mentioned above are just few out of the many such incidents where the apologists have played an extremely debilitating role that provides a defensive shield to extremism and terrorism. Such statements facilitate the radicalization of vulnerable and impressionable young minds by the religious extremist and fundamentalist organizations. Often such statements are misquoted and vigorously used by extremist forces. Various Jamaat-e-Islami WhatsApp groups in Kashmir quote Arundhati Roy's views on Kashmir and seek intellectual justification for their hate-mongering. At the same time, there is also the phenomenon of deniability regarding the radicalization going at the grassroots level. Barring a few newspaper reports and cover stories, the author did not come across any robust academic work on radicalization, while researching for this book. These newspaper reports have also started coming out only lately, especially after individuals from Kerala started joining ISIS. The issue of deniability and the negative role of the media and intellectuals have also been discussed in the case study on Kashmir that comes later in this book.

While interviewing some prominent security expert, the author came across the idea of "competitive secularism" that emerged after the demolition of Babri mosque in 1992. These elements maintain that after the Babri mosque demolition, the constitutional ideal of secularism was made into a political weapon to garner minority votes. Although it was used earlier also, there was an implied understanding in the political class that certain red-lines were not to be crossed in the interests of national security. However, in the post-Babri phase, the "red-lines" were violated with impunity and the phenomenon of "competitive secularism" became a dominant trend. It led to a kind of unhealthy competition between political parties to appease the minorities by going to unimaginable lengths. Extremist clerics were not only tolerated but also given public recognition and political platforms. Prominent politicians had shared dais with the now absconding extremist preacher Zakir Naik, on several occasions in the past. Legitimate security operations were questioned as fake encounters and many dedicated and honest cops were jailed. It led to strong demoralization of the security apparatus and the security forces. In the states of Bengal and Kerala, the practice of "competitive secularism" went to extremes for electoral gains and the results can be seen in the form of active jihadi hubs thriving in the two states. Ultimately, it nurtured a very robust pillar of the ecosystem of Islamism (discussed in detail in the Kashmir and Kerala case studies) constituted by the political class, intellectuals, media and civil rights activists. The dominant intellectual narrative was set by this "ecosystem" which discouraged an open-minded and honest inquiry into the evils of radicalization and religious extremism, in the academic and public space. Even the sane voices feared raising the issue of radicalization for the fear of being bracketed with the so-called right-wing extremist organizations.

These led to the neglect of systematic research in the field of radicalization. Even in the higher echelons of intelligence agencies, the attitude of denial prevailed. Most of the senior officers were trained in the cold-war era intelligence culture and were active in 1980s. They had an interface with conventional issues such as LTTE and Pakistan's nuclear program. The lack of field and scholarly insights into the new phenomenon of Islamic extremism and terrorism coupled with the deliberate appeasement policy followed by the political and intellectual class hindered the growth of a serious security and academic narrative on Islamic extremism and terrorism.

In India's academic world, now there is a frank recognition of the problem of radicalization as a result of the devastating terrorist attacks after 9/11 and our own experience of 26/11 that established the rise of transnational jihadist organizations such as Al Qaida and ISIS. However, primarily driven by the political agenda, there is a tendency to explain increasing Islamic extremism as a product of the communal politics of Hindu organizations and the ruling Bhartiya Janta Party (BJP) coupled with the alleged heavy-handedness of security forces against individuals suspected of involvement in terrorist activities. The perception prevails that after the National Democratic Alliance

(NDA) government was voted to power in 2014, the process of radicalization has increased as a reaction to current government's faith in the ideology of nationalism.

However, the matter is not as simple as it looks superficially. First of all, it's not the first time that the BJP has been voted into power. BJP-led NDA was in power at the Center from 1999 to 2004 and in several states of India, for last three decades. There was never a major drifting away from the Nehruvian consensus which essentially implied a governance model firmly rooted in the ideals of socialism and secularism (though in practice it always turned out to be minority appeasement for electoral gains). India's bilateral relations with Islamic countries remained strong and have even improved further under the current NDA rule. Further, the sheer size of the Muslim minority in India is so large (176 million and 14.6 per cent of India's population[40]) that no political party can even imagine of antagonizing or alienating the entire community. Given this, what is being touted as Hindu nationalism by the elitist-left-liberal cabal for dubious political and economic reasons is nothing more than the assertion and at times, aggression to correct the historical wrongs in myriad domains like politics, society, and the academic world. Furthermore, democracy in India has taken such strong roots and the institutions of state machinery are so powerful that any political party would always find it impossible to affect a sea-change in the tone and tenor of the basic model of governance. Secularism is embedded in the basic structure of the constitution and it is almost impossible to tamper with that as there are strong checks and balances.

Hence, the phenomenon of radicalization in India needs to be analyzed beyond the frame of reaction to the rise of Hindu nationalism. It has largely been the result of domestic religious reform movements like Deobandism and the influence of global Jihad. MJ Akbar in his seminal work "Tinderbox: The Past and Future of Pakistan" observes that radicalization in India dates back to 1740s, i.e. the decades immediately following the demise of Mughal king Aurangzeb. According to Akbar, Shah Waliullah in 1740s advocated that Muslims should isolate themselves from Hindus. He believed that Muslims lost power in India because of their going astray from the path of true Islam and adopting the practices of non-believing Hindus. MJ Akbar further informs in his book that Sir Syed Ahmad Khan, the great Islamic reformer, and scholar of the 19th century was the first one to visualize a separate homeland for Muslims.

In fact, India was the place where the Khilafat movement to restore the Caliphate was begun by none other than Mahatma Gandhi himself in 1919. The Muslim League, which demanded separate electorates for Muslims in 1908 and later demanded a separate homeland for Muslims, was formed in the year 1906, much before the RSS was formed. Jihadi outfits like Students' Islamic Movement of India (SIMI) and Popular Front of India were formed in 1977 and 2006, respectively, even before the BJP came into power. And, the Kerala Navdathul was active in the 1950s. If incidents of communal riots and terrorist attacks and the busting of the sleeper cells of terror outfits are taken as any measure of radicalization, then it is noteworthy that no any such major incident has taken place after 2014. In fact, India faced most lethal terror attacks before 2014, during the governments led by the Indian National Congress. The sleeper cells of Indian Mujahiddin (IM) and SIMI, both terrorist groups were busted during the Congress rule. After 2014, only 75 Indians[41] are known to have so far joined ISIS despite India having world's second/third largest Muslim population. Most of them come from non-BJP–ruled states like Kerala and Andhra Pradesh. Intelligence agencies have confirmed that the radicalization of these ISIS sympathisers was the result of the online propaganda. Surprisingly, non-BJP states like Kerala, Andhra Pradesh and West Bengal (WB) have witnessed events which indicate an increasing trend towards radicalization. Interestingly, the staunch anti-Modi regimes in Kerala and WB (Malda and Nadia districts)[42] have emerged as the hub of jihadi activities. In WB, the majority community has been officially restricted from celebrating the traditional festival "Durga Puja"[43] by the state authorities which appears more like an appeasement to Islamic extremism.

As expected, the central government has adopted a nuanced, cautious and balanced approach in dealing with Muslim matters. The government has initiated some courageous and reformist steps such as the banning of the Islamic practice of "triple talaq"[44] and the promotion of scientific education. Such steps are being opposed by a minuscule of orthodox Muslim clergies, communal leaders and dubious civil society activists with the support of "politico-intellectual complex" which includes some mainstream political parties and left-leaning intellectuals of India.

It deserves to be mentioned that India's large Muslim community is being held back from economic and educational progress by the orthodox and fanatic religious clerics because they want to maintain their hold over the community intact. However, to unravel the community's huge potential, the above-mentioned reformist measures are largely supported by the progressive elements within the community as timely and acutely needed.

The Prime Minister's efforts to popularize the relatively liberal Sufi Islam as an alternative to extremist ideologies of Islam has received a great backing from India's Muslims because a majority of them have been traditionally following Sufi practices. Initiatives like a bill against Islamic practice of "Triple Talaq" (divorce law), which is very derogatory to Muslim women, have received a strong support from the Muslim women.[45] The banning of Haj subsidy[46] (pilgrimage subsidy given to Muslims) has been seen as an end of appeasement politics of the past. While initiating these measures, the government has taken care not to make any changes or make overtly anti-Muslim decisions out of any bias or hatred.

In foreign policy arena also, contrary to everyone's expectations, the government voted in the favor of the UN resolution condemning US transfer of its embassy from Tel Aviv to Jerusalem.[47] Government's tough stand against terrorism and extremism witnessed in its tough approach against Pakistan, in Kashmir, in the crack-down on terror financing networks and effective actions in the matters of "love-jihad" (a phenomenon in which Muslim men marry Hindu women to convert them to Islam) and extremist clerics like Zakir Naik[48] have not been viewed as anti-Muslim in the popular perception. They appear more like part of the government's policy of zero tolerance on terrorism.

Interestingly, over the last four years, Shia-Sunni differences seem to have intensified in India. The Shia community has supported the government on the "triple talaq"[49] issue and shown a conciliatory gesture to solve the dispute over Babri mosque. It is also noteworthy that, in India, Shia community is relatively better off economically and educationally.

However, it must be admitted that the overtly communal rhetoric of some Hindu fundamentalist outfits and their leaders, and its portrayal by the mainstream media and intellectuals as a conspiracy against Islam generate a fear of sorts among the Muslims. The government's tough stance against terror, and reformist approach in the matters like "Triple Talaq," the stray incidents of murders of Muslims over beef-eating and love-jihad make it easier for the extremist religious clerics and communal politicians of the community to sound alarm-bells of a threat to their faith. Such espousal of fear by portraying the government as a threat to Islam, by a section of media, intellectuals, and politicians has led to the meteoric political rise of the hitherto fringe Muslim communal leaders.

In future, it is feared that further polarization of the Muslim community may happen in the electoral politics. But, will all this lead to jihadi extremism or not is still a debatable question. Only time will provide answers to such questions. And, we also need better measures and indicators to study the phenomenon of radicalization in India.

Conclusion

The caliphate is not something that is created in a vacuum. It is an end result of the long-drawn process of radicalization, with Wahhabism, Salafism, Deobandism and other hardline ideologies representing its different stages. Hence, it is high time for India to act and address the challenge of radicalization. This would need a well-coordinated and systematic approach with a sensible balance of centralization and decentralization in law-enforcement, intelligence-gathering, advocacy, community policing and special operations and in the overall counter-terrorism strategy. Involvement of different stakeholders from the intelligence community, civil society, law-enforcement machinery, academia and religious institutions could make the counter-radicalization initiatives more effective.

NOTES

1 Mahaprashashta, Ajay Ashirwaad, "Wahhabi Impact," Frontline, November 29, 2013, Accessed October 1, 2018, https://www.frontline.in/cover-story/wahhabi-impact/article5338336.ece? homepage=true

2 Jayshankar, Dhruva andPelangeli, Sara, "Assessing the Islamic State threat to India: It is a serious but manageable challenge," *Times of India*, May 6, 2017, Accessed October 3, 2018

3 "Wahhabi or Deobandi: Dead body exhumed from grave by the members of another Muslim sect," *The Siasat Daily*, February 14, 2016, Accessed October 1, 2018, https://archive. siasat.com/news/wahabi-deobandi-dead-body-exhumed-grave-members-another-muslim-sect-916715/

4 Barelvis, Wikipedia, https://en.wikipedia.org/wiki/Barelvi

5 http://www.barelwis.com/

6 "Deoband School," Encyclopedia Britannica, Accessed October 4, 2018, https://www.britannica.com/topic/Deoband-school

7 Ibid

8 Ibid

9 "Islam in India," Global Security.org, Accessed October 10,2018, https://www.globalsecurity.org/military/world/india/religion-muslim.htm
10 Nanjappa, Vicky, "How Saudis funded Rs 1700 crore for Wahhabi influence in India," *One India*, June 25, 2015, Accessed October 10, 2018, https://www.oneindia.com/india/wikileaks-how-saudi-funded-rs-1-700-crore-wahabi-influence-india-1787820.html
11 Jayshankar and Pelangeli, op. cit
12 Jaffrelot, Christophe, "Saudi connection," *The Indian Express*, July 5, 2017, Accessed October 10, 2018, http://carnegieendowment.org/2017/07/05/saudi-connection-pub-71444
13 Mahaprashashta, Ajay Ashirwaad, "Wahhabi Impact", *Frontline*, November 29, 2013, Accessed October 1, 2018, https://www.frontline.in/cover-story/wahhabi-impact/article5338336.ece? homepage=true
14 Mahurkar, Uday, "Why are Indian Wahabbis angry with Modi for promoting Sufism?" Dailyo, April 7, 2016, Accessed October 8, 2018, https://www.dailyo.in/politics/muslims-narendra-modi-islam-world-sufi-forum-wahhabi-shia-sunni-deoband-rss/story/1/9961.html
15 Dhulipala, Venkata, "How the Jamait-Ulama-i-Hind fought against the partition of India?" *The Caravan Magazine*, March 2015, Accessed October 8, 2018, http://www.caravan magazine.in/vantage/madani-jinnah-muslim-league-partition
16 Mahurkar, op. cit
17 Stewart, Scott and Burton, Fred, "Tablighi Jamaat: An indirect line to terrorism," STRATFOR, January 23, 2008, Accessed October 8, 2018, https://worldview.stratfor.com/article/tablighi-jamaat-indirect-line-terrorism
18 Madhan, Kuhan, "India's pluralistic Islam under seige," *The Diplomat*, April 29, 2016, Accessed- September 27, 2018, https://thediplomat.com/2016/04/indias-pluralistic-islam-under-seige/
19 Stewart and Burton, op. cit
20 Alexiev, Alex, "Tablighi Jamaat: Jihad's stealthy legions," *Middle East Quarterly*, January 1, 2005, Accessed October 8, 2018, https://www.meforum.org/articles/2005/tablighi-jamaat-jihad-s-stealthy-legions
21 Akbar, MJ, "Tinderbox: The Past and Future of Pakistan," 2005, Accessed October 8, 2018
22 Allen, Charles, "Hidden Roots of Wahhabism in British India," World Policy Journal, 2005, Accessed: October 10, 2018
23 Akbar, op. cit
24 Wood, Greame, "What ISIS really wants?" The Atlantic, March 2015, Accessed: October 8,2018, https://www.theatlantic.com/magazine/archive/2015/03/what-isis-really-wants/384980/
25 Nanjappa, op. cit
26 Jaffrelot, op. cit
27 Jayshankar and Pelangeli, op. cit
28 Nanjappa, op. cit
29 Ibid
30 Ahmad, Tufail, "India must urgently act against Wahhabi organizations," *The Muslim Times*, December 17, 2015, Accessed October 8 2018, https://themuslimtimes.info/2015/

12/17/india-must-act-urgently-against-wahhabi-organisations/

31 Ibid

32 Ibid

33 Wood, Greame, "What ISIS really wants?" *The Atlantic*, March 2015, Accessed October 8, 2018, https://www.theatlantic.com/magazine/archive/2015/03/what-isis-really-wants/384980/

34 Gall, Carlotta, "How Kosovo was turned into fertile ground for ISIS?" *The New York Times*, May 21, 2016, Accessed October 8,2018, https://www.nytimes.com/2016/05/22/world/europe/how-the-saudis-turned-kosovo-into-fertile-ground-for-isis.html

35 Vidino, Lorenzo, "The roots of the Barcelona attack," *Foreign Affairs*, October 11, 2018, Accessed October 11, 2018, https://www.foreignaffairs.com/articles/spain/2017-08-25/roots-barcelona-attack

36 "Why Pakistan's jihadists are joining ISIS, deserting Hafiz Saeed's Jamaat-ud-Dawa?" Zee News, December 30, 2015, Accessed October 8, 2018, http://zeenews.india.com/news/world/why-26/11-mumbai-attacks-mastermind-hafiz-saeeds-jihadists-are-joining-isis_1839893.html

37 "Hafiz Saed entering Pakistan's politics is part of army's plan to bring militant groups into mainstream," *First Post*, September 16, 2017, Accessed October 8, 2018, https://www.firstpost.com/world/hafiz-saeed-entering-pakistan-politics-is-part-of-armys-plan-to-bring-militant-groups-into-mainstream-4050193.html

38 *Asian Age*, "Historian Irfan Habib Likens RSS with ISIS," November 2, 2015, Accessed September 27, 2018 http://www.asianage.com/india/historian-irfan-habib-likens-rss-isis-149

39 Pandya, Abhinav, "In search of a credible opposition," *HW News Network*, June 2, 2018, Accessed September 27, 2018, https://hwnews.in/columnist/abhinav-pandya/search-credible-opposition/43827

40 "Islam in India," Global Security.org, Accessed October 10, 2018, https://www.globalsecurity.org/military/world/india/religion-muslim.htm

41 Tacimer, Natalie, "India and the fight against Islamic State, "*The Diplomat*, June 14, 2017, Accessed October 8, 2018, https://thediplomat.com/2017/06/india-and-the-fight-against-islamic-state/

42 Dutta, Saikat, "Is West Bengal becoming a new Jihadi terror hub?" IDR, October 17, 2014, Accessed October 8, 2018, http://www.indiandefencereview.com/news/west-bengal-is-a-new-jihadi-terror-hub/

43 "Durga puja, Muharram", *Indian Express*, September 21, 2017, https://indianexpress.com/article/india/mamata-baerjee-durga-ouja-west-bengal-durga-idol-immersion-muharram-calcutta-high-court-4852938/

44 Saif, Khalid, "What is triple talaq or instant divorce?" *Al Jazeera*, August 22, 2017, Accessed October 8, 2018, https://www.aljazeera.com/indepth/features/2017/05/tripple-talaq-triple-divorce-170511160557346.html

45 Kulshreshtha, Parul, "Majority of women support abolition of triple talaq," *The Citizen is Hopeful*, February, 19, 2017, Accessed October 8, 2018, https://www.thecitizen.in/index.php/en/NewsDetail/index/7/9970/Majority-of-Muslim-Women-Support-Abolition-of-Triple-Talaq

46 Ghosh, Avantika, "Haj subsidy discontinued: credit for phasing it out goes to supreme

court," *Indian Express*, January 17, 2018, Accessed October 8, 2018, https://indianexpress.com/article/opinion/haj-subsidy-haj-india-modi-mukhtar-abbas-naqvi-5027434/

47 Mitra, Devirupa, "Indian government to earlier line, backs UN Resolution against Trump's Jerusalem call," December 22, 2017, Accessed October 8, 2018, https://thewire.in/diplomacy/india-unga-resolution-jerusalem-trump-us-israel-palestine

48 Saif, Khalid, "Why India wants to arrest the preacher?" *Al Jazeera*, May 21, 2017, Accessed October 8, 2018, https://www.aljazeera.com/indepth/features/2017/05/india-arrest-preacher-zakir-naik-170521055023564.html

49 Roy, Debayan, "Shia personal law board for Triple Talaq ban, issues Fatwa against cow slaughter," News 18, April 6, 2017, Accessed October 9, 2018, https://www.news18.com/news/india/shia-personal-law-board-issues-fatwa-against-cow-slaughter-bats-for-triple-talaq-ban-1368547.html

3

Radicalization Case Studies in Kerala and Udaipur, and Mapping ISIS and AQ in India

After the cases of Indians joining ISIS and AQ came to light, there has been a surge in academic studies, journalistic inquiries and policy documentation into the phenomenon of radicalization. However, the prism of investigation has been very narrow. Serious scholarly research into jihadi radicalization in India has primarily focused on studying the footprints of transnational and domestic terrorist organizations affiliated to them, terrorist attacks, terror modules and Pakistan's proxy support to such activities. It may however be emphasized that jihadi radicalization is a social problem, a religious issue and at its roots, a psychological problem. It has a critical dimension of age; mainly, it is the youth who are coming under the grips of radicalization. The phenomenon of terrorism comes much later. ISIS, AQ, Hizbul Mujahiddin, LeT and Indian Mujahiddin are the final end products of the entire process of radicalization. The process of jihadi radicalization may happen as a result of Islamization, as it happens through the ecosystem of Islamism (graphical representation provided in the Kashmir case study). Radicalization is also, therefore, a near-final stage of the idea of Islamism in practice.

In the following case studies, an attempt has been made to explore the social, political and religious forces aiding processes of jihadi radicalization at the grassroots level. The focus in these case studies is the operational dynamics of the ecosystem of Islamism in Kerala and Udaipur (Rajasthan). The case studies will be followed by an overview of the ISIS phenomenon in India.

CASE STUDY 1: KERALA

In any random guess, Kerala, the God's own country will be the least likely state to send the largest Indian contingent to Syria and Afghanistan to join ISIS. However, in 2016, when 21 residents of Kerala suddenly escaped to join ISIS in Syria and Afghanistan, it took everyone by surprise. The land of lagoons, beaches, spices, economic prosperity, impressively high-literacy rates and decades of atheistic-communist rule, was beyond anyone's imagination to emerge as a stronghold of Islamic extremism and terrorism.

Before delving deeper into the fertile ground of Islamic extremism and terrorism that was nurtured in the state over the last three decades, it would be useful to state a few simple manifestations of radicalization happening at the social and individual levels:

1) For past several years, the young Muslims have been migrating to Yemen and Sri Lanka to live a life of piety, learning and peace. In Sri Lanka, those who are trained in Islamic studies establish communes of Salafi Muslims and encourage the residents to live a life of learning and piety. The motivation behind such migrations is the religious injunction that a true Muslim should migrate from Dar-ul-Harb (meaning house of war) to Dar-ul-Islam (meaning house of peace/ Islam/Deen).[1]
2) In Malappuram district (70 per cent Muslim population), during Ramazan, not only the Muslim shops but also shops owned by Hindus and Christians remain closed during the day. Non-Muslims complain of being threatened and intimidated if they try to open the eateries during Ramazan.[2]
3) Ansiba Hasan, a Muslim actress, faced abuse from Islamist trolls for posting a photograph with a Buddhist monk, and actor Asif Ali was abused for posting a picture from Lords with the caption, "Lord's— The Mecca of Cricket."
4) During 2015, Ramazan, mid-day meals were stopped in Kozhikode after some Islamic clerics issued a fatwa. Indian Union Muslim League, which calls itself a secular party and had been a member in UPA government, did not oppose the fatwa.[3]
5) In recent years, several cases have been reported of public transport not running on Eid-ul-Fitr and Eid-ul-Azha. Public spaces like shopping malls have separate prayers rooms for Muslims (not for the

other communities). Muslim houses have their names in Arabic whereas the non-Muslim houses have their names in Malayalam. Muslims pray in offices and schools.[4]

6) Overt religiosity is witnessed in the form of an increasing number of people keeping beards and donning skull-caps and burqas. Strong Arabic influence in dress patterns, lifestyle, eating habits and other cultural traits can be seen in places like Malappuram, Palakkad and Kasargod. Ironically, there is a street named Gaza in a Kasargod municipality.[5] Salafi communes have been set up in Kozhikode, Kasargod, where the inhabitants stay aloof from modern lifestyle. There is no electricity and television. They rear goats and camels and endeavor hard to replicate the 7th-century Arab world of prophet's times.
7) The installation of the statues of Tunjethu Ezhuthachan (father of the Malayali literature) and actor Prem Nazir had to be abandoned because of opposition of the Kerala Jammah Council and the local Muslim inhabitants. Even the bust of Mahatma Gandhi could not be installed in Lakshadweep because of opposition of the local Muslims. In Cochin University, breasts of a plant figurine had to be pruned after the members of Jamaat-e-Islami (JeI) became influential in the teachers' organization. This reflects the same mentality which Taliban exhibited while destroying Bamiyan Buddha.[6]
8) In 2010, a professor's hand was chopped off by Popular Front of India (PFI) members in Ernakulum for setting up a paper that allegedly insulted Prophet Muhammad.[7]
9) With strong petro-dollar funding, Wahhabis have established control over 40 mosques.
10) In the neighboring state of Tamil Nadu, an Islamic congregation was held at Tiruchirapalli by Tamil Nadu Thowheed Jamaat which passed 18 resolutions declaring "dargah worship," astrology and other syncretic rituals as shirk. It was held in complete secrecy and projected as a religious reform initiative. Such movements of the "oneness of Islam" have become very common in Kerala and Tamil Nadu.[8]
11) The cadres of religiously inclined JeI (6158 in 2008 to 8753 in 2016), PFI (45,000 in 2009 to 120,000), Kerala Navdathul Mujahiddin (25,200 to 65,200 till date) and Tamil Nadu Thawheed Jammat (20,000 to 100,000 in the last decade) have risen in large numbers.[9]

12) In Malappuram, school students approached the principal to change biology teacher because she was a woman. On several occasions, children have refused to go to schools because they did not want to mix up with students of other faiths. Young men have been indulging in bitter fights with sisters over the Islamic way of dressing and living.[10]
13) Large-scale conversion camps are being run in the state by PFI, Niche for Truth and Peace International Foundation. NIA has brought forth cases of love-jihad in which Hindu and Christian girls are wooed to convert. Among those 17 individuals who suddenly disappeared from Kasargod and Palakkad to join ISIS, many were new converts.[11] Clear links between such conversions and terrorism can be deduced.
14) Community leaders like Abdul Nasir Madhani, accused in Coimbatore and Bangalore blasts, command huge popular support in Kerala. According to senior journalists, Abdul Nasir Madhani is politically and socially so powerful that it is almost impossible to arrest him. The political parties resort to appeasement of Islamic extremists for the fear of losing votes.
15) Intelligence agencies have reported that ISIS middlemen hired the services of two religious centers in two northern districts and one southern district of Kerala to recruit impressionable and vulnerable youngsters. As on March 30, 2018, 90 Keralites were thought to have joined ISIS. Of this, 16 have been killed in raids by US and other forces fighting ISIS in various countries in the Middle East, since 2016. Of the 90, 21 were from Kasaragod and 38 from Kannur. At least 12 Keralites had joined ISIS from Bahrain.[12]

A Look at the History

Having examined some of the overt manifestations of jihadi radicalization in Kerala, a look at the history of Islam in Kerala can be helpful in understanding the current dynamics of radicalization.

Unlike North India, Islam in Kerala came directly via sea along with the Arab traders. It was a peaceful arrival without large-scale forcible conversions, plundering activities, genocides and temple destruction. It did not interfere in the then existent social customs and the culture. Due to its mild and somber nature, the king of Calicut Zamorin allowed any newborn on Friday in a Hindu family to convert to Islam. However, unlike North India, Islam in Kerala was almost the same version that prevailed in the Arab world. Since it came directly via sea route, it was not diluted in its journey to Kerala. In the North, it took nearly 400 years for Islam to establish itself in the heartland of North India. The conquerors occupied many territories on the way; faced fierce resistance from the local population at every level, i.e. social, cultural and political, and in the process the nature of Islam was transformed. The interface with non-Islamic cultures and the compulsions of ruling over non-Muslim majorities convinced the Islamic rulers that stringent dictates of the faith would have to make way for political and cultural accommodation.

In Kerala, the arrival of Islam did not lead to any communal frictions with the Hindu population. The naval commanders of Zamorin were all Muslims because Hindus considered it "impure" to travel across the seas. The first signs of conflicts surfaced after the arrival of Portuguese under Vasco-da Gama in 1498 AD. His arrival brought the Islam-versus-Christianity conflict to India. Indian Hindus supported Muslims in the conflicts because of their years of peaceful co-existence and the reasons of trade.

The phase of aggressive and violent Islam began with the invasion of Hyder Ali and his son Tipu Sultan, in Malabar in 1771 and 1789, respectively. Those invasions were turning points in the history of Islam in Kerala. Hyder Ali plundered and desecrated the Hindu temples for gold. His son forcibly converted Hindus and Christians, made Hindus eat beef and gave lands of Hindus to the new converts to Islam. With that, the Hindu-Muslim relations strained in Kerala.

In 1921, Malabar rebellion against the British and Hindus had clear overtones of communal conflict between the Hindus and Muslims. In the Marxist historiography, the movement is depicted as an agrarian issue, hiding the inconvenient fact that British efforts to rehabilitate the Hindus displaced from Malabar led to fierce resistance from Moplah Muslims. There were violent and brutal clashes between the two communities. The Moplah leader Kun Muhammad Haji declared a caliphate and even issued passports. He is still regarded as the hero of Sunnis in Kerala. Many Keralites supported the Khilafat movement of 1920. The roots of global Islamism were strongly present in the Kerala of 1920s also.

After 1973, the petrol prices quadrupled and the Salafi/Wahhabis flourished with the huge petro-dollar funding. Their activities in the state intensified in the field of proselytization, education and social work. The demolition of Babri mosque played a significant role in an upsurge in Islamic radicalization in Kerala.

Lately, the activities of Islamic extremist organizations have also received a boost from the growth of Hindu nationalism. There have been bitter clashes between the Rashtriya Swayamsevak Sangh (RSS) and fundamentalist and anti-national activities. Popular Front of India (PFI) cadres in Kerala. Cases of beef-lynching, communal riots and ghar-vapsi movement have been vigorously used by extremist organizations to recruit and radicalize young minds.

The Ecosystem of Islamism

There are broad parallels between the patterns of the ecosystem of Islamism in Kerala and Kashmir. However, there are two significant differences: in Kashmir, the Kashmiriyat stood as a firm guard against radicalization, while entities based in Pakistan drove the financial, political and ideological engines of the ecosystem.

The core of the ecosystem in Kerala comprises a network of several self-funded Salafi charitable organizations—the schools, orphanages and hospitals run by them, extremist Islamic clerics and the large-scale conversion drives. The core also includes radical Islamic social and political movements like PFI and its political front, student-wing affiliates and branches spread across the country. Besides, the sleeper cells and terror modules of domestic and transnational terrorist organizations also find their place in the core. Large-scale foreign funding from the gulf countries through hawala channels and donations and the private local funding (zakat donations) supply the necessary fuel to the core.

The middle layer is constituted by (a) lay followers, (b) mainstream political parties resorting to the appeasement of extremist organizations for vote-bank politics and (c) the social media. The last layer comprises pseudo-human rights activists, intellectuals/academicians and media professionals who either sit silently on such issues or provide an intellectual shield to extremism in the name of promoting diversity, minority rights and the freedom of expression. It also comprises heavily politicized state intelligence and police machinery, the narrative of global Islamism, contemporary geopolitical and religious events in West Asia, and the fringe Hindu extremist groups. Furthermore, robust historical, economic and cultural ties with the Gulf region promote rampant Arabization, facilitating a cultural "disconnect" from the indigenous cultures. It nourishes the financial base, extremism and the puritanical roots of the ecosystem, thus providing an overarching umbrella for the growth and expansion of the ecosystem, domestically and internationally.

Popular Front of India[13]

Formally, PFI is an organization that claims to engage in social work. However, in essence, it is an Islamist organization which firmly believes in political Islam. It is based in Kerala but rapidly expanding to the other states of India such as Karnataka, Tamil Nadu, Maharashtra and Manipur. PFI came into existence in 2006 but its origins go back to 1993. After the demolition of Babri mosque, National Development Front (NDF) was created in Kerala to protect the interests of the Muslim community. In public domain, NDF portrayed itself as an organization devoted to socio-economic reform work for Muslims, but its extremist and violent nature was exposed when some of its members were arrested for rioting and murdering eight Hindus on Marad beach in Kozhikode in 2003. There were allegations of it having links with foreign intelligence agencies, but these could not be proved.

NDF's activities were limited to Kerala. It was decided to create a nation-wide organization. In 2006, PFI was established by merging like-minded Karnataka Forum for Dignity and Manitha Neethi Pasarai (Tamil Nadu). Over the next three years, Goa Citizen's Forum, Rajasthan's Community for Social and Educational Society, West Bengal's Nagarik Adhikar Suraksha Samiti, Manipur's Lilong Social Forum and Andhra's Association for Social Justice merged with PFI. However, it remained most active in Kerala. PFI's other units are (1) All India Imam Council (Religious Scholars' unit) and (2) Satya Sarini, educational and charity organization based in Malappuram, actively engaging in conversions.

PFI's links have been established with the banned terrorist outfit Students' Islamic Movement of India (SIMI), an extremist organization formed to counter western materialistic influences in India and to encourage Muslims to live according to the Islamic code of life. A large number of PFI office bearers had strong links with SIMI, before it was banned in 2001.

PFI has been strongly communalizing the social space in Kerala. Intelligence sources maintain that PFI actively promotes jihad through campaigns and lectures in jihad. It encourages its cadres to kill right-wing Hindu activists in return for the rewards in afterlife. However, it has not staged large-scale terrorist attacks against civilians like Indian Mujahiddin. It is still regarded as an extremist outfit, not a terror outfit.

Involvement of PFI in Attacks and Murder Cases

1) In 2010, Professor TJ Kurien's hands were chopped off for setting up a paper, allegedly offensive to the Prophet Muhammad. In this case, a charge-sheet was filed against 37 PFI members.
2) According to a Kerala government report submitted to the Kerala High Court in 2012, PFI cadres were involved in 27 murder cases, mostly of RSS and CPI-M cadres.
3) Another report of the Kerala government (2014) stated that 86 "attempts to murder cases" were registered against PFI.
4) Furthermore, PFI members have indulged in the murders of RSS cadres in Mangaluru, Bengaluru, and Mysuru (all in Karnataka).

Forced Conversions and Links to Terrorism

A "sting" operation by a national television channel claimed that AS Zainaba, President of National Women's Front (PFI's Women Wing) facilitated and organized forced religious conversions to Islam at Satya Sarini, a charity trust run by PFI. A Kerala police report submitted to NIA alleges the involvement of PFI in 97 cases of forced conversions. NIA is conducting investigations into the cases of forced conversions.

In the course of interrogation of Shahjahan, an IS sympathizer from Kajiranghode in Kannur (deported from Turkey after a failed attempt to cross into Syria), it was revealed that ten members of PFI had gone to Syria to participate in the jihadi wars of ISIS. Later, PFI clarified that its members who had joined ISIS had left PFI as the organization had differences of opinion with them.

According to an National Investigation Agency (NIA) report[14] (Kannur PFI Case, Case No. RC-05/2013/NIA/KOC), PFI had organized a terror training camp in the forest of Kannur. NIA seized swords, country-made bombs and ingredients for IEDs. PFI has actively aided the emergence of Kerala as the breeding ground of terrorists, extremists and radicals. The well-known Wagamon camp of SIMI was held in Kerala in 2007[15] and PFI backed it. The camp charted out the strategy to beat the ban on SIMI, and after the meeting, Indian Mujahiddin was born.[16]

Since 2017, Ministry of Home Affairs has been considering banning PFI because of the number of cases against PFI under Unlawful Activities Prevention Act (UAPA). However, PFI has categorically denied any links with terrorist organizations.

Nevertheless, the organization is under heavy scrutiny for its alleged involvement in suspicious terror activities. However, it has been difficult for the intelligence agencies to substantiate its allegations against PFI with concrete and admissible evidence. Besides, the PFI and its political wing Social Democratic Party of India (SDPI) have substantial social and political clout in the state. With a dedicated cadre of 25,000 members and 300,000 sympathizers, it can swing the Muslim vote.[17] Mainstream politicians in the state have either been in an appeasement mode for electoral reasons or in the denial mode. Recently, CPI (M) maintained silence on the SDPI's alleged involvement in the murder of student leader Abhimanyu. On the question of banning PFI, CM Pinrayi Vijayan stated that it is not the policy of the government to ban any communal or terrorist outfit. "Any outfit that creates riots in India and divides society, then it should be banned and that organization is the RSS,"[18] he said. Furthermore, he argued that organizations like PFI could not be dealt with a ban, but with legal action. However, India's legal arsenal to tackle radicalization and extremism is woefully inadequate.

Columnist Vicky Nanjappa, an expert on Islamism in Kerala, in a telephonic conversation stated that PFI was infiltrating into the feeder outfits of the mainstream political parties. Their clear agenda was propagation of Political Islam, and that they are trying to run a parallel government. In July 2009, PFI's Dar-ul-Khada asked Muslims to approach only Sharia courts, not the judicial courts. In the pursuit of the agenda of Political Islam, PFI has intensified its activities in the university campuses, through its student wing Campus Front of India (CFI).

In the above context, a review of Rashid Abdullah's[19] video-tape on PFI can be very useful in understanding the real intent and nature of the organization and its operations. Rashid Abdullah was the chief recruiter of IS in Kerala. Currently he is believed to be in Afghanistan with IS Khorasan. He hails from Kasargod and was the mastermind of the mass escape of 16 people from Kasargod and Palakkad to join IS.

In the 70th edition of the voice message, he informed that NDF, the precursor of PFI was formed to wage jihad against the oppressors of Muslims in CPI (M) and RSS. The aim of NDF was jihad-fi-Sabillah (jihad in the path of Allah) and the lectures of the NDF classes included exposure to alleged instances of tortures that Muslims underwent in different parts of the country. NDF lectures also prepared the cadres to make sacrifices and pledge strong loyalties to the organization.

However, according to Rashid, NDF lost its Islamic character after the formation of SDPI, the political wing, which wanted to bring Sharia rule through democracy. He added that due to the dilution of its Islamic character, many PFI cadres shifted loyalties to IS. Currently, there are many IS supporters in PFI, but they are lying dormant. PFI leadership knows about it and is trying to bring them back or prevent them from joining IS by issuing circulars stating that PFI will return to its original Islamic nature. PFI leadership is also convincing them by saying that PFI will join IS later, and that PFI is the Islamic State of India.

From the views of Rashid, it becomes clear that the real agenda of PFI is political Islam and the organization is inherently at the crossroads with liberal values, secularism, democracy and multiculturalism. It also becomes clear that the boundaries between non-violent and violent extremism in PFI are very fluid. Furthermore, it also becomes clear that in the event of any major religious upheaval in West Asia or the rise of a transnational terrorist organization like IS, PFI can be a reliable and effective platform for its induction in India. With its expanding network across the country, PFI was likely to emerge as an efficient conduit for the dissemination of religious/ideological extremism across the country.

Its efficiency is also strengthened by the fact that it has strong links with Maoist and Dalit organizations, and it has many front organizations doing social work in the form of NGOs. One such entity, the Green Valley Foundation, was used for secret meetings for planning anti-national activities.[20] As already mentioned, PFI's camouflaging as an entity working for social welfare and human rights imparts it a robust shield of deniability.

Finances and Gulf Links

A 19-page dossier prepared by the NIA[21] and submitted to the Home Ministry gives in-depth information about the financial networks of PFI. PFI has collected funds from various frontal and religious organizations based in Gulf countries. It has used organizations like India Fraternity Forum (IFF) and Muslim Relief Network (MRN) to receive funds from Gulf countries. The dossier also mentions that PFI leaders like Abu Backer A. Sayed and EM Abdul Rahman camouflage their visits to Gulf countries as visits undertaken for Haj/Umrah or meeting their expatriate relatives, but the real aim is to collect discreet funds. MRN, a PFI NGO received funds from Islamic

Development Bank (Jeddah) and has links with World Assembly of Muslim Youth (WAMY) and National Confederation of Human Rights Organizations. Besides, PFI has also received donations from Muslim business people in Karnataka and Kerala. PFI also collects membership fee (INR 10-1,000) and Ramadan donations. The funds raised were used for setting up its studio "Thejas" at Bangalore PFI office and to publish books and magazines. The funds were also used for organizing terror training camps and train its cadres in martial arts, indoctrination camps, religious conversions, IEDs and making crude bombs.

Other Religious, Semi-religious and Muslim Political Organizations

The organizations like Kerala Navdathul Mujahiddin (KNM)[22] (1950) have been active for seven decades. KNM has several feeder organizations such as

1) Ithihadu Shubbanil Mujahideen (ISM)
2) Mujahid Students Movement (MSM)
3) Muslim Girls & Women's Movement (MGM)

KNM calls itself a Muslim reform organization with the objective of a social and religious renaissance. KNM runs many educational institutions (schools and colleges), nursing colleges, medical colleges, hospitals, and clinics and generously funds various social welfare programs for Muslims. KNM started with the objective of cleansing the Sunni Islam in Kerala of the corrupt practices like polytheism and bringing back the Islamic practices and traditions of the Arab world. The ideological line of KNM is Salafism.

It has already been discussed in the previous chapter that Salafism is a puritanical school that believes in a rigid and literal reading of the Quranic injunctions, and is against all kinds of syncretic practices that result from the interaction with other cultures. It believes in very strict interpretation of Sharia. However, KNM categorically rejects IS as a representative of Muslims. KNM calls itself a reformative organization. Its reforms include steps like allowing a woman to lead the prayers in the mosque, and conduct the prayers in Malayalam. However, nowadays, KNM is facing opposition from those Salafi Muslims of Kerala who returned from Saudi Arabia after their religious education. They find the Salafi groups and practices of Kerala to be a deviation from the original Arab version. As a result of such dialectics, organizations like KNM are compelled to gravitate towards a higher degree of puritanism to keep their survival intact. Also, it can happen if they claim and portray themselves as the most austere Salafis.

KNM does not have direct links with any terror organization and it does not have any proven role in radicalization. KNM was the first organization to take the lead in the campaign against the religious fascism of SIMI and Abdul Nasir Madhani, according to Dr. Abdul Majid Salahi,[23] President of KNM's youth wing. KNM took a firm stand against IS. However, the fact that it believes in Salafi ideology raises many concerns. The people in Kerala who joined IS have strong Salafi leanings.

Regarding Salafism in Kerala, it may be noted that the strong cultural and economic linkages with Gulf brought an early exposure of Salafism in Kerala. With that, came vigorous Arabic influence in belief systems, culture, eating habits, social customs and dress patterns. In the previous chapter, data about large-scale Saudi funding of Wahhabism in India through investments in schools, colleges and social work is also mentioned.

However, it needs to be highlighted that there is a tendency of vague generalization in the academic and security establishment's approach towards Salafism, not just in India, but across the world as well.

Saudi Arabia is a Wahhabi country and ISIS also believes in Wahhabism. However, Saudis have categorically rejected IS and called it a terrorist organization. In India, Salafis follow the Saudi line, so jumping straight away to categorize anything remotely associated with Salafism as terror-related may not be a rational approach. In various interactions with Salafi clerics, it was found that none of them was advocating any radical/extremist violent action (the Salafi definition of Jihad is discussed in the Kashmir case study and in Chapter I). It appears that Salafism is the most misrepresented and abused ideology and the reasons are inherent. Salafism has rejected schools of jurisprudence like Shafai, Hanfi, and Hanbali. Their emphasis is on the rejection of any middlemen who interpret the original Quranic texts. For them, there is no intermediary between Allah and a Muslim. Such an attitude rules out the possibility of enlightened and intellectual guidance in matters of religion. Secondly, they believe in literal interpretation and want to bring back the Islam of the times of the Prophet and the first four Caliphs. Now, when it comes to practical matters of life, re-living history is very difficult. The whole idea is very vague and vulnerable to use and abuse according to personal whims and fancies, and political and religious interests. Thirdly, Salafis emphasize a great deal on ritualistic aspects and the external symbols of religion like skull-caps, ways of worshipping and beards as compared to the spiritual essence of Islam. It ends up in Salafism projecting a very standard and uniform version of Islam. There is no place for diversity, local beliefs and local cultures. Often, it happens that the ground realities and local customs are at odds with the literalist Salafi interpretation. The literalist interpretation of Salafis ends up in developing a very exclusivist and a fundamentalist mindset, as a result of which the lay followers under the influence of Salafism tend to shun away any intermingling with those who do not subscribe to their belief systems. In Kerala, one can find several Salafi individuals setting up Salafi communes where Salafi-only Muslims get to practice their version of Islam in the company of like-minded people. However, the distorted understanding of the instruments of Salafi theological apparatus—jihad, caliphate, political sovereignty of Allah and divine duty—turns such communes anti-national and against pluralistic societies.

All the traits mentioned above may actively facilitate in nourishing a mindset that is prone to violent extremism. One can find several incidents showing that wherever Salafism has gone, it coincided with the rise of violent extremism. For example, advent of Wahhabis in Kosovo in 2000s led to the rise of Islamic extremism and one can see that once a liberal country, Kosovo sent a large number of foreign fighters to IS. However, there is no necessary causal link between Salafism and terrorism. Hence, an attitude that generalizes all Salafis as extremists and terrorists may be fallacious.

In India, there is a tendency to pass the entire burden of extremism and terrorism on Salafis. No doubt, Salafism has generated a "disconnect of sorts" with the local syncretic and liberal traditions of Islam, but there is also a need to realize that even with the so-called liberal and syncretic schools of Islam, there has been a problem of extremism, bigotry and orthodoxy in social matters. Communal tensions between the Hindus and Muslims have existed for long, much before the so-called Salafi storming of the Islamic citadel. Even among the local Muslim community and religious organizations, the tendency to equate extremism with Salafism is strong. The reasons for such identification are also due to the doctrinal differences with Salafis, rivalry for social space or rather power struggles (the loss of social and political clout). The local schools try to garner the support of state establishment in an unequal battle to counter Wahhabis who usually have more financial, political and intellectual heft as compared to the local Islamic schools.

Hence, an objective investigation into radicalization and terrorism needs to have a nuanced understanding of the doctrinal aspects of the different schools of Islam and the socio-political and economic dynamics of the entire matrix. Academics and policy experts need to understand the religious/doctrinal roots and then transcend into the other domains of radicalization such as the role of new communication technologies, psychological factors and the demographic factors.

Indian Union Muslim League[24] (IUML) of Kerala, which has been partner in the former UPA and the Congress-led governments in Kerala, alleges that there has been a concerted attempt to target Salafis in the state whereas the problems of extremism, communalization and violence emerge from Political Islamist organizations like JeI, PFI and SDPI. PFI leader P Koya[25] categorically refuted the claims of IUML, stating that individuals who joined IS were all having Salafi leanings. Here, it needs to be highlighted that JeI is not a subscriber of the Salafi line of thought (JeI believes in Hanafi School of Islamic law). JeI's agenda is one of political Islam based on the teachings of Maududi and Saiyyid Qutb. However, this needs to be seen in the light of the analysis of PFI mentioned above. Furthermore, it also needs to be mentioned that IUML is linked with Indian National Congress (main political rival of left-based parties in Kerala) and the JeI and PFI have managed to gain the support of left-sympathizers in Kerala with their strong anti-imperialistic stand.[26]

Salafi radicalization is done through the unquestioned use of theological apparatus whereas the SDPI and JeI radicalize the youth psychology through politicization. JeI intends to transform Islam into a political movement. The spiritual leaders of Kerala like Sayyid Alawi are appropriated into the political domain by selectively reading and citing their teachings. JeI focuses on the most radical segments of their teachings. Sufi scholars and their teachings are employed by JeI for more radical political ends. JeI has always argued that government jobs are *shirk* (apostasy) for Muslims and they must resign from them. Even on public issues affecting Muslims, JeI proposes radical solutions rather than democratic methods. JeI's ideology and modus operandi does not align well with plurality and the idea of secular nationhood. This is the reason why youths under its influence are attracted to jihadi extremism. Though JeI in Kerala was publicly forced to disown the Maududi ideology, internally it has never been able to abandon it entirely.

Furthermore, JeI uses Marxist frameworks to politicize Islam. It places

Islamic socialists like Malcolm X, Franz Fanon, Ali Shariati and Alija Muhammad on a higher pedestal than the traditional scholars like Al-Imam-Shafi, Abu Haneefa-Al-Kufi, Al-Imam-Malik and Ahmad-Ibn-Hanbal. JeI has even called the Muslim socialists like Malcolm X, Al Usthad which implies that it gives them a spiritual status. As a result of this, the young followers of JeI are lured to the Marxist thinkers mentioned above and they adopt the latter's methods and thinking without considering the context.

In the words of the scholar Anwar Haneefa,[27] "while the Salafis engender radicalization through the socialization of theology engendered through lucid canonical readings, non-contextual approach to histories and linking themselves to *shahadat* (martyrdom) and *jannah*, the Jama'at-e-Islami tries to radicalize the community through more politically-oriented creations of allegories, histories, and textual readings."

Another node in the ecosystem of Islamism in Kerala is the Peace International Schools, a chain of schools run by Peace Foundation headed by a physics teacher–turned evangelist MM Akbar. Among the 21 missing individuals of Kerala, five were associated with Peace International Schools, including Abdul Rashid, the chief recruiter of IS in Kerala, currently with the IS Khorasan, in Afghanistan. Peace International has been accused of inducing forced conversions to Islam. Mariyam, Yahya, Esa, Fathima and Ayesha (Indian nationals who escaped from Kerala to join IS) were all associated with Peace International and were all recent converts to Islam. There are notions that the organization encourages "love-jihad" where Muslim men woo the girls of other faiths to convert them. However, MM Akbar has denied his involvement in conversions. He said that those who want to covert willingly could contact him through an organization called "Niche of Truth" but Peace International does not actively encourage conversions.

Having reviewed the various religious and political nodes of the ecosystem of Islamism, it becomes essential to understand the technological nodes of the ecosystem. The advent of rigid and reactionary ideology of Salafism has been accompanied by the opening and strengthening of the global/international dimension of Islam in Kerala. Since Salafism has its roots in West Asia, naturally the focus of spirituality and divinity for a Salafi follower lies in West Asia, and not anymore in the local Sufi shrines. This generates a strong bond of affinity with the global Islamism. Plus, Salafism comes as a rich, affluent, modern and tech-savvy version of Islam. All the events in the global Islamic movement are communicated through internet and social media. Salafis have innovatively used social media to engage the youth. The popularity of Zakir Naik is largely due to his methods of communication. The youngsters who follow Salafism often abandon the traditional Sunni scholars for religious guidance and depend entirely on the internet for religious education and enlightenment. Internet is full of distorted interpretations of religious injunctions. Impressionable minds fall prey to them. Besides, IS propaganda videos are very innovative and imaginative in engaging youth. In one of the videos, Rashid Abdullah, the chief recruiter of IS, lured the young men of Kerala by mentioning that life was very comfortable in IS territories. Everything from chocolates to meat and biscuits was available. He further said that everything that Sharia allowed was permissible in IS territories. In other propaganda videos, the interviews of Indians who joined IS were shown and even members of Indian Mujahiddin were interviewed in some videos.

Some Observations

Islamist radicalization in Kerala is multidimensional. For those with purely theological yearnings, religious lectures and classes are there providing justification of Jihad and caliphate. And for young minds with intellectual yearnings and interest in political philosophy, JeI gives a political and Marxist framework to Jihad. For those young minds seeking thrill in technology and adventure, engaging social media content is there and for those weak and vulnerable young minds searching identity and anchorage, there is a strong infrastructure for conversions and indoctrination. Some important points to note are as follows:

1) Most of the radicalized minds are young minds. They come from well-to-do families (upper middle class) and are well educated. The 21 individuals who escaped from Kasargod and Palakkad to join IS were doctors, engineers and IT professionals, and management graduates.
2) If one analyses the statements of the young Keralites who joined IS, they appear as individuals with strong religious convictions. For example, Ayesha said in her YouTube video, "This whole life is a test... I had to break my mother's heart, my father's heart... But what matters most is Allah." The message sent by the 21 escapees said, "We reached our destination. There is no point in complaining to Police... we have no plans to return from the abode of Allah."[28]

3) Furthermore, many of the radicalized ones were new converts to Islam. One often comes across the narrative of migrating from Dar-ul-Harb to Dar-ul-Islam[29] among the radicalized segment. In Salafi communes, the tendency is to create 7th-century Arabia. The residents rear goats and camels. Interaction with non-Salafis is shunned away. They have a firm belief that in the first place, Salafi battle is with those Muslims who have deviated from the path of Quran, and then with the infidels. From the facts mentioned above, it becomes clear that there is a strong use of religion and the theology of Islam in radicalizing. Hence, the statements by senior politicians that radicalization in Kerala has nothing to do with religion are completely baseless and an exercise in denial. Additionally, it also becomes clear that the problem of radicalization has deep psychological roots. Rich, young men and women appear to be searching for an identity. They are trying to find spiritual anchorage by opting for over-religiosity. Their weak and vulnerable mental state forms a perfect ground for extremist indoctrination, online or in person.

   Hence, counter-radicalization and de-radicalization policies should have multiple ways and multiple levels of engagement. Broad-based and generic policy measures are also needed, but along with them, zeroing in on the individuals susceptible to radicalization can be immensely helpful.

   The intelligence agencies focused on individuals who were on the verge of radicalization. Such individuals were subjected to constant surveillance and social media monitoring. Their operations were highly successful as they prevented many youngsters from joining IS. Such radicalized individuals were immediately contacted and their parents were also informed about them. Then, through counseling many of them were brought back to the mainstream.
4) Mainstream political parties and the religious organizations try their best to downplay the threat of radicalization. Few cases have already been mentioned earlier in the chapter. The IUML, which claims to oppose extremism of PFI and IS, supported Zakir Naik because of his belief in Salafi ideology. These inter-organizational and inter-sectarian differences on religious narratives and the appeasement policy of politicians are extremely detrimental to the communal harmony of the state. In the long run, the interplay of these organizations will

only help in creating confusion, hindering the clarity in understanding and realizing the gravity of the threat posed by Islamic radicalization in Kerala.

5) So far, no major terrorist incident has taken place in Kerala in spite of the modules of IS, AQ and Indian Mujahiddin working in the state. According to informed sources, major terrorist incidents have not occurred in Kerala because the extremist elements want to protect Kerala as a safe haven. They want to keep their sleeper cells active and use the immunity and peace in the state for organizational work, strategic planning and meetings, and seeking shelter.
6) The youngsters also get attracted to Wahhabism because of its opulence. The prosperity of the Salafi muslims returning from the Gulf attracts the youngsters. Salafis have strong presence in education, medical sector and social work. The youngsters also get lucrative financial, career and educational opportunities from their Salafi affiliation. Besides, by associating with groups like PFI and SDPI, the youth feels politically and socially empowered. The rise of Hindu right-wing in the state has also emerged as a factor strongly aiding the growth and expansion of organizations like PFI and SDPI.

Conclusion

1) Firm and effective action against the ecosystem of Islamism in Kerala is needed. Especially organizations like PFI need to be banned. There arises a concern that if PFI is banned, its activities may become more secretive and lethal and the security agencies may not have sufficient capabilities to suppress them. One would like to recommend that such organizations need not only to be banned but rendered ineffectual or rather neutralized by taking strong military, financial and legal measures. All instruments of statecraft must be employed to liquidate such radical organizations.
2) The problem is one of serious national security issue and merits urgent attention. If avoided or delayed, it will become a menace for Indian establishments in the near future.

CASE STUDY 2: UDAIPUR

The Udaipur case study presents a strange cocktail of nascent Hindu radicalization and the early footprints of global Islamism.

The analysis presented below is based on interactions with the state police officers, intelligence officers, local politicians and community leaders and academicians. It also includes author's experience as the Strategic Advisor to an NGO based in Udaipur (2016-2018). Besides, before 2004 through 2010, he worked at the grassroots level in the development sector in Rajasthan. These provided him with rich experience and exposure to the state's political, social and security dynamics.

Udaipur is a Tier-2 sleepy town located in South Rajasthan. It is a historical city and a famous tourist destination known for its rich medieval history and robust forts. Every year lakhs of foreign and domestic tourists visit the city to get the feel of history which is very well preserved.

To understand Islamic radicalization in Udaipur, a brief overview of its history can be immensely helpful. In fact, such an approach should be recommended for almost every district and region selected for study of this nature. Since India has a huge diversity in culture, religions and social systems, an effective counter-radicalization policy has to be decentralized to the extent of imaginatively engaging the diversities mentioned above. To that end, the local histories and socio-cultural patterns need to be studied by policymakers and those tasked with implementation. It would surely help them in addressing the challenges of radicalization.

Udaipur was a center of Sisodia Rajputs of Mewar in Rajasthan. The Sisodias of Mewar were powerful Rajput rulers who even laid claims to the throne of Delhi. The famous legend of Jauhar of Padmini, the queen of Rana Ratan Singh of Mewar, is said to have taken place in Chittor, the capital of Mewar. Rana Sanga defeated the Muslim ruler Bahadur Shah of Gujarat. Rana Sanga had also defeated the Lodi King Ibrahim Lodi of Delhi (1518, Battle of Khatoli) and emerged as the strongest contender to the throne of Delhi.

When Babur invaded India, Sanga expected him to return to Kabul after defeating Ibrahim Lodi. However, Babur decided to stay back and emerged as Rana Sanga's rival. Sanga fought with him in the Battle of Khanwa (1527 AD) near Agra. He had a huge army (80,000-100,000), and in numbers, Babur's army of about 12,000 soldiers was no match to his. However, better technology, generalship and military skills led to Babur's victory. In the battle, Babur had taken the title of Ghazi and invoked all his *Begs* (nobles) to support him in the religious war against an "infidel" king.

Babur's grandson Akbar sent Mughal armies against Udai Singh, the king of Mewar. In the battle of Chittorgarh, 30,000 farmers were butchered by the Mughal armies in the fort of Chittorgarh (1567 AD). Jaimal and Fatta of Udai Singh's army fought bravely and died on the battle field. Udai Singh's son Maharana Pratap continued the Rajput battle with Akbar. The famous battle of Haldighati was fought in 1576 AD. Rana Pratap used guerilla tactics in the battle. Though he could not win a decisive victory, Mughal armies under Man Singh suffered heavy losses. However, recent research by Dr. Chandra Prakash Sharma of Mohanlal Sukhadia University, Udaipur, suggests that Rana Pratap had actually won the battle. Akbar's army could not subdue Maharana Pratap in his lifetime. After his death in 1599, the battle continued in the reign of Jehangir and Pratap's successors.

The jauhar of Padmini, the battles of Sanga and Pratap (mentioned above), and the valiant Rajput resistance against the Mughal armies are deeply embedded in the sub-conscious of the people of Mewar. The influence can still be felt strongly in the folklore, social customs and rituals. Furthermore, the battles are also remembered as the brave and heroic Hindu struggle against Muslim armies. The prime motivations were political but there was an element of communal-cum-religious identity as well. It is still a matter of academic debate as to what extent the battles mentioned above had the element of communal pride and identity. Simultaneously, there were incidents of Muslim warriors fighting alongside Rajput armies against Mughals. Pathan warrior Hakim Khan Soor was the commander of Rana Pratap. Later, Pathan mercenaries were brought and settled in the villages of Mewar. In Kumbhalgarh village, right outside the robust fort of Kumbhalgarh, Pathans were settled. They were employed in military services by the local chieftains.

Today, in almost every village, one can find Muslim households. Besides Pathans, which are considered of superior status (almost similar to Rajputs), there are Muslims from the lower castes also. The Dawoodi-Bohra Shia Muslims are also settled in Udaipur and the neighboring Vagad region. They are economically affluent and mostly engaged in business. Religiously, they are orthodox and conservative, but in social matters and inter-faith relations they are believed to be very cordial and liberal.

Rajputs have been dominant in the region since 8th century AD. The relations between Hindus and Muslims were friendly. There were many common deities that both the communities worshipped. In villages, the relations were more than friendly. Though there were incidents of minor communal frictions, those were exceptions. After Babri mosque demolition in UP (1992), the scenario began to change in Udaipur. Communal riots became frequent and violent. The connectivity of the local population and the local politics with the national and international politics enhanced and the results of the national and international issues concerning Muslims had their impact in Udaipur also.

It is informally learnt that these days there is a heavy influx of Deobandi preachers in Udaipur. One can find numerous Tablighi Jamaat cadres visiting Muslim households in cities and villages and convincing the local Muslims to subscribe to their views and stop worshipping Mazaars (tombs of dead ones). When asked, the surprising response of one of the security officials was that Barelwis are "common Muslims looking similar to ordinary Indians whereas Deobandis have more Arab like looks and they appear intimidating." Later, one found out that even senior police officers were hardly aware of these two schools of thought.

According to local intelligence officials, over the last decade, Deobandis have found some social space in Udaipur. Along with the religious missionary work, Deobandi cadres also help poor Muslims financially in setting up small businesses. Karawada town in the district has emerged as a hub of Deobandi activities. Furthermore, Deobandis have an edge in getting access to the local Muslim populace. They recite Namaz in Barelwi mosques after the Barelwi Imams whereas the Barelwis would not do that. The increasing popularity of Deobandis has led to frequent clashes with Barelwis. There was an incident in which a Deobandi's dead body had to be exhumed from a Barelwi graveyard! Such tensions are increasing these days. But the number of Deobandi followers is still small in comparison to the Barelwis. So far only around 150 Muslims have joined TJ. However, this data was not accurate and the knowledge of ground reality of the officials was rather superficial. During a field study, it was found that new mosques were coming up not just in Udaipur city but also in the rural areas.

Activities of the Ahle-Hadith sect have also come to notice in Udaipur. A lavish new mosque built in Saudi style has come up in Udaipur. A total of 99 per cent of the local Muslims are Barelwi Sunnis and their economic conditions do not vouch for the construction of such a large mosque unless there is a mass shift from Barelwi school to Ahle-Hadith. However, such a shift has not yet taken place. Besides, there is a Bohra community which is economically affluent but they are Shias and not expected to finance a Salafi mosque. In a small village in the nearby Dungarpur district, a lavish Salafi mosque has come up in the last few years. Interestingly, the local Muslims are from Ghanchi community and their economic status is very poor. Hence, financing of such mosques, silently coming up in small cities of North India, is a serious issue. Additionally, it is worrying that local intelligence and police officials and the district administration in general are not even vaguely aware of these developments. In most cases, they had no idea and they showed little interest in the issues of Salafi and Deobandi activities in the region.

Over the last decade, the visits of clerics from puritanical Islamic schools have become more frequent. The local Muslim residents listen to their lectures in the mosques. The trend of watching Islamic religious television programs on PTV and Gulf-based TV channels is on the rise. Along with these developments, incidentally some more disturbing trends have come up in recent years. The principal of a local Christian missionary school complained that Muslim students have started asking for long holidays on Eid on the pattern of Diwali and winter breaks. They are also pressuring to allow them to keep beards, create a separate prayer room in school for them and adjust the school schedule according to their religious requirements. Furthermore, in many cases they refused to sit with girls and Shia students. Some of them even objected to girls wearing jeans and western clothes. The school principal was extremely worried because these things never happened earlier in Udaipur. Besides, in social spheres the healthy interaction between Muslims and Hindus evident in the form of joint celebration of festivals like Diwali, Holi and Muharram, which was a norm earlier, appears to be on its last leg, these days. The large segment of Muslim population, influenced by better educated Islamic clerics coming from abroad, UP and Bihar, has started believing that all such syncretic practices are shirk (apostasy).

The social media platforms and WhatsApp are also radicalizing the Muslims in a major way. A remote city like Udaipur is slowly coming under the creeping influence of global Islamism. Recently, the local Muslims staged a protest asking the government to offer shelter to Rohingya refugees. In 2017, an inflammatory anti-Hindu post on Facebook went viral and created a communally tense situation. Finally, 8 to 10 local youngsters were arrested and the local administration had to shut down the internet for four days.

The city is also witnessing a huge influx of migrant labor from Malda in West Bengal. Locals sources suggest that around 150 to 200 laborers from Malda have arrived in the city, but their numbers might be much more. All of them register themselves as Bengalis and not illegal Bangladeshi immigrants that they most likely are. Interestingly, they carry all certified documents of identity. The police maintain that even if they are illegal immigrants, it is difficult to prove that because they have the right documents. It is quite possible that the authorities in Malda, and other border districts help them in forging the documents in return of monetary rewards.

However, the matter of concern in this study is that Malda and Nadia have emerged as the hubs of Jihadi terror. Besides, in Bangladesh, AQIS and ISIS affiliates like Jamaat-ul-Mujahiddin have found a strong foothold. While interviewing the migrant laborers in Udaipur, it was found that they were living in illegal colonies, being frequented by extremist clerics from outside Rajasthan.

There is no serious Shia-Sunni problem in the city but frictions do exist and are serious in a very subtle manner. The problem of extremism is also present in the Barelwi sections. This is contrary to the commonly held belief that the problem of extremism is with Deobandis and Wahhabis only. Furthermore, during the Hindu-Muslim communal frictions, Muslims of all sects unite. The mutual differences do not prevent them from fighting and acting in unison. In such cases, the larger identity of belonging to Islam dominates their sub-identities.

Furthermore, the city's Muslim individuals from the poor background are also involved in the crime. Drug addiction is a major problem among the youth. It also needs to be noted that radicalization is an issue with the youth in Udaipur. Their elders have strong leanings towards Sufism and are liberal in nature. Their local roots are strong. However, the new generation is coming under the grips of extremist ideologies. Because of this, they are having sharp differences with their elders.

In addition to the facts stated above, it also needs a mention that the local cyber-monitoring infrastructure to check online radicalization is in a bad shape. Even the most basic equipment and technology like mobile trackers and laptops are not there in adequate numbers. The technological infrastructure, training and skill-sets are lacking and the awareness of global terrorism issues is minimal.

Udaipur is also witnessing rapid Hindu radicalization and that is adding fuel to the fire of radicalization among Muslims. Young Hindu boys wielding lancets, machetes and swords shouting inflammatory communal slogans are common sightings these days. Few months back, Shambhulal Regar[30] of the nearby district Rajsamand killed a Bengali Muslim laborer in a matter that was revealed to be a case of either love-jihad or a love triangle. He released a video of the killing which had blatant communal content. Next day, local Muslims of Udaipur staged a protest in which anti-national slogans threatening massive violence were shouted. The whole thing turned into a major communal conflict. Next day, the whole city was flooded with Hindu youngsters wearing saffron robes and wielding weapons. The people were obviously brought in droves from the nearby villages. They were all armed and shouting slogans like "Jai Siyaram" and "Har Har Mahadev." Fortunately, nothing serious happened, but it could have turned into a violent communal riot claiming many lives.

Observations

1) So far, no open links of local residents with SIMI, IM or PFI have come to notice. But that possibility cannot be ruled out. There is a strong possibility of the city being used by sleeper cells for strategic planning, surveillance, shelter and managing logistical aspects of the terrorist operations. Furthermore, the migrant laborers and the local radicalized segment of the population may be used for facilitating the smooth presence and movement of the sleeper cells.
2) As regards Hindu radicalization, it must be noted that it is a serious problem in the city. However, ideological and theological elements are almost missing in the case of Hindu radicalization. The problem of radicalization is majorly due to (a) unemployment, aimlessness and un-employability of the youth, (b) reaction to global Islamism and jihadi terrorism, (c) social media and WhatsApp propaganda and/or (d) activities of the Hindu extremist/fringe groups.

   Hindu radicalization can result in (a) violent communal riots, (b) shrinking of the social spaces of communal harmony, (c) strengthening of radicalization among Muslims and (d) increase in the appeal of the ideology of transnational terrorist organizations like ISIS and AQ among the local Muslims.

3) Case studies of cities like Udaipur can be very useful in developing a national-level counter-radicalization programme for smaller cities which would be significantly different from that for the metros and larger cities.

Mapping ISIS Phenomenon in India

India is often regarded as an "outlier case" as far as the influence of ISIS is concerned. Home to world's third largest Muslim population (after Indonesia and Pakistan), and with a long history of communal tensions between Hindus and Muslims, it was expected to have sent a large number of foreign fighters. However, contrary to the prevailing narratives in the strategic community, the number of foreign fighters from India has been miniscule as compared to the number of foreign fighters sent by Europe, America, Russia and Central Asian Republics, let alone Middle East and North Africa.

First, only 142[31] (132 named) Indians have been conformed to have affiliated with IS in some way, with the liberal estimates ranging around 200 to 300. The number of Indians who finally reached West Asia and Afghanistan between 2014 and 2016 is only around 10 to 15.[32] However, this should not lull us into complacency because there have been several worrying trends also. The number of Indians linked to IS has steadily grown since 2014.

Year	No. of Indians linked to ISIS
2013	1
2014	6
2015	35
2016	75
2017 (first four months)	25

Source: Times of India.[33]

Furthermore, India has been at the receiving end of the jihadi terrorism for about three decades now. There are enough fault lines in social, cultural, political and religious domains making India highly susceptible to the forces of Jihadi radicalization. Alongside, there are strong forces of resilience also. Following questions may arise in strategic circles:

1) Has IS failed in India?
2) How strong were its efforts in finding roots in India?
3) What kind of threats will be posed by IS in its post-territorial phase?

Hence, understanding ISIS phenomenon in India becomes essential for framing a strategy to counter the threat of jihadi radicalization in future.

Research and analysis on the subject is largely based on the data generated by various local and international think-tanks, central and state investigation agencies, media stories and interviews conducted with strategic analysts, scholars of religion and counter-terrorism officials.

A Look at Some High-Profile IS Cases in India

From 2011 until 2013, Indian agencies held IS to be a West Asian phenomenon. There was a false sense of security that Indian Muslims would not respond to the calls of global jihad by IS, and as a result, one does not come across any substantial effort and awareness in India to understand IS phenomenon, its strategy, long-term objectives and attempts to gain global outreach through internet.

In October 2014, six top commanders of Tehreek-i-Taliban Pakistan (TTP), including Shahidullah Shahid, declared their allegiance to ISIS. In the following months, ISIS named TTP chief Hafiz Saeed Khan as the "wali" (governor) of the Khorasan province which includes India.[34] Islamic Movement of Uzbekistan (IMU) also defected to ISIS and Indian Mujahiddin (IM) split into two factions: Sultan Armar formed Ansar ul-Tauhid fi Bilal ul-Hind which became the chief recruitment wing of ISIS, while Riyaz Bhatkal faction continued its loyalties to AQ.[35] Next is a timeline of events.

1) 2011-2014: Two childhood friends, Haja Fakkurudeen Usman Ali (40), a grocery store manager in Singapore and Gul Muhammed Maracachi Maraicar (37), a software professional, were radicalized, and decided to join IS in Syria. Both of them were born and brought up in Cuddalore and were radicalized by the plight of Muslim suffering in Syria. Images of Muslim suffering and the mainstream media coverage played an important role in their initial radicalization. After that, they accessed the ISIS online propaganda material. They planned to move to Syria to join IS. Gul, the one with stable job and earnings, is said to have motivated Haja. They also planned to seek permission from the family members in India (visited India twice between November 2013 and January 2014). During these visits, he held several conspiracy meetings with Khaja Miodeen and Shakul Hamid in Tamil Nadu and Karnataka with the intention of recruiting more persons

for ISIS. Haja's parents opposed his decision but he moved to Syria in January 2014 with his family against his parents' wishes (via Turkey, but still there is no clarity). In the meantime, Singapore authorities arrested Gul and deported him to India.[36] In the interrogations, he revealed that both of them had planned to intensify ISIS recruitment in the universities and educational institutions in Chennai. Later, in 2017, five individuals were arrested in Chennai for involvement in ISIS-related activities. One of them, Ansar Meeran had financed Haja and his family's journey to Syria (Data Source: ISIS Tracking Project by ORF).[37]

2) 2014: Four young men, Arif Majeed, Fahad Tanveer Sheikh, Aman Naeem Tandel and Shaheem Tanki, from Kalyan (Mumbai) successfully made it to Syria as a part of the 22 pilgrims "making a religious trip to Iraq." Then they fled to Falujah and joined ISIS. Arif was a son of a Unani doctor. According to intelligence agencies, the four young men were radicalized through internet. Later, Majid surrendered and was brought back to India. The other three were reported killed.[38]
3) December 2014: Mehdi Biswas,[39] a software engineer was arrested in Bangalore. He was running the Twitter handle of ISIS under the name of "Shami witness." It was a successful propaganda outlet that helped ISIS in recruitment in India. The account had a strong international outreach. He was also reportedly in touch with the assailants of Dhaka terrorist attack in 2016.
4) In July 2016, 21 people disappeared from Kasargod and Palakkad in Kerala to join ISIS. Rashid Abdullah was the chief recruiter. Five of them were connected to Peace International School chain of Kerala. Many were new converts. Ayesha, Rashid's wife was a Hindu convert. All the families in Kaasargod knew Rashid and the three families were known to each other. Rashid also knew two Christian brothers Bestin and Bexen from Palakkad who converted to Islam. Rashid introduced Bexen to a Hindu girl Nimisha who converted to Islam and married him. Bestin and his girlfriend Merrin also converted to Islam.[40] All of them were highly educated with degrees in management and engineering.
5) 2016: Muhammed Mosiuddin (alias Abu Musa), a 26-year-old grocer from Burdwan (West Bengal) was arrested on the charge of planning

lone-wolf attacks in the name of ISIS against local and Western targets. Mosiuddin's interest in ISIS developed through online networks where he met with other ISIS enthusiasts to discuss future strategy and planning operations. He came in touch with Shafi Armar (alias Yusuf al-Hindi, founder and self-appointed Amir of Junud al-Khalifa-e-Hind). Shafi, a resident of West Bengal, was a former Indian Mujahiddin operative and was one of the chief recruiters of ISIS in India. During this period, Mosiuddin also came in contact with Abu Sulaiman, a former member of Jamaat-ul-Mujahiddin, Bangladesh (JMB). Their initial communications were on Facebook, but later they switched to other platforms like Nimbuzz, Surespot and Trillian. In 2015, JMB joined these conversations. Abu Sulaiman travelled to India from Bangladesh to visit Mosiuddin to discuss the establishment of ISIS' foothold in India. Meanwhile, Mosiuddin tried to arrange finances and passport for traveling to Syria with Armar's help.

Mosiuddin, at the same time also recruited Saddam Hussain (a 25-year-old unemployed man) and Shaikh Abbasudin, a 22-year-old daily wage plumber. Mosiuddin, Abu Sulaiman and the two new recruits commenced efforts to build ISIS' base in India. Their activities included surveillance trips to Srinagar and Delhi in 2015 (train trips sponsored by JMB). Attempts were made to disseminate ISIS ideology in the Valley by fomenting protests with ISIS flags and YouTube video clips. But Mosiuddin's ultimate dream of travelling to Syria was never fulfilled because he could not arrange finances and passport.[41] The rich and educated lads from Kerala and Maharashtra could get passport and travel to Syria whereas the poor and comparatively illiterate Mosiuddin could not. Furthermore, to what extent Shafi Armar was interested in him also gives a clue to ISIS' recruitment policy which apparently focuses more on educated and rich ones.

6) October 2016: Ansar-ul-Khalifa, ISIS module, was busted in Kannur, Kerala, by the NIA. Six persons were arrested. The group was led by Manseed Omar al Hindi, who developed ties with ISIS while working in Qatar. The group had 12 members. The group was planning a Nice-style attack on a JeI meeting with truck as a weapon.[42]
7) There have been several cases of the waving of ISIS flags during agitations in Kashmir but these cannot be accepted as substantial evidences for the official presence of ISIS in Valley. They appear more

like teasers. Eisa Fazli killed a policeman in Srinagar in the name of ISIS. Later, ISIS' Amaq News agency legitimized it as its operation. But no militant organization in Kashmir has pledged official allegiance to ISIS which is also the case with its other "wilayats" (provinces).[43] However, ISIS mindset is taking strong roots in Kashmir, and Zakir Musa's Ansar Ghazwat-ul-Hind (AGUH) openly talks about Islamic State in Kashmir (details discussed in the case study on Kashmir).

State	No. of ISIS cases	State	No. of ISIS cases
Kerala	37	Gujarat	4
Telangana	21	Uttarakhanda/Bengal	3 each
Maharashtra	19	Andhra	1
Karnataka	16	Bihar	1
UP	15	Delhi	1
MP	6	Rajasthan	1
TN	5	J&K	2

Source: Times of India.[44]

Observations

1) Kerala, the most literate state has the highest recorded number of ISIS cases, i.e. 37. The Wahhabi/Salafi religious and ideological bond created and nurtured over the years by economic links with the Gulf created a fertile ground for radicalization and the results are quite expected. Maharashtra, West Bengal and Telangana have also witnessed worrying levels of radicalization.
2) All those who joined ISIS are youngsters. Most of them come from affluent economic background, and had advanced educational qualifications in the field of engineering, medicine, information technology, medicine, dentistry, and management studies. Many of them were anglicized in personal lifestyle. For example, the case of Mehdi Biswas may be an interesting one: Mehdi adored Hollywood movies, American actresses, and American superhero movies and attended Hawaiian theme parties. Before his arrest, he posted on Twitter, "May Allah guide, protect, strengthen and expand the Islamic State ... Islamic State brought peace, autonomy, zero corruption, low crime-rate."[45]
3) Furthermore, except UP, the majority came from the more prosperous, developed and networked states of India. This trend is quite similar

to the trends in other parts of the world with relatively liberal societies most vulnerable to ISIS radicalization: Morocco, Tunisia (comparatively liberal in the Arab world), Australia, Nordic countries, France and Belgium.

4) There were several cases of online radicalization. One-third of the total numbers were already affiliated with the domestic terror organizations like SIMI, IM and Junud al-Khalifa-e-Hind and PFI. It shows that ISIS' strategy is very flexible and can successfully tap into the existing jihadi infrastructure. In most of the cases, the transition from the local jihadi set-up to global jihadi set-up was very smooth.
5) ISIS radicalization in India was not a faceless process, nor was it entirely online, happening on its own with a multiplier effect. Well-trained ISIS recruiters like Shafi Armar and Rashid Abdullah have been arrested. They were running ISIS terror modules in West Bengal and Kerala. Similarly, in Kannur (Kerala), an ISIS module with 12 active members and a leader was busted. The recruiters were trained by ISIS to become efficient recruiters. They were trained in convincing the probable candidate by using online content and distorting theological texts. Even the Twitter handlers of ISIS such as Mehdi Biswas and Muhammad Sirajuddin[46] (IOC official, arrested in Jaipur) were highly tech-savvy and efficient in using social media platforms like Facebook, for publishing online contents and encrypted applications like telegram and WhatsApp. This study, because of paucity of data, does not aim at a concrete analysis on the nature of the exact relationship and the frequency of contacts between the ISIS recruiters in India and the core ISIS leadership. However, it is emphasized that ISIS represents a different model of organizational structure and command and control systems. Therefore, investigating ISIS from the conventional prism of locating a centralized leadership and control system may not be a sound idea. In fact, ISIS' strategy of roping in educated and tech-savvy young men and women suggests that the organization's training strategy focused on self-radicalization and self-training through online mediums.
6) Besides, other vectors that played an important role in radicalization are family ties, marriage/relationships, group ties and conversions. An important pattern that comes forth from the analysis of pro-ISIS

individuals in India is that they preferred to work in groups and moved to Syria and Afghanistan in groups. This pattern has strong parallels with cases in Europe. The ISIS attack in Paris in 2015 was an effort of a group of individuals who came from Belgium's Muslim-populated ghetto town of Molanbeek.[47] Many of them were childhood friends.

7) India has also been an anomaly in so far as there has been no case of lone-wolf attack so far. The general trend in South Asia is to work in groups. The reason for this may lie in the fact that the institutions of collective social identities like families, caste, communities are still very powerful in India. However, this cannot be a reason to rule out the possibility of such attacks in future. Mosiuddin and the Kannur ISIS module wanted to organize lone-wolf attacks. It must be noted here that local socio-cultural factors may have an influence on the strategy and modus operandi, but largely they are guided by the religious injunctions on such things, as conveyed by the ISIS leadership. When ISIS spokesperson Adnani urged ISIS Jihaids to use any weapon—knives, machetes, cars and trucks—to attack, then it did figure in the ISIS modules as a potential strategy to be employed.
8) Regarding radicalization in India, some unique features come to light. As mentioned earlier, the Singapore group of pro-ISIS individuals was seeking approval from their families before joining ISIS. One of them, Haja, moved to Syria with his family. Similarly, in Kashmir also, the militants continue their contacts with their families and friends even after joining a terrorist organization. As discussed in the Kashmir case study, they have been found talking to their families before encounter deaths or fidayeen attacks. This phenomenon is inconsistent with the prevailing notions that a radicalized individual gets disconnected from his friends and family as he finds a virtual community of like-minded people.
9) The radicalized individuals came from diverse backgrounds. Many of them came from affluent backgrounds with high education (Kerala modules); there were others like Mosiuddin from a humble economic background and poor education. Many of them were previously associated with IM, PFI and SIMI. In many cases, convicts cited the rise of Hindu extremism, beef-lynching as reasons for their radicalization. Some others stated that the conditions of Muslims in the post-9/11 world and Muslim suffering in ME at the hands of

foreign powers radicalized them. Almost 95 per cent of them refer to online ISIS content as the motivating factor. Furthermore, Olivier Roy's theory (from his study of radicalization in France) that homeless, drug addicts and second-generation Muslims who faced integration problems in society were more prone to radicalization does not find much resonance in India. Most of the ISIS cases had no family issues. In fact, they had a good family support system. Muslims in India have been living for almost 1,000 years now, so there are no integration problems as such.

The inconsistencies mentioned above make it extremely difficult to derive a standard logic for radicalization. However, in all the cases analyzed, theology and the geopolitics of global Islamism emerge as common factors. Many of them displayed pronounced religiosity before making a move to Syria. The over-religiosity manifested in keeping beards, wearing skull-caps, advocating dressing restrictions on their sisters, and despising television and cinema. This needs to be taken into consideration for the future policy-making. Until now, the role of religion in radicalization has been downplayed in intellectual and security circles. Politically, it may be an uncomfortable zone to enter. But if the problem is to be addressed seriously, an objective and honest assessment of the role of religion needs to be carried out. Greame Wood,[48] an expert voice in terrorism, studied more than 100 ISIS recruiters and concluded that religion plays an extremely important role in ISIS' strategy, and ISIS has made jihad religious again. For further details, the readers may refer to the essay "Post-ISIS: Future of Global Jihad."[49]

Did ISIS Fail in India?

Stanford University's counter-extremism project, "Spiders of Caliphate" studied the social media networks of ISIS and found that in South Asia, there were two nodes of ISIS (Facebook community of ISIS followers): one in Afghanistan-Pakistan and the other one in Bangladesh. India is more or less missing in that network of nodes. The counter-extremism project has concluded that ISIS cannot be called a success in India. The total number of Indians who subscribed to ISIS was miniscule. Even a small entity such as Maldives sent 200 fighters to ISIS. There was no large-scale sophisticated ISIS-led attack in India and not even a proper lone-wolf attack, typically characteristic of ISIS. What hindered the progress of ISIS in India? An exploration will bring forth several reasons:

1) Firstly, it appears that ISIS did not accord the same level of priority to India and South Asia as was accorded to the Western and the Middle Eastern world. In Kashmir, the organization named Islamic State in Jammu and Kashmir (ISJK) existed but it did not find much traction. As already mentioned previously, no group in Kashmir has announced official allegiance to ISIS, just the way Abu Sayyaf of Manila or the TTP of Pakistan did. Kabir Taneja[50] (ORF) in his detailed study on the ISIS phenomenon in South Asia opines that ISIS deliberately did not include Kashmir in their "quest of Caliphate" in al-Hind because it feared that the jihadi terrorist organizations in Kashmir like HM and LeT have nationalist or patriotic orientations and hence, would never accept merger with ISIS. He further says that ISIS has tremendous brand value, so militant outfits find it suitable to use their brand name to gain popularity and recognition which was evident in the case of massive popularity which Zakir Musa achieved after stating his idea of establishing Islamic state in Kashmir. However, during field research, it was found that the ISIS, as an organization, cannot be said to have achieved any major success in Kashmir, but the ideology and the caliphate narrative of ISIS has captured some degree of popular imagination. The details are discussed in the chapter carrying the case study on Kashmir.
2) ISIS' brutal tactics and killing of fellow Muslims did not rhyme well with the socio-cultural ethos of South Asia. India's strong family values and a robust national and cultural identity cutting across religious lines was also an effective deterrent.[51] The ISIS narrative also did not align well even with local extremist organizations such as PFI and JeI. In South Asia, Muslims have lived in a democratic set-up and evolved in a multicultural environment. As a result, fanaticism and extremism advocated by ISIS did not find a fertile ground here. Secondly, majority of Muslims in South Asia follow Barelvi and Deobandi Islam. Barelvi school is comparatively tolerant and allows the syncretic Sufi practices. ISIS' Wahhabi line of Islam is at odds with the Barelvi and Deobandi belief systems. Furthermore, the causes of radicalization in India are highly localized and communal in nature. Dominant jihadi narrative is over the Hindu-Muslim communal frictions. Being a minority, the prevailing threat perception among Muslims is from the rising Hindu assertiveness, and not from the fellow non Wahhabi Muslims, whereas

the ISIS' prime targets were non-Wahhabi Sunni Muslims and Shias first and then the Kafirs.

3) Jihadi terrorism in South Asia, India in particular, is largely controlled by Pakistan's ISI. ISI does not have any ideological fixation. It uses terrorist organizations for its narrow geopolitical ends, certainly not in the cause of Islam. Therefore, in the Indian context, transnational terror outfits like AQ and ISIS have to face stiff competition from Pakistan-backed, highly organized, disciplined and well-funded terrorist groups like HM, LeT, JeM and Harkat-ul-Jihad-al-Islami (HuJi). Self-radicalized and untrained ISIS sympathizers are no match for such a well-trained and organized Jihadi infrastructure.
4) Many Indian ISIS fighters were not treated with dignity by the Arab ISIS fighters. Indians were rarely given military assignments. They had to face Arab racism. A report[52] by MI6 and CIA revealed that ISIS considered Indians, Bangladeshis and Pakistanis inferior to Arab fighters so they were used as canon-fodder for suicide bombings. They were used for menial jobs.
5) Indian Muslims have a fair representation in politics, bureaucracy and the financial world of India. They have high stakes in Indian democracy and the peaceful functioning of the state.
6) In India, the state and its security infrastructure gave a robust checkmate to ISIS activities at all levels—operational, strategic and psychological. There was strict monitoring of social media outlets and the individuals on the verge of radicalization were identified and the prompt action was taken and 60 per cent[53] of the 142 ISIS sympathizers were arrested and interrogated.

Al Qaeda in Indian Subcontinent

While the US was downsizing its military contingents in Afghanistan, AQ leader Ayman Al Zawahiri, in September 2014, announced the creation of the regional affiliate of Al Qaeda in Indian Subcontinent (AQIS), to harness the potential of the vast sanctuaries in Pakistan, Afghanistan and Bangladesh.[54] Asim Umar, an Indian terrorist associated with HuJI, a Pakistan-based terrorist group with its network spread across India, was made the chief of AQIS and Abu Zar as his deputy. Asim Umar is said to be a religious scholar who taught in a madrasa in Karachi and wrote four books encouraging Jihad.[55] The group's core leadership and activities are centered in Pakistan but according to the intelligence sources, it has serious ambitions in Kashmir and India which is further substantiated by the fact that an Indian with a strong network in India was appointed as its chief.

AQIS has several former AQ-affiliated groups working under its umbrella. There is no precise information but some prominent names include Afghan Taliban (Afghanistan), TTP (Pakistan), HuJI (Bangladesh and Pakistan); Harkat-ul-Mujahideen or HuM (Indian state of J&K), Harkat-ul-Mujahideen al-Alami or HuMA (Pakistan); LeT (Indian state of J&K), and JeM.[56]

There are various reasons for setting up of AQIS. Some experts argue that it was established to counter the rival organizations like ISIS from gaining ground in South Asia. If one goes by the views expressed in AQ's online mouthpiece "Resurgence," it appears that the AQIS was created to reclaim the territory it operated before the US-led invasion of Afghanistan before 2001. It remained weak after its formation in 2014. But in 2017, it started getting momentum. American strategic expert Seth G Jones[57] observed in his congressional testimony that AQIS had become very active by 2017 and "boasted of several 100 fighters by 2017, with its cells mostly active in Afghanistan (Helmund, Kandhar, Ghazni, Nuristan and Zabul provinces) and Bangladesh." He attributed this revival to the Taliban advances in Afghanistan and the relation that AQIS has with Taliban and other outfits like TTP and Lashkar-i-Jhangvi. AQIS operatives have been active in conducting attacks in Bangladesh and online propaganda work through its media arm Al-sahab.

In an August 2016 message, AQIS attempted to use the death of HM activist Burhan Wani in an encounter in Kashmir, to mobilize Muslim youth in South India for Jihad. AQIS released leaflets in local languages also. In June 2017, AQIS released a document titled, "Code of Conduct."[58] Its focus was on Kashmir and the document clearly suggests that police, military, intelligence agencies and the leaders of right-wing Hindu organizations will be its prime targets. Soon after that, AQIS lent support, through its media wing al-Hurr, to AGUH, a new militant outfit led by HM renegade Zakir Musa (details mentioned in the Kashmir case study). The formation of AGUH was announced on July 27 by Global Islamic Media Front, an AQ-affiliated information network. However, many of its prominent commanders like Abu Dujana and Rashid Bhatt have been killed in police encounters. But the group and its ideology are gaining ground in Kashmir.

Base Movement[59]

In South India, AQ affiliate "Base Movement" (BM) captured public attention with a series of bombings in 2016. There is no precise information about the origins of the group but it has been active since 2015, after the Charlie Hebdo attacks in Paris. The group sent a threatening letter to Tamil daily, "Dinamalar" which read "Yesterday Paris – Charlie Hebdo, Tomorrow Dinamalar" indicating a possible attack similar to the Charlie Hebdo. As no attack happened, authorities raised doubts on the authenticity of the letter.

In 2016, BM sent threatening letters to state authorities in Karnataka and Tamil Nadu warning of attacks in the southern states. Five low-intensity blasts targeting law courts did occur in 2016: in Chittoor, Andhra Pradesh (April 7); Kollam and Mysore, Karnataka (June 15 and August 1, respectively); Nellore, Andhra Pradesh (September 12) and Malappuram, Kerala (November 1). The letters had mentioned of avenging the hanging of Yakub Memon (Mumbai Blast Case), killing of LeT operative Ishrat Jahan and atrocities on Muslims in India. The letters were traced to Singanallur in Coimbatore. Later, NIA investigations led to the arrest of four suspects, Abbas Ali, Suleiman Muhammad Abdullah, Samsun Karim Raja and Mohamed Ayub Ali. The probe revealed that most of the court blasts were linked to the judicial trials of SIMI cadres. All the incidents were said to be linked to remnants of the banned Al-Umma militant group, active in South India since the late 1990s, and SIMI members, reorganized under BM. The investigations and other corroborative evidence also suggested that the now defunct Al-Umma group had pledged allegiance to AQIS in 2015. Intelligence sources claim that Al-Umma leader Abu Bakr Siddhique heads BM.

Future Threats

Recently, 22nd report[60] of the Analytical Support and Sanctions Monitoring of the UN says that AQIS is "ideologically" inclined to carry attacks inside India but its capability is limited and it is lying low because of the increased security measures in the region. The report further says that AQ is closely allied to Taliban. It is efficient in adapting to the local context and can easily tap into the local grievances and socio-political fault lines. It can easily embed into the local struggles. The report also says that although the immediate threat remains from ISIS, AQ is an "intellectually stronger" group and remains a longer term threat. AQ has tried to revive its activities in India when the main focus of security agencies is on the ISIS-related activities. Though AQIS's strike capabilities in India are still limited, it should not be underestimated. AQ has proved itself as highly resilient and survived almost a decade-long war on terror. Its diffused network and ability to mingle and accommodate the local extremist organizations into its fold is its strength. Moreover, it has a high brand value. Informed sources suggest that AQIS has strong penetration at the grassroots level in India. Its sleeper cells working in Bangladesh and India are active on the radicalization front. And, whether one agrees or not, AQIS has led to the consolidation of jihadi extremist elements in the Indian hinterland, despite its limited capabilities.

As regards ISIS, it is in a post-geography state. It is now a self-proclaimed caliphate with no territory. But there is a likelihood of it transforming into an AQ-like diffused network. ISIS brand is still strong and attractive, especially amongst youth. It may leverage its brand value to promote lone-wolf attacks in its name. Furthermore, its most sophisticated cyber-jihad infrastructure disseminating highly extremist and violent Islam remains the biggest threat. It must, however, be highlighted that for India, ISIS was never a threat in the sense of a territorial power as India is too strong a country. For India, threat will always be in the ideological arena and it is likely to increase in the future. The notion of caliphate, awareness of global jihad and sentiments for caliphate are stronger than ever.

ISKP has entrenched itself in Afghanistan. It has significant presence in the eastern provinces of Kunar, Nangarhar and Nuristan, and is also active in Jowzjan, Faryab, Sari Pul and Badakhshan provinces in the north. The group has plans to expand into Ghazni, Kunduz, Laghman, Logar and Uruzgan provinces. The UN report cited above also says that "In Kabul, Herat and Jalalabad, ISIL already has sleeper cells and has committed disruptive, high-profile attacks, including against both government and Taliban targets during the Eidul-Fitr ceasefire."

The UN report further noted that that ISIL has between 3,500 and 4,000 members in Afghanistan, including between 600 and 1,000 in northern Afghanistan (with both sets of numbers on the increase). It is led by Abu Sayed Bajauri who is not listed; majority of its members and leaders were formerly members of TTP and it may represent an emerging threat to the Central Asian states. Many Indians from Kerala have also joined ISKP in Afghanistan.

With the support of some state actors, the ISKP can attempt to create a strong footprint in the Kashmir Valley by tapping into the caliphate narrative (Azadi baraye Islam) which has, of late, gained serious traction in the area. However, despite a better brand value of ISIS, it is assessed that AQ has better chances of finding a niche in Kashmir. AQ has been present in the Af-Pak region for long now and AQIS core leadership has a robust base there. Besides, it has an institutionalized approach, a long history of jihad operations, expertise in survival tactics and highly efficient organizational structure. Additionally, a Council on Foreign Relations report,[61] discussing in detail about AQ reorganizing itself, had predicted its resurrection. There is also a possibility of AQ and ISIS uniting, according to a Council on Foreign Affairs essay by Bruce Hoffman.[62] It appears possible because ISIS was a breakaway group from AQ and the differences between the two were more on ego issues and minor differences in ideology and strategy.

This essay was drafted in September 2018 and the assessment of IS threat has been in line with its status and forecasting done at that time. Earlier, in the chapter, the author has discussed in brief about the links between Salafi followers of Kerala and Sri Lanka. The author also discussed the visits of Keralite Salafi followers to Sri Lanka for training in Wahhabi theology and setting up of Salafi communes in Sri Lanka and Kerala. After the recent suicide bombings in Kerala, such links have figured prominently. Sri Lankan army chief has categorically stated that suicide bombers of the Colombo attack visited Bangalore, Kerala and Kashmir,[63] possibly for training. Furthermore, National Tauheed Jamaat of Sri Lanka has historical links with Tamil Nadu Thowheed Jamaat. Much lies to be unearthed and explored about the said links and emerging networks. However, it appears that IS is far from dead. Also, it is building a South Asia wide grid exploiting local grievances and extremist organizations. Harsh V Pant and Kabir Taneja write in *Foreign Policy*, "This poses a greater challenge for South Asia in particular, with its political tensions often crossing religious lines, as the Islamic State rebrands as a global insurgency.... The Islamic State functions as brand name now a days, with those adopting its image creating instant narratives, gaining immediate attention and reaching the front pages around the world. A lax approach after the territorial defeat of Islamic State is no longer an option-instead nations worldwide have to adapt to battle a hydra-headed insurgency."[64]

As seen in the case of recent bombings, the threat emerges from foreign fighters[65] who return to home countries in South Asia from the battle fields of

Syria and Iraq. With advanced training in communication technologies, weapons and explosives, they are likely to play an instrumental role in training local cadres, logistics and planning and executing operations. It may result in more suicide bombings, vehicular attacks and routine terrorist attacks including the lone-wolf attacks. Also, with respect to IS, it has to be kept in mind that the organization has been evolving in techniques and sophistication, be it communication or terrorism. The IS has displayed a unique ability and attitude in adopting new technology. In this view, it is highly likely that it may resort to innovative techniques of terror aiming at mass causalities. Such innovations may include cyber-attacks, inciting communal riots, and acts of bio-terror. The author learned in an interaction with an informed interlocutor from Srinagar that ISIS modules in Maharashtra were in touch with Hizbul Mujahiddin leadership in Kashmir and were encouraging them to associate with ISIS. Furthermore, he also told that ISIS modules were exploring new ways such as getting control of the key players and centers of India's economy, and effect economic sabotage to India. For example, targeting key business centers, tourist destinations and high-end hotels may be aimed at targeting country's economy and tourism. Targeting India's economic heft and growth is not a new phenomenon. It has always been there. It is one of the most prominent aims of Pakistan behind its proxy war in Kashmir. ISIS may attempt it in future, with more disastrous effects and at a much larger scale.

A Brief Note on Online Radicalization

It may be mentioned that 95 per cent of the identified pro-ISIS cases of individuals in India referred to the online content disseminated by the ISIS propaganda machine. The "weaponization of the internet" has emerged as a robust pillar of global jihad. The social media and the internet have truly democratized[66] jihad and emerged as the most powerful channels of spreading the jihadi ideology and radicalizing young minds. ISIS made the most sophisticated use of social media and internet in recruitment, conducting operations and exporting extremism. However, it also needs to be mentioned that online radicalization cannot happen in vacuum. There has to be a context, an overall socio-cultural, religious and political milieu nurturing and aiding radicalization in which online radicalization/social media acts as sophisticated and efficient channel for radicalizing young minds by disseminating radicalizing content to a large audience at an unimaginable speed. Thus, social media is a technological tool to speed up and intensify the process of radicalization. For example, in Kashmir, social media has emerged as the most potent channel of radicalization. But, it is just a tool which has made the process efficient and faster in an already prevalent milieu of radicalization. Previously, what clerics were doing at a much slower pace in mosques and seminaries is now being done through WhatsApp and Facebook, at a much faster pace and on a larger scale.

Terrorist organizations use internet for recruitment of the radicalized individuals (otherwise difficult to contact in the real world), propaganda, religious indoctrination, terror-financing through crypto-currencies, training in using weapons available in day-to-day life such as knives and machetes, and making IEDs, training in cyber-warfare, communicating instructions and psychological warfare. ISIS online propaganda material included text documents, videos of executions, lectures by extremist clerics and militants and magazines like Dabiq (later renamed Rumiya after the fall of Dabiq).

Rand Corporation's project "Radicalization in Digital Era"[67] examined 15 cases of terrorism and found empirical evidence to suggest that internet creates more opportunities to get radicalized by being available to many people and enabling communication with like-minded people 24/7 from across the world. The study confirmed that internet may act as "echo-chamber" for extremist beliefs, i.e. it may provide more and better opportunities to confirm extremist beliefs than offline interactions. The report goes on to suggest that internet radicalization is not a substitute for in-person radicalization through physical contact. Rather, it complements the in-person radicalization. Furthermore, internet cannot be said to have enhanced the opportunities for self-radicalization as all the 15 individuals were in contact with other individuals either physically or virtually.

Pro-ISIS individuals use WhatsApp and telegram for communication. Initially, they use social media platforms like Facebook and Twitter, and then move to the encrypted communication applications. The use of internet makes it very easy to get in touch with the like-minded people from across the world. For instance, ISIS recruiter Muhammad Sirajuddin had built an online group[68] that included like-minded people from Mauritius, Indonesia, Sri Lanka and Argentina. ISIS has been the most tech-savvy in the use of internet. It has used many techniques to counter freezing of its accounts. ISIS uses the technique of "reverse shout-out" to reestablish their accounts. There was an account called "Baqiyashoutout" that provided instructions to reestablish accounts.

Emphasis was on reclaiming the network of followers. Furthermore, ISIS asks its followers to main strict anonymity. The instructions include not to turn on the GPS and instead use Virtual Private Networks (VPN). ISIS supporters were instructed to download Hola VPN or a similar programme on a mobile device or Web browser. Once installed, users could select an Internet Protocol (IP) address for a country outside the US, and thus bypass email or phone verification.[69]

ISIS used cyber-sphere to spread its ideology and shape thoughts by setting the dominant discourse that Muslims around the world needed a holy caliphate and it is their divine duty to migrate to the caliphate. According to Haroro J Ingram,[70] the research designs of ISIS messaging focused on the pragmatic aspect of the propaganda, i.e. "stability, security and livelihood" and the second focus was on "perceptual aspects," tapping into the person's identity by projecting themselves as the sole protectors of Sunni Muslims. This type of messaging was to coax the audience to make identity-choice–based decision-making. ISIS was projected as the only solution to the crises Sunnis were facing and the enemy identities were projected as the cause of that crisis. First a narrative of identity insecurity was created and then the audience was encouraged to make decisions that will suit his or her identity.

In India's case, local terrorist organizations such as JeM, Indian Mujahiddin, HM and LeT have also started making intensive use of internet for radicalization. In Kashmir, internet (WhatsApp, signal, telegram, Twitter, Instagram and Facebook) has emerged as the most powerful channel of radicalization (details discussed in the Kashmir case study). These days, militant commanders in Kashmir periodically release video-lectures that are quite popular on the social media. Such videos and audio clips have explicit jihadi and extremist content and they get viral on WhatsApp, Facebook and Instagram, within seconds. They are immensely helpful in radicalizing and motivating young individuals to join militant organizations.

In comparison, Pakistan-based terrorist groups follow a slightly traditional approach and do not put much premium on the online learning of Islam. Most of the LeT cadres are from the seminaries of North Punjab (Pakistan) and Jaish cadres are from the seminaries of South Punjab. In this regard, ISIS has been the most advanced one on the frontiers of technology. Recruitment process in Kashmir valley is more through personal contacts. Like-minded extremists are approached through personal contacts, socialization with militants and peer network or in the Ijtemas/classes of organizations like JeI.

But groups like LeT have been reported using internet-based COMSAT technologies—in Mumbai attacks (26/11), they used GPS technology. Furthermore, AQIS has a strong presence on the internet. Its YouTube channels like Al Firdaws and Ansar AQIS were banned. It also has many online magazines such as *Nawai Afghan* and *Statements*, published in Urdu, English, Arabic, Bangla and Tamil. Its blocked Twitter accounts, Ansarul Islam and Abna_ul_Islam_media, had a following of over 1,300. Its Telegram accounts are said to have a member count of above 500.[71]

The role of internet technology in radicalization is being underappreciated by India's security experts, both practitioners and professionals. It needs to be understood that social media and internet-based communication technologies connect very strongly to the young minds and the sheer force of their impact in shaping thoughts, attitudes and behavior of the young generation needs to be recognized with complete objectivity, awareness and strategic foresight. The social media and internet are likely to emerge even more powerful in the future as the society is becoming more and more individualistic and the institutions of collective social identity such as family, caste and kinship are on decline. With weak family and support systems, and the decline of spiritual values with rising materialism, an impressionable young mind is more likely to seek anchorage in virtual communities of online networks.

India's security apparatus needs to invest in training and capacity building to counter the online radicalization. The cyber-security infrastructure and the skill-sets in the police departments are inadequate and need to be significantly enhanced.[72] The expertise of the private sector can be roped in through public-private partnerships in setting up a robust infrastructure to combat online radicalization. Also, there is an acute need of a robust legal mechanism to check online radicalization. This may include regulating social media platforms like Facebook and Twitter. "Spiders of Caliphate,"[73] the counter-extremism project, studied the ISIS' global support network on Facebook. Their findings suggest that "IS's online networks, in particular on Facebook, are growing and can be utilized to plan and direct terror attacks as well as mobilize foreign fighters for multiple areas of insurgency." Furthermore, the report also concluded that "IS has developed a structured and deliberate strategy of using Facebook to radicalize, recruit, support, and terrorize individuals around the world." Though Facebook has taken several measures to stop fake news and address online radicalization, and given assurances to policymakers and governments, ISIS' presence on Facebook is pervasive and highly professionalized.

A robust understanding of the operational dynamics of ISIS on platforms like Facebook and Twitter can be immensely helpful to the policymakers in the security establishment in identifying potential recruits. As already highlighted in the earlier chapters, Indians joining ISIS preferred to work in groups. Hence, nuanced understanding, surveillance and analysis of these group dynamics on Facebook and twitter communities can be extremely useful in identifying and busting terror modules/cells. Besides, regular monitoring of online behavior and expression of thoughts by individuals through Twitter and Facebook posts can be useful in understanding individual's journeys, pathways of radicalization and the trigger points (stage when an ideologically radicalized individual decides to become violent).

To sum up, India needs to invest heavily in creating a technical and legal infrastructure to combat online radicalization.

NOTES

1 Ahmad, Tufail, "The Roots of Islamic Radicalization in Kerala," *New Age Islam*, September 30, 2016, Accessed September 27, 2018, http://www.newageislam.com/radical-islamism-and-jihad/the-roots-of-islamic-radicalisation-in-kerala/d/108722

2 ibid

3 ibid

4 ibid

5 Nanjappa, Vicky, "Kerala, a State Which Has No Answers to Islamist Radicalization," *One India*, September 30, 2017, Accessed September 27, 2018, https://www.oneindia.com/india/kerala-a-state-which-has-no-answers-to-islamist-radicalisation-2553780.html

6 ibid

7 Shaju, Phillip, "13 Guilty of Chopping Kerala Professor's Hand," *Indian Express*, May 1, 2015, Accessed September 27, 2018, https://indianexpress.com/article/india/india-others/13-guilty-of-chopping-kerala-professors-hand/

8 Madhan, Kuhan, "India's Pluralistic Islam Under Seige," *The Diplomat*, April 29, 2016, Accessed September 27, 2018, https://thediplomat.com/2016/04/indias-pluralistic-islam-under-seige/

9 Singh, Rakesh, "Caliphate Radicalization Rising in India," *The New Indian Express*, April 9, 2017, Accessed September 27, 2018, http://www.newindianexpress.com/thesundaystandard/2017/apr/09/caliphate-radicalisation-rising-in-india-1591542.html

10 Nanjappa, op. cit

11 Rajendran, Dhanya and Varier, Megha, "Kerala's Missing 17: How a Complex Web of Conversion and Radicalization Led Them Out of India," *The News Minute,* July 9, 2016, Accessed September 27, 2018, https://www.thenewsminute.com/article/keralas-missing-16-how-complex-web-conversion-and-radicalization-led-them-out-india-46218

12 Shreenath, J, "Has Kerala Become the Most Preferred Recruitment Hub After J&K?," *The Week*, June 27, 2018, Accessed September 27, 2018, https://www.theweek.in/news/india/2018/06/27/has-kerala-isis-preferred-recruitment-hub.html

13 Dev, Arun, "Explained: Why Does the Government Want the Popular Front of India Banned?", *The Quint*, November 24, 2017, Accessed September 29, 2018, https://www.thequint.com/explainers/explainer-why-government-wants-pfi-banned-popular-front-of-india

14 National Investigation Agency, NIA Cases, Case No. RC-05/2013/NIA/KOC, 2013, Accessed July 17, 2018, https://nia.gov.in/case-detail.htm?102

15 Nanjappa, Vicky, "Revealed: How IM was Formed at Terror Camp in Kerala?," Rediff.com, August 5, 2013, Accessed July 17, 2018 https://www.rediff.com/news/report/revealed-how-im-was-formed-at-terror-camp-in-kerala/20130805.htm

16 Nanjappa, Vicky, "Kerala's Love for PFI and Why the State Will Not Ban the Outfit?," *One India*, July 17, 2018, Accessed September 29, 2018, https://www.oneindia.com/india/keralas-love-for-the-pfi-and-why-the-state-will-not-ban-the-outfit-2736316.html

17 ibid

18 ibid

19 Menon, Prasanth, "PFI Taught Jihad to Kerala Muslims: Rashid," *Times of India*, May 29, 2018, Accessed September 30, 2018, https://timesofindia.indiatimes.com/india/pfi-taught-jihad-to-kerala-muslims-rashid-abdulla/articleshow/64367951.cms

20 Sandhu, Kamaljit Kaur, "Kerala-based Islamist Organization PFI's Gulf link Exposed; NIA Claims It Collected Funds from Expatriates," *India Today*, September 27, 2017, Accessed September 30, 2018, https://www.indiatoday.in/india/story/na-kerala-islamist-organisation-popular-frot-of-india-1053512-2017-09-27

21 ibid

22 Wikipedia, KNM

23 Aravind, Indulekha, "Why a Section of Kerala's Muslim Youth is Treading a Radical Path?," *The Economic Times*, July 31, 2016, Accessed September 30, 2018, https://economictimes.indiatimes.com/news/politics-and-nation/why-a-section-of-keralas-muslim-youth-is-treading-a-radical-path/articleshow/53468470.cms

24 ibid

25 ibid

26 ibid

27 Haneefa, Anwar, "Theological and Political Radicalization: Salafi and Jamaat-i-Islami Influence in Contemporary Kerala," August 30, 2016, Accessed September 30, 2018, https://cafe dissensusblog.com/2016/08/30/theological-and-political-radicalization-the-salafi-and-jamaat-e-islami-influence-in-contemporary-kerala/

28 Safi, Michael, "How ISIS Recruiters Found Fertile Ground in Kerala, India's Tourist Gem," *The Guardian*, November 29, 2016, Accessed September 30, 2018, https://www.theguardian. com/world/2016/nov/29/isis-recruiters-fertile-ground-kerala-indias-tourist-gem

29 Aravind, op. cit

30 Outlook, "Shambhu Lal Regar Gave Afrajul's Murder A Love Jihad Angle To Hide His Affair, States Police Chargesheet," January 15, 2018, https://www.outlookindia.com/website/story/shambhu-lal-regar-gave-afrajuls-murder-a-love-jihad-angle-to-hide-his-affair-sta/306866

31 Jayshankar, Dhruva and Pelangeli, Sara, "Assessing the Islamic State Threat to India: It is a Serious but Manageable Challenge", *Times of India*, May 6, 2017, Accessed October 1,

2018, https://blogs.timesofindia.indiatimes.com/toi-edit-page/assessing-the-islamic-state-threat-to-india-it-is-a-serious-but-manageable-challenge/

32 "Tracking ISIS' Influence in India," ORF, Accessed October 2, 2018, http://trackingisis.orfonline.org/

33 Jayshankar and Pelangeli, op. cit

34 Sherazi, Zahir Shah, "Six Top TTP Commanders Announce Allegiance to Islamic State's Baghdadi," *Dawn*, October 14, 2014, Accessed October 2, 2018, https://www.dawn.com/news/1137908

35 Rasheed, Adil, "Jihadist Radicalization in India: Internal Challenges, External Threats," *Journal of Defense Studies*, July 2018, Accessed October 2, 2018, https://idsa.in/jds/jds-12-2-2018-jihadist-radicalisation-in-india

36 "Singapore deports Indian Man for Syrian Links", *Indian Express*, March 24, 2014, Accessed October 2, 2018, https://indianexpress.com/article/india/india-others/singapore-deports-indian-man-for-syrian-links

37 "Tracking ISIS' Influence in India," op. cit

38 ibid

39 Channel 4 News, "ISIS Propagandist Shami Witness: Man Charged in India," June 2015, Accessed October 2, 2018, https://www.channel4.com/news/isis-shami-witness-medhi-masroor-biswas-charged

40 The News Minute, "The Men and Women Recruited by Islamic State from Kerala: NIA Releases Pictures," July 2017, Accessed October 2, 2018, https://www.thenewsminute.com/article/men-and-women-recruited-islamic-state-kerala-nia-releases-pictures-73661

41 Taneja, Kabir, "Uncovering the Influence of ISIS in India," *ORF Publication*, July 12, 2018, Accessed October 2, 2018, https://www.orfonline.org/research/42378-uncovering-the-influence-of-isis-in-india/

42 Abraham, Bobins, "Ansarul Kahlifah: The IS Module Busted in Kerala was Under NIA Scanner for Four Months," *The News*, October 4, 2016, Accessed October 2, 2018, https://www.indiatimes.com/news/india/ansar-ul-khilafah-the-isis-module-busted-in-kerala-was-under-nia-scanner-for-four-months-262950.html

43 Taneja, Kabir, 'Perils of Humoring ISIS in Kashmir", ORF, June 30 2018, Accessed October 2, 2018, https://www.orfonline.org/expert-speak/42014-the-perils-of-humoring-isis-in-kashmir/

44 Jayshankar and Pelangeli, op. cit

45 Channel 4 News, op. cit

46 Singh, Mahim Pratap, "Indian Oil Corporation Manager in Jaipur arrested for Islamic State Links", *Indian Express*, December 11, 2015, Accessed October 3, 2018, https://indianexpress.com/article/india/india-news-india/indian-oil-corporation-manager-in-jaipur-held-for-islamic-state-links/

47 *Reuters*, 'How Captured Paris Attacks Suspect Abdelsalam Hid in Molanbeek," March 19, 2016, Accessed October 3, 2018, https://www.cnbc.com/2016/03/19/captured-paris-attacks-suspect-abdeslam-hid-in-belgiums-molenbeek.html

48 Wood, Graeme, "True Believers," *Foreign Affairs*, October 3, 2018, Accessed October 3, 2018, https://www.foreignaffairs.com/reviews/review-essay/2017-08-15/true-believers

49 Pandya, Abhinav, "Post-ISIS: Future of Global Jihad," *VIF Publications*, November 28, 2017, Accessed October 3, 2018, https://www.vifindia.org/article/2017/november/28/post-isis-future-of-global-jihad

50 Taneja, Kabir, op. cit
51 Pandya, Abhinav, "Why ISIS Can't Make Much Headway with Muslims in India?," *Huffington Post,* December 2015, Accessed October 3, 2018, https://www.huffingtonpost.in/abhinav-pandya/why-isis-cant-make-much-h_b_8824410.html
52 NDTV, "ISIS Considers Indian Recruits Inferior to Arabs, Treats Them as Cannon-fodder: Report," November 23, 2015, Accessed October 3, 2018, https://www.ndtv.com/india-news/indian-recruits-inferior-to-arab-fighters-treated-as-cannon-fodder-report-on-isis-1246695
53 Jayshankar and Pelangeli
54 *The Economic Times,* "Al Qaeda in Indian Subcontinent Getting More Active: US Experts," July 12, 2018, Accessed October 3, 2018, https://economictimes.indiatimes.com/news/defence/al-qaeda-in-indian-subcontinent-getting more-active-us-experts/articleshow/59589905.cms
55 Rasheed, op. cit
56 ibid
57 *The Economic Times,* op. cit
58 "Code of Conduct: Al Qaeda in Indian Subcontinent," *As Sahab Media Subcontinent,* June 2017, https://azelin.files.wordpress.com/2017/06/al-qacc84_idah-in-the-indian-subcontinent-22code-of-conduct22-en.pdf
59 Roul, Animesh, "Al-Qaeda's Quite Resurgence in India," *Terrorism Monitor,* August 15, 2017, Accessed October 3, 2018, https://jamestown.org/program/al-qaedas-quiet-resurgence-in-india/
60 "Al-Qaeda in Indian Sub-continent 'Ideologically Inclined' to Carry Out Attacks in India," *First Post,* August 14, 2018, Accessed October 3, 2018, https://www.firstpost.com/india/al-qaeda-in-the-indian-subcontinent-ideologically-inclined-to-carry-out-attacks-in-india-reveals-un-report-4960521.html
61 Hoffman, Bruce, "Al-Qaeda's Resurrection," March 6, 2018, Accessed October 3, 2018, https://www.cfr.org/expert-brief/al-qaedas-resurrection
62 Hoffman, Bruce, "The Coming ISIS–al Qaeda Merger," *Foreign Affairs,* October 3, 2018, Accessed October 3, 2018, https://www.foreignaffairs.com/articles/2016-03-29/coming-isis-al-qaeda-merger.
63 "Suicide Bombers Visited Kashmir, Kerala and Bengaluru: Sri Lankan Army Chief," *The Hindu,* May 5, 2019, Accessed May 6, 2019, https://www.thehindu.com/news/international/suicide-bombers-visited-kashmir-kerala-bengaluru-sri-lankan-army-chief/article27036863.ece
64 Pant, Harsh V, Taneja, Kabir, "ISIS's New Target: South Asia," *Foreign Policy,* May 2, 2019, Accessed May 6, 2019, https://foreignpolicy.com/2019/05/02/isiss-new-target-south-asia/
65 Pandya, Abhinav, "Jihadi Terror Enters Sri Lanka," *VIF Publications,* April 25, 2019, Accessed May 6, 2019, https://www.vifindia.org/article/2019/april/25/jihadi-terror-enters-sri-lanka
66 Pandya, op. cit
67 von Behr, Ines, Anais Reding, Charlie Edwards, and Luke Gribbon, "Radicalisation in the Digital Era: The Use of the Internet in 15 Cases of Terrorism and Extremism," Santa Monica, CA: RAND Corporation, 2013, https://www.rand.org/pubs/research_reports/RR453.html.

68 Taneja, op. cit

69 Rasheed, op. cit

70 Ingram, Haroro. "Islamic State's English-language Magazines, 2014-2017: Trends & Implications for CT-CVE Strategic Communications," The International Centre for Counter-Terrorism – The Hague 8, no. 15, 2018).

71 Rasheed, Adil, "Jihadist Radicalization in India: Internal Challenges, External Threats," *Journal of Defense Studies*, July 2018, Accessed October 2, 2018, https://idsa.in/jds/jds-12-2-2018-jihadist-radicalisation-in-india

72 Pandya, Abhinav, "Cryptocurrencies: A New Scourge of Terror Financing," *VIF Publications*, August 27, 2018, Accessed October 3, 2018, https://www.vifindia.org/brief/2018/august/27/cryptocurrencies-a-new-scourge-of-terror-financing

73 Waters, Gregory and Postings, Robert, "Spiders of the Caliphate: Mapping the Islamic State's Global Network on Facebook," May 2018, Accessed October 3, 2018, https://www.counter extremism.com/sites/default/files/Spiders%20of%20the%20Caliphate%20%28 May%20 2018%29.pdf

4

CASE STUDY ON KASHMIR AND CALIPHATE 2.0: TURKISH EFFORTS TO WOO INDIAN MUSLIMS

KASHMIR: A CASE STUDY

In this case study on Kashmir, a range of qualitative and quantitative tools were employed including, group interviews, semi-structured interviews, literature review, survey and casual interactions with a diverse range of people. The interviewees included youth groups from South, Central and North Kashmir (40), university and college students from Srinagar (100), residents of downtown Srinagar, security officials, intelligence experts, NGO workers, artists, separatists, former militant commanders, over-ground workers (OGWs), school students, government officials, religious clerics, mainstream politicians, youth political leaders, ordinary civilians, teachers, tour operators, tourism fraternity, traders and shopkeepers. The data so collected provided a rich mix, representing a very broad range of ideas.

Kashmir in many ways is a unique case study for radicalization because traditionally it has been a liberal society. Gandhi Ji saw a ray of hope in Kashmir when India was burning in the inferno of post-partition communal riots (1947). However, that reality existed long-long time back. Over the years, the Kashmiri society has witnessed a gradual process of Islamization creeping into the society, politics, and culture, resulting in the emergence Islamic doctrine of Jihad as a dominant narrative of the so-called Tahreek or Kashmiri political movement. Various factors have played their roles in this process of gradual unfolding of religious extremism and exclusivism in Kashmir. In this chapter, it is intended to analyse in detail, the complex dynamics of radicalization in Kashmir in a historical context.

Kashmir is a 5,000-year-old civilization and an inherent part of the idea of India's civilizational, cultural, social and political evolution. Vedic tribes inhabited the area. Kashmir has been mentioned in Greek accounts and Neelmat Purana, and was a part of Mauryan Empire. In the 1st millennium BC, Kashmir was an important center of Buddhism and Shaivism and the 4th Buddhist Council was held here during the reign of Kushana king Kanishka in which scholars like Vasumitra, Ashwaghosha, and Nagarjuna participated. Karkota king Lalitaditya Muktapida defeated Tibetans, Arabs of Sind, and ruled over Magadha, Kamrup, Kalinga and Gauda. His empire extended into Central Asia. India's first original work of history "Rajatarangini" by Kalhan comes from Kashmir. The Muslim phase of Kashmir began with the Buddhist ruler Rinchana's conversion to Islam in 1300 AD.

From 1586 to 1751, Mughals ruled Kashmir, followed by Afghans from 1747 to 1819. The Sikhs ruled Kashmir until 1846 (first Anglo-Sikh war). After the Sikh defeat, Dogras of Jammu ruled over Kashmir, and in 1947, the last Dogra king Maharaja Hari Singh signed the instrument of accession, making the state an inalienable part of India by legally and politically merging with the new Republic, not only its land but also, more importantly, its civilizational roots and ethos.

Over the centuries, Kashmir has been the center of different religious traditions-Hinduism, Buddhism, Sunni Islam, and Shia Islam. During the Muslim rule, there were phases of religious bigotry and attempts were made to ruin the Catholic, spiritual and scholarly traditions of Kashmir. Muslims kings like Sikandar levied Jaziyah and forcefully converted Hindus.

However, parallel to this, there also were developments that saw the amalgamation of the Shaivite-Buddhist mysticism with the Sufi mysticism of Islam. Central Asian Naqshbandi Sufi saints like Nuruddin Wali emphasized upon religious harmony and love. Hindus worshiped him as Nand Rishi. Hindu mystics like Lalleshwari were revered by Muslims also. The beautiful cultural intermingling gave rise to Kashmiriyat—the syncretic culture of Kashmir that symbolizes religious harmony, tolerance and focusses on the spiritual essence of the religions rather than the exclusivist undertones of ritualistic differences. It found its most beautiful expression in rich culture, music and peaceful co-existence of Kashmiri Pundits, Sikhs and Muslims in the valley.

In contrast, today's Kashmir presents a starkly different picture. The generation born in the 1990s hardly had any exposure to Kashmiryat as it grew up in the environment of conflict, military presence, and terrorist violence. There is strong resistance to resettling of Kashmiri Pundits (they were ousted in 1990), and a vast chunk of Kashmiri youth openly talks of Caliphate and Islam as the only destiny of Kashmir. The process of Islamic radicalization in Kashmir has been parallel with the unfolding of the political and social events in the state. Therefore, rather than leap-frogging to the near-final stage of the more extensive process of Islamization, i.e. radicalization, it becomes imperative to understand the evolutionary dynamics of the all-pervading ecosystem of Islamism in Kashmir.

In the current scenario, Islam and to a large extent Islamism more or less animate every aspect of life, and hence it becomes essential to know the extent of Islam's penetration and the operational dynamics. This chapter will review the impact, likely future scenario and some case studies to understand the pathways of radicalization, followed by some specific features of radicalization in Kashmir, concluding with some concrete policy recommendations.

In Kashmir, Islam as an identity had existed for about seven centuries and by its inherent nature, its default or fundamental presence in the socio-political and cultural aspects was an accepted fact. It also had its spells of extremism, bigotry and forced conversions even before 1947. However, as mentioned previously, the Islam in Kashmir was very different from its West Asian counterpart. Also as compared to the Islam in other parts of India, the Kashmiri version of Islam was quite tolerant, accommodative and liberal. As compared to the different regions of the Indian subcontinent, the history of Hindu-Muslim relations in Kashmir has been far more cordial and smoother. Until the late 1980s, in Kashmiri villages, the teachers were always the Kashmiri Pundits. Both the communities jointly participated in festivals like Kheer Bhawani, Amarnath Yatra, and shrine celebrations at Batmalu Saheb and Charaar-e-Sharif. There were several common customs and rituals in marriages. There is no record of large-scale communal riots or the destruction of Hindu temples in the valley, despite the fact of the violent separatist movement plaguing the state for three decades.

The situation began to change in the 1980s. The death of Sheikh Abdullah in 1982 created a political vacuum. The ensuing political developments led to the intensification of the mistrust between the Indian establishment and

Kashmir. It created space for Islamic organizations which had hitherto been functioning on the margins and confined more or less to the social aspects of life. The mainstream secular leaders occupied the political space. In the 1987 elections for the State Assembly, an ensemble of religious groups led by Jamaat-e-Islami (JeI) participated in the polls for the first time under the banner of Muslim United Front. The rigged elections and political mismanagement provided an ideal platform in 1989 for the Pakistani dictator, General Zia-ul-Haq to fulfill his ambition of giving "a 1,000 cuts" to India. Pakistan unleashed a proxy war in Kashmir. There was a massive influx of Mujahiddin fighters (financed, nurtured and trained by the US and Pakistan in the 1980s) from Afghanistan, rendered jobless after the withdrawal of Russians (after the end of cold war) and with that began Kashmir's connection with the global Islamism. Separatist and extremist elements ousted the Pundits by threats and intimidation in 1990, and since then Kashmir has seen a rapid rise of Islamic extremism and a more than a proportionate decline in Kashmiriyat.

The core of Islamist ecosystem of Kashmir is today, constituted by hardline religious and fundamentalist organizations such as Jamaat-i-Islami(JeI), Hurriyat Conference, Jamiyat Ahle-Hadith (JAH), Tablighi Jamaat (TJ), Tahreek-ul-Mujahideen (TuM); local-cum-Pak–sponsored terrorist organizations like Hizbul Mujahiddin (HM), Al Badr, Laskhkar-e-Toiba (LeT), Jaish-e-Muhammad (JeM), Islamic State of Jammu and Kashmir (ISJK), Ansaar Ghazwat-ul-Hind (AGUH); transnational terrorist groups like Al Qaida (AQ), ISIS and Pak-based "charity" groups like Jamaat-ud-Dawa (JuD) and Pakistani establishment controlled by ISI. The second layer comprises mosques, social media, extremist literature, prisons, a vast network of OGWs, Gulf-based charities and individual donors, Zakat collections, educational and charity institutions, lay followers, and cadres present in the state's institutions (academia, civilian administration, and the police forces).

The last layer facilitating and aiding (knowingly or unknowingly) the success of the first two segments comprises the national and the local mainstream political parties, domestic and international civil society groups and human rights activists, mainstream national and the local media, global geopolitical actors and events, events in the Middle East (ME) and the broader Islamic world, the Hindu extremist organizations, absence of a rational counter-narrative, inadequate secular educational infrastructure, rampant corruption and poor governance, atrocities by armed forces, trust deficit between Delhi and Kashmir, neglectful or instead appeasing attitude of the state apparatus and last but not the least, incompetent handling of the political and security situation in state, short of any strategic foresight.

All these elements of the ecosystem of Islamism in Kashmir work in perfect harmony with each other, one feeding into the other and ultimately strengthening the entire ecosystem, for example, radicalization leading to militancy and militancy leading to more radicalization. The ecosystem is internally dynamic and continuously evolving in sophistication. Externally, it is expanding. For example, it has adopted the use of social media and internet technologies in a very aggressive and innovative way. Over the years, the intra-system harmony has refined and it has emerged as a highly complex matrix. Therefore, policymakers need to understand this complex matrix first and then have a holistic approach rather than a piecemeal one.

Jamaat-e-Islami (established in 1942 AD)

In the current scenario, the most severe threat concerning radicalization leading to terrorism comes from JeI. As said by Mr. Shiv Murari Sahay, the veteran counter-terrorism official of J&K (Pultizer Project, November 5, 2012), JeI is a South Asian version of the Muslim Brotherhood of Egypt. Keeping in mind, the considerations of space, it may not be possible to delve deeper into the factual details of the origins of JeI (more on JeI, later in the section "How to deal with Jamaat-e-Islami?"). However, suffice it to say that JeI believes in political Islam. It follows the teachings of Maulana Maududi, Syed Qutb, and Hasan Al Banna—that the society and politics should be conducted in line with the divine law of Sharia. It is an extremist organization that dehumanizes non-Muslims, Shias, and Sufi Muslims. In social domains, it is conservative, fundamentalist, exclusivist and orthodox. Though like Etaqadis or Barelwis, they follow the Hanafi school of thought, they do not believe in Shrine worship and see many syncretic Sufi practices as blasphemy—the impurities borrowed from the Hindu idolatry. They agree with Ahle-Hadith in their rejection of shrine worship, and attitude towards the Shia and Ahmadiya Muslims and non-Muslims.

In the political domain, JeI supports Pakistan's claim on Kashmir. It is member of and ideologically aligned with the separatist Hurriyat Conference (APHC). JeI's de facto militant face is HM. Its agenda is pro-Pakistan and it openly talks about that in its Ijtemas (religious-political discussions). Informed interlocutors during the interviews maintained that from 2002 through 2008, the peace period in Kashmir, JeI strongly entrenched itself in the Kashmiri society through proselytization, social service, Ijtemas (religious gatherings), threats, terror, and intimidation. The result of their heightened efforts was seen in the unrest that erupted in 2008, and continuing since then. According to informed sources, JeI is said to have played an instrumental role fomenting the fires of 2016 post–Burhan Wani agitation. Today, in most of the social and political circles of Kashmir, it is firmly believed that not a single targeted and political killing happens in Kashmir without JeI's approval. JeI has strong presence in education and the social service sectors. Hundreds of schools run by the Falai-Aam (FA), trust of JeI, are better than the government schools in infrastructure and the quality of teaching. These schools combine modern scientific education and Islamic teachings. Local newspaper, *Greater Kashmir* reported that the Trust has helped spread education over the last 30 to 40 years to areas that had remained even beyond the reach of the government.[1] Incidentally, government-run schools are viewed poorly by the local people. There aren't enough non-religious private schools. In such a scenario, where the state, private sector, and the secular non-profit sector do not have a strong presence in the field of school education, JeI and Ahle-Hadith have intervened effectively, earning social legitimacy. JeI also did impressive rehabilitation work during the disastrous floods of 2014.

JeI generously distributes Islamic literature in the form of books, pamphlets, and brochures in colleges, universities, jails and social circles. The original Arabic literature is translated in Urdu and English in Pakistan and sent to India. Tons of literature on political Islam is available in all the bookshops in Srinagar. These include books of Maulana Maududi, Syed Qutb, and Hasan Banna. The quality of printed versions is excellent and at first glance, one gets an impression that they are political science or IR books. The objective appears to be to motivate the youth and capture their intellectual imagination in the early impressionable years.

These books are widely read in universities and colleges. Prof. Muhammad Rafiq Butt, professor of Sociology in Kashmir University (native of Ganderbal) who joined HM and was killed in police encounter only three days after leaving home was an avid reader of Maududi literature. According to the police officials who closely observed his case, he was blending political Islam with sociology in his classroom lectures. According to informed interlocutors, Jamaat acts as a conduit for militancy. JeI functions as a socio-political wing of HM and its cadres function as OGWs of HM in providing infrastructure/logistic support, organizing protective shell in which militants operate. JeI has substantial penetration even in the state's lower and middle-level civil administration, civil secretariat, colleges and universities, jails, legal fraternity, powerful financial institutions, political groups, and the police department. Allegedly, they also help in arranging logistics, weapons, and shelter for the Foreign Terrorists and in facilitating their movements. One can clearly see the evidence of extended JeI presence on the ground. According to a former LeT militant whose religious radicalization started after association with Islamic Jamiyat-ul Talba, or IJT, the student wing of JeI, Jamaati association facilitates easy entry into militancy. The cadres, in the beginning, are asked to perform their religious duties. Later, if someone expresses a strong inclination for joining a militant group, he is asked to resign from JeI at least a year before his formal induction into the militant wing, i.e. HM. This is done to feign innocence later with a justification that as soon as JeI spotted radicalization tendencies, it expelled the concerned individual.

Getting formal membership of JeI is rather tough. It begins with participation in Ijtemas, followed by an active association with its youth wing and after attaining the age of 40, one can apply for the basic membership. In a district of 500 villages, on an average, there could only be about 400 active memberships of JeI. They have a very dedicated cadre and strong grassroots presence.

Their modus operandi involves the use of persuasion, threat, violence, and intimidation. People in the rural areas are scared of cooperating with the state and armed forces for fear of JeI to the extent that they would not even like to be seen publicly with high-ranking government officials. They fear that JeI OGWs also act as an intelligence arm of militant organizations reporting the movements of ordinary rural and urban folk. The informers of security forces and others who want to collaborate in development work with the government are dealt with threats and violence. Furthermore, JeI has an expertise in psychological harassment and pressuring the opponents. For example, they keep intelligence of those citizens who vote during elections. After that, they indulge in intense character assassination of such individuals. They are branded as traitors. For them, following phrases are often used, as reported by one of the victims: "X ne Shahido ka sauda kiya" (X betrayed the

The Ecosystem of Islamism: Internally Evolving and Externally Expanding

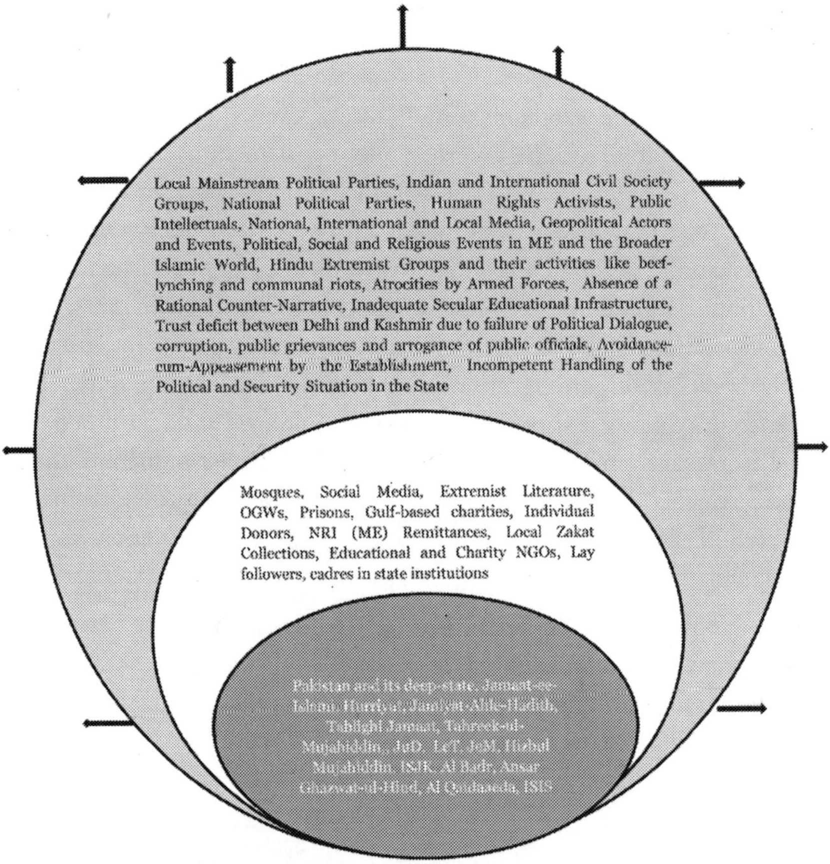

cause of martyrs, i.e. the militants who died), "Y ne shahido ki lasho par paav rakhkar vote kiya" (Y trampled upon the corpses of martyrs and voted for India). Those who do not agree with their ideology have to face character assassination in Universities, government offices, social and political circles. His or her prospects of promotion and growth are crushed by Jamaat cadres. And, those who support their ideology receive a strong support in business, jobs, employment and other social and political platforms. For example, if there is an upstart lawyer or a doctor from Jamaat, Jamaat cadres will work actively to popularize him to boost his clientele and income. In return, Jamaat gets a stronger hold and donations for its cause.

Furthermore, according to informed sources, Jamaat and HM have been sending boys to PoK since 2012 for the required training. Moreover, 2014 onwards, Jamaat has strengthened itself at the ground level in South Kashmir, and Peoples Democratic Party (PDP) that has a strong electoral base in South Kashmir is widely known to have turned a blind eye for obvious reasons. Moreover, the result can be seen in the current phase of bloody militancy in South Kashmir. It may be emphasized that more than any other Tanzeem, the JeI symbolizes strongly entrenched Pakistani footprint in Kashmir. It is the gravest threat to India's national security.

However, these days, it appears that the young generation has become a little disillusioned with JeI. The reasons are their threats and terror tactics. They are seen as fulfilling the agenda of foreign players and less concerned with the grievances of Kashmiris. Their malicious political machinations and complete disregard of Kashmiriyat further infuriate the local Kashmiris. The young generation also sees JeI as a corrupt organization. In many quarters, it is alleged that during 2016 unrest, JeI got its cadres, arrested in stone-pelting, released through influence and bribery. There are also stories doing rounds that JeI siphoned off funds sent for the rehabilitation of the "pellet" victims.

The intellectual class disagrees with the ideology and activities of Jamaat. In South Kashmir, ordinary citizens even maintain that if JeI did not have the word "Islami" in its name, people would not even look at it!

Within JeI, ideological differences have existed since 2001. The moderate and the intellectual section favour a more non-violent political action and therefore want JeI to distance itself from HM. The remaining radicalized and hardcore Pakistan supporters seem to have captured the organization.

The youth finds JeI archaic and orthodox. Ahle-Hadith, which has better financial resources, now attracts the younger generation, with profound linkages with global Islam. It projects itself intellectually and logically. It engages in prolific use of the modern communication technologies and internet which is instrumental in luring young impressionable minds.

Lately, Jamaat has increased its operations in Central Kashmir. This can be seen in the form of weekly invitations being sent to individuals in rural areas inviting them to participate in Ijtemas. Recently, the leadership has also been charged with a mandate to go on a high recruitment drive. Over the last few months (April 2018 onwards), JeI-administered WhatsApp groups are being created in large numbers. It appears that some dominant long-term strategy is being designed to capture the current youth unrest.

Jamiyat Ahle-Hadith

It believes in the Wahhabi/Salafi school of thought. Wahhabi line is followed by many diverse entities such as ISIS, AQ, and Saudi Arabia, UAE and Qatar. However, there are vast differences in the versions adhered to by ISIS/AQ and states like Saudi and UAE (refer to Chapter I for more details on this). Kashmir-based journalist Tariq Mir has, for the US-based Pulitzer Center, carried out an intensive study of the growth of Salafism in Kashmir. In his essay, "Kashmir: From Sufi to Salafi," he contends that introduction of the Salafi thought in Kashmir "goes back nearly a hundred years but such was the belief in local traditions of Sufi Islam that the Puritans remained on the remote fringes of Kashmir's religious and cultural life. That began to change as the insurgency gathered force from 1989."[2]

The Salafist reject the Sufi shrine/tomb worship and other syncretic rituals and practices. They find them the pernicious influences of Hindu and Greek mythologies. Their line of thought is fundamentalist in nature as compared to Sufi traditions. The corruption in shrines and the dogmatic practices of Sufi are also a substantial factor for the rise of Ahle-Hadith and other fundamentalist jamaats. Salafis have a significant following among the youth. The present generation of Kashmiris was born in the early 90s, and grew up in an environment of violence, religious radicalization, and political turbulence. As a result, they already have a radicalized mindset to some extent. They have no memories of the Pundit-Muslim syncretic social culture of Kashmir. With such a basic cognitive framework, they are not much interested in Sufi practices. In the present times, the post-90s generation perceives the Indian military presence as an onslaught on their Islamic identity. They look for an anchorage—a belief system that provides them an empowering Islamic identity. Where the dominant narrative is militancy, conflict, and violence, the peaceful Sufi meditative religion does not align well with the sentiments of the youth. The current generation believes that Sufism imbibed meekness, pacifism, and tolerance in the society which led foreign invaders to occupy Kashmir in the past. In such disturbing times, going back to the fundamentalist and puritanical belief system gives them a sense of anchorage, strength, and security. The overarching conflict scenario and unrest since 2010 have actively aided the growth in the popularity of Ahle-Hadith in youth, and there has been a terrific increase in its adherents.

The Salafis have substantial petro-dollar funding. They also generate sources through individual and organizational donations from Gulf-based charities, income from plazas, malls, colleges, hospitals, and travel agencies. Impressive network of mosques, in Arabic style with minarets and huge domes are coming up fast in different parts of Kashmir. Once with a marginal presence in the valley, Ahle-Hadith now claims to have around a million followers in the Valley of six million people, and they have approximately 700 mosques.[3] Their mosques have better heating systems, hamams, and superior quality of construction. The imams in Salafis mosques are paid somewhere around INR 60,000 to 70,000 per month in comparison to the Maulvis in Etaqadi mosques who are paid just around INR 5,000 to 6,000. The Imams in Salafi mosques are better educated (many of them get their Islamic degrees in Saudi Arabia), refined and sophisticated. The duration of Friday prayers offered in Salafi mosques is very short as compared to the Etaqadi mosques where it is around one and a half hours, another tactic to lure youth.

Interestingly, according to Tariq Mir, "it isn't just the doctrinal primacy that is alluring but the chances of social mobility."[4] The rise of Maulana Al-Kindi, the Salafi poster boy in Kashmir is a testament to it. He was born and brought up in a poor and remote area of southeastern Kashmir where he spent his childhood in tough conditions. After the Madrasa education in Srinagar, he was recommended by a Salafi leader for higher studies in Saudi Arabia where he earned his PhD in Islamic Studies. It opened the gates of opportunities for him. After having taught in Saudi for 12 years, he is back in Kashmir. He still gets a considerable pension from his previous employers. According to his local followers, Al-Kindi still wields strong influence with access to the highest echelons of power in Saudi Arabia. Besides, the author observed that many local Muslims from lower castes like cobblers, shikarawalas (boats men) sweepers and butchers are joining Ahle-Hadith sect because it promises true Islam to them, putting an end to their low-caste status. It can also be seen in the fact that a large number of Salafi followers are not using their caste names. Instead, they use Salafi as their last name. Hence, the desire to seek equality and social status also leads many Etaqadi Muslims to follow Salafism.

Salafis are modern in their approach. They rely on intensive use of advanced communication technologies, the internet, and social media. Absconding preacher Zakir Naik is immensely popular amongst the Salafis of Kashmir. Ahle-Hadith mosques and seminaries have doubled in the last 27 years. According to the FCRA reports, their top donors are from UAE, Saudi Arabia, and Qatar.[5] The state receives crores of rupees in donation each year over the decade. The Salafis are actively engaging in religious conversions and moral policing. According to informed sources, the extremist and separatist leader Asia Andrabi, presently booked by NIA, actively encourages and facilitates the conversions of Sikh and other non-Muslims girls to Islam. Tourists are also approached with an intense religious propaganda. Videos of such proselytization activities are easily available on many social media groups in the valley. The Salafis are ahead of others in their non-religious social presence. They run orphanages, clinics, colleges, schools, and madrasas. A great deal of Salafi literature has been freely distributed in Kashmir over the last 30 years. However, with home to 2.8 million internet users, the spread of Wahhabi influence is more dangerous through social media messaging platforms.[6] The religious overdose is generating fundamentalism and exclusivism, eventually leading to the extremism of thoughts and actions.

The organizational structure of Ahle-Hadith includes four sub-schools: Jamiyat Ahle-Hadith (Gawkadal-based and puritan), the main body, Difai (ultra-puritan), Guraba (religio-political ultra-puritans like Masarrat Alam) and Sout-ul-Haq (ISIS mindset). It believes that a non-conformist is wajib-ul-qatl (eligible for murder). Informed sources confirmed that radical suspects are in the range of 1 per cent to 5 per cent in Kashmir. Ahle-Hadith split with Hurriyat in 2003. It is now associated with TuM which has links with LeT (it believes in Salafi ideology). TuM is a part of PoK-based United Jihad Council, led by Syed Salahuddin, the HM commander who in 2014 supported the entry of AQ in Kashmir[7].

Unlike JeI and Barelwis, they refrain from discussing the domestic political issues in their mosque lectures. Tariq Mir informs that the Ahle-Hadith mosques have long sermons on Palestine, western aggression against the Islamic world but they are silent on the local Kashmiri issues. In fact, in one of the interactions with an Ahle-Hadith, Imam Maulvi Razzak of Srinagar mosque (Nishat mosque) informed that the ongoing militancy and the activities of JeI are un-Islamic. He said that the Jihad is waged for the cause of Allah, not out of personal revenge or for attaining political power. However, informed sources believe that they are establishing an ideological base for themselves at this stage.

However, not everything is quiet on the Salafi front. Lately, some Ahle-Hadith scholars like Mushtaq Veeri have praised IS and Baghdadi and propagated caliphate code in Kashmir. In a video released, he vehemently declares,[8]

> "Dekha Salafiyon ka kamal, jab salafi maidan men utarte hain to wapis naam lene ka kabhi sochte hi nahi. Ham Islami hukumat qaim karke rahenge. Iraq men dekho Abu Bakr naam ke salafi ki hukumat... Kashmir men anqareeb insha Allah Islami jhanda gaad diya jaega...."
>
> (See the achievement of the Salafis! When the Salafis embark on their mission in the battlefield, they do not back out. Look at the state of the Salafist by the name of Abu Bakr Baghdadi in Iraq... God willing, we will be hoisting the Islamic flag soon in Kashmir....)

Mufti Shabbir Ahmad Kasmi,[9] a Deobandi (ideologically, a close cousin of Ahle-Hadith) has expressed support for Zakir Musa and his AGUH. Extremist narratives of puritan Sunni schools have also raised fears among the Shia community. As a result, even the Shias are exhibiting early signs of radicalization.

Minor incidents of sectarian rivalries have already started emerging. Clashes between Barelwis and Ahle-Hadith are becoming prominent. In October 2011, an ugly brawl erupted between the Salafis and Barelwis in the Palpora.[10] The town of Palpora had become a vibrant Salafi center. It invited opposition from the local Barelwi population (the Hanafi followers) when the new Salafi converts questioned the authenticity of the Barelwi customs and traditions. Police had to intervene, and ultimately the Salafis broke away from the community and built a make-shift mosque in a nearby apple orchard.

The Barelwis allege that Ahle-Hadith followers are not respectful to their elder saints. Ahle-Hadith, however, accuses them of shirk and indulgence in shrine corruption. They claim that Sufis are devoid of the spiritual essence and are exploiting the religion for financial gains and social clout. Tussles have been reported between Barelwis and Ahle-Hadith relatives of a dead man in the Nishat area over funeral rites. The conflict became extreme, and both the groups performed the funeral prayers (janaze ki namaz) separately. Later, Barelwis accused the Ahle-Hadith group of possessing weapons and allegedly (as per the Ahle-Hadith sources) attempted to get them involved in fabricated charges.

If there are scholars like Kindi who prefer to maintain silence on political issues, there are also leaders like Masarrat Alam who openly talk about political Islam. For many followers, the gradual acceptance of the doctrine of Takfiri (a heretical belief held by some Salafis calling for excommunication and, in extreme cases killing of Muslim thought to have deviated from the path) is alarming. Allegedly, according to informed sources, the Budgam shrine was burnt by the hardline Soit-ul-haq faction. Maulana Shawkat Ahmad Shah, a famous Salafi cleric, was boycotted by the extremist Salafis for cooperating with the security forces in ushering in the peace process. He was shot dead by LeT in April 2011.[11]

The incidents of shrine burning by Salafis in Pakistan may have a debilitating impact on the religious harmony of Kashmir also, as the state is home to several Sufi shrines. Sources confirm that if the shrines are not heavily guarded as they are now, there can be several incidents of vandalizing shrines. In casual conversation, ordinary Kashmiris do express their fears that violent sectarian rhetoric of the ME is finding resonance in Kashmir. The state already has the history of the traditional Shia-Sunni rift, but lately, brawls have been reported between the clerics belonging to Salafi and Deobandi and Barelwi sects.[12]

The government of India's Chief Interlocutor and a steady Kashmir hand, Dineshwar Sharma has categorically stated that the biggest challenge in Kashmir is to de-radicalize its youth and militants. He observed, "I am worried about the people of Kashmir. If all this picked up, the situation will be like Yemen, Syria and Libya. People will start fighting in so many groups. So, it is very important that everybody, all of us, contribute so that suffering of Kashmiris ends."[13]

Emerging Salafi-Kashmiriyat Conflict

In the long run, the Salafi spread will threaten the remnants of Kashmiriyat and it may completely disconnect Kashmir culturally from India. This is so because Salafism generally brings with it, Arabization of the social and cultural system. In essence, it aims at a very standardized version of Islam which would be in conflict with the local culture, language and even the idea of a nation-state. If in future, the Salafi followers will reject the concept of democracy, elections, and a secular nation, how will India engage them? It will be an altogether different language and will strengthen the roadblocks in the journey towards peace and political dialogue.

Barelwi/Etaqadis

Having given the detailed account of the meteoric rise of Ahle-Hadith and active presence of the JeI, the question arises, "What is the status of Barelwis vis-à-vis radicalization?"

Though the majority of the population is still "Etaqadi" (Barelwi local Muslims), their roots in Sufism have lost the spiritual essence. Only rituals like worshipping shrines have remained intact with strong overtones of religious extremism and communalism, conditioned by the overall milieu of religious and political radicalization. The general perception prevails that Barelwis/Sufis are not extremist. However, statistics tell a different story. A study conducted by the intelligence agencies reported that there are 7,000 mosques in the valley. Ahle-Hadith has 700 mosques, and with the JeI, the total number of mosques goes up to 1,000. Deobandis have 1,500 mosques, and the rest are Sufis. The study further reveals that 79 per cent of the militants have an Etaqadi background, 16 per cent have Jamaat background, 3 per cent are from Ahle-Hadith, and the remaining 3 per cent are from the Deobandi school of thought. Also, in the overall milieu of strong anti-India sentiment, strengthened by religious extremism and exclusivism of puritanical Sunni schools, even the Etaqadis have become extraordinarily fanatic and extremist in their attitude. Maulana Abdul Rashid Daudi, a prominent Barelwi cleric of Kashmir, declared fatwa against those Muslims who paid tributes to former PM Atal Bihari Vajpayee.[14]

Hence, the oft suggested and widely prevalent notion in policy circles of encouraging Sufism in Kashmir fails to reflect the ground reality. At best, it could be wishful thinking because the dominant sentiment is of going back to puritanical and a fundamentalist version. With such a zeitgeist, the Salafi School is more aligned. The conflict over the last two decades has taken the most massive toll on Kashmiriyat. Its essence of communal harmony and tolerance manifested in social events like shrine worship and fairs is on a rapid downward trajectory. The leftovers of Sufism or the outer trappings are competing in extremism and fundamentalism with organized and well-funded ideologies like JeI, Deoband, and Ahle-Hadith. No doubt, they stand a poor chance in this highly uneven battle. Their task is made even more difficult by the forces of globalization and advanced communication technologies which put the Muslims of Kashmir in an easy "connect" with the sectarian, religious and political events of the ME.

Militancy, Religion and Afterlife

The militancy itself is a big causal factor in religious radicalization. An individual who joins a militant organization is given rigorous training in religious studies. Religion becomes a critical weapon to get rid of the fear of death. An ex-militant of LeT revealed that religion is the most crucial factor in radicalizing Muslims in Kashmir. It is used to dehumanize the enemy which rids the militant of any guilt-feeling while killing anyone.

Furthermore, it gives the individual the strength of faith in the face of adversities. In an interaction with a police officer with vast experience in interrogating terrorists, it was mentioned that LeT terrorists utter only religious justifications for their actions during interrogations. They are a highly brainwashed lot.

There is no fear of death. During Cordon and Search Operation (CASO), ordinary civilians march in hundreds to the encounter site for stone-pelting. The current sentiment of glorifying death and becoming a Mujahid has its roots in the concept of afterlife in Islam. In Islam, death is seen as an investment for attaining the reward of Jannat in the afterlife. Also, Kashmir already has a rich history of worshipping tombs and graves. The concept of afterlife gets a boost from the material conditions prevailing in the society. When there is conflict all around, the faith in religious injunctions promising a paradise after death gets certified, in a way. Hence, the religious narrative feeds into overall feelings of resentment and passion for joining militancy.

Thus, the Islamic concept of the afterlife is a strong motivator for militants. The whole social system supports it. The families of dead militants command huge respect as the families of the Shaheed. The mothers of militants killed hardly have any sense of remorse. They have a feeling of satisfaction of having sacrificed a son in the cause of religion. In villages, their graveyards have become revered places of social unions and mobilizations. Funerals have emerged as places of community mobilization. The whole society seems to be in a grand state of mourning with strong religious overtones. Such a milieu can be a fertile ground for the next stage of individuals volunteering as suicide bombers.

Similarly, stone-pelting also has strong religious symbolism. During CASO, mosques are used to give a call to people on loudspeakers to assemble at the encounter site. Also, in Islam, the concept of stoning a Satan is very pious. This kind of religious imagery is being used in a very disruptive manner to manipulate young minds. Informed sources maintain that separatist Hurriyat leader, Masarrat Alam, managed to distribute in the schools in 2008-09, CDs teaching Intifada through stone-pelting. The CDs showed video clips of Palestinians pelting stones at Israeli forces. The message was clear: stone-pelting is a holy exercise, with a religious sanction and hence could be used in jihad. The Palestinian example was instrumental in inspiring the local populace. Since then, stone pelting has evolved as a robust tactic to shield militants and disrupt security operations.

After the encounter death of militant Burhan Wani, the state witnessed a vigorous upsurge in militancy. Every month, 18 to 20 young men join a militant organization. By August 2018, the count had already crossed 130. It is said that in South Kashmir, 10,000 men are waiting to pick up arms. More individuals joining militancy means more CASO operations, stone-pelting and encounter deaths, followed by religiously charged funeral processions—a perfect combination of all the conducive factors for the radicalization of more young men. Such funerals have also emerged as hunting grounds for militant commanders to recruit new cadres.

The detailed analysis of different militant organizations is beyond the purview of this chapter. However, suffice it to mention that since the 1990s, the terror Tanzeems have become more Islamized, extremist and exclusivist. Though the subtext of the Kashmiri movement since 1950s has been Islam, from 1990s onwards, lately, it has increasingly occupied the central position giving way to religious fanaticism and ultra-extremism. Earlier terrorist organizations like Jammu Kashmir Liberation Front (JKLF) were not very overt in emphasizing Islam, though it did exist as an undercurrent. JKLF got replaced by Jamaat-backed HM which was avowedly Islamic in its proclamations. Then, LeT and JeM, inspired by Wahhabism and Deobandi school of thought respectively, arrived in Kashmir. Along with them, transnational terrorist organizations like AQ and ISIS, believing in the radical notions of Takfeeri, have also made inroads in Kashmir. According to a senior counter-terrorism official, in the current conflict situation in Kashmir, only the most radicalized ones survive—it is the survival of the fittest, i.e. the most radical one.

Furthermore, it can also be seen that with the rapid growth of Sunni fundamentalist thought over the last decade, there is a spectacular rise in the following of the notions of the caliphate and sharia-law governed society. New organizations like AGUH (led by former HM commander Zakir Musa) that are ideologically affiliated to AQ have a significant following in universities where Ahle-Hadith followers are sitting in prominent positions. It may not be appropriate to cite the incidents of the waving of ISIS flags by stone-pelters as a strong evidence for the existence of ISIS in Kashmir. However, under no circumstances, the fact of the increasing popularity of the ISIS mindset in Kashmir can be denied. Security forces have neutralized several militants of ISJK, last being Daud Salafi. Burhan Muzaffar Wani, the poster boy of Kashmiri militancy, had openly talked of the caliphate in his videos. A group of masked youth waving IS flags (IS supporters) even tried to vandalize the pulpit of Mirwaiz Umar Farookh (Etaqadi Muslim and the chief Imam of Jamia Mosque).[15] In today's Kashmir, there is a massive following of Zakir Musa who wants an Islamic Kashmir. If AGUH had sufficient funds, weapons, and organization, by now, there would have been a "Musa army" determined to establish Sharia rule in Kashmir. Young boys in the 9 to 18 age group find a role model in Zakir Musa. These young boys actively participate in stone-pelting. In middle-class homes and upmarket private schools, faculty members have strong sympathy with militants like Zakir Musa. There appears a strong possibility of school administration facilitating the participation of young boys in stone-pelting, directly or indirectly. Many of these young boys are booked in police cases and face harassment at the hands of police. Their radicalization begins at the early age of 8 to 9 years. By the time they are 18, they are ready to join militants groups. Even the PhD scholar like Mannan Wani, in his famous letter before his encounter, categorically endorses the Islam as a complete system encompassing ways and methods to run society, politics and economics. In effect, he is supporting the idea of political Islam. He also says that wherever Islamic model of governance has been given a chance, people have seen an era of peace and justice. Interestingly, he was the member of HM which is an ideological opponent of Zakir Musa's AGUH which believes in Caliphate ideology. It shows that the ISIS mindset is making inroads into the traditional militant groups like HM which have been using the concept of Jihad but confined it to fight against India. They have not ventured into the territory of global Islamic caliphate. It is likely that in the future, the youth joining organizations other than AGUH may also be heavily under the influence of the notions of caliphate and political Islam. Furthermore, Mannan's letter reveals him as a political scientist who talks about the secular concepts of occupation, democracy, minority rights, human rights and the nature of parliamentary candidates. However, ironically, he is comfortable with political Islam and sharia-governed society, at the same time. It clearly exposes the duplicity and schizophrenic nature of his claims of being democratic and secular. It also shows that the modern rational education may not be the perfect guard against the ISIS mindset. The vulnerability of intellectuals like Mannan to the extremist ideology of political Islam is alarming, and a worrisome development.[16]

There are people in Kashmir who claim knowledge of Kashmiri boys having participated in the ISIS battles of Mosul and Falujah. Furthermore, they also informed that ISIS recruits from Nasik (Maharashtra) were in touch with some Salafi followers in Kashmir and through them they tried to rope in HM for their operations. The future appears grim because AGUH, ideologically affiliated to AQ, has a rising popularity profile. The Islamic State in Khorasan (ISKP), currently entrenched in Jalalabad (Afghanistan), may try to become active in Kashmir through local sympathizers. The declining fortunes of ISIS in West Asia may also drive it to become more active in Kashmir.

Even the separatists have expressed concern over the growth of ISIS mindset in Kashmir. Zakir Musa openly threatened to kill Hurriyat leaders[17]. He openly declared that Kashmiris' jihad is for Islam and not for any Azadi. He even disapproved and condemned Hurriyat's ways as un-Islamic. Seeing his popularity, the hardline and staunch anti-India separatist Hurriyat leader Syed Ali Shah Gilani had to admit that Zakir Musa's methods and ideology are akin to the ideal Islamic way of Jihad. The deceased ISJK militant Daud Salafi had said that Hurriyat leaders have no right to visit his funeral. Local sources have reported clashes between the groups supporting a merger with Pakistan and the ISIS followers.[18]

The Sense of Alienation and Mistrust

Years of political instability, conflict, presence of security forces and consistent failure of the dialogue processes have led to a deep sense of mistrust and insecurity among the youth. The mainstream political parties have lost credibility. In the popular perception, mainstream parties are seen as neck deep in corruption, political opportunism, and nepotism. Public grievances have been mounting and have remained unaddressed. There is a profound "disconnect" between the masses and the civil administration. People complain that district-level civil servants and high-ranking officials are arrogant and supercilious. It is very tough to access them even for redressal of routine grievances. Lack of outreach to the ordinary people is very obvious, even to a lay observer. Infrastructure development work has been crumbling. Even the high-profile constituencies like Beerbah (Omar Abdullah) and Ganderbal (Dr. Farukh Abdullah) present a sorry state of affairs about roads, public services, and amenities. Academic infrastructure of the state is in bad shape. Colleges lack quality infrastructure and quality teaching.

As mentioned above, religious organizations like JeI have a strong presence in academia. In such a scenario, the absence of a secular and intellectual narrative is more than obvious. Besides, not only the mainstream political parties, even the separatist Hurriyat has lost social legitimacy. They are perceived as foreign agents (which they are) fulfilling the agenda of Pakistan and having least concern for the local Kashmiris. They are also accused of high-level corruption-accepting monetary benefits from India and Pakistan both.

The overbearing presence of security forces leading to interference in the day-to-day lives of the common people has made things worse. Barricades, checkpoints, and scrutiny are very humiliating for the ordinary people. Young men complain of security personnel seizing and checking their mobile phones. Often, there are incidents of humiliating and high-handed behavior by security personnel even in routine matters. Allegedly, Burhan Wani joined militancy to seek revenge because he was harshly beaten by cops. People complain that even if an individual's picture is seen with a stone-pelter, he is fabricated in false cases and has to pay huge bribes to the police officials. The police are said to have extracted large sums in bribes for setting the stone-pelters free.

The overall conflict situation makes normal democratic governance extremely difficult. All this has led to a deep sense of distrust, alienation, and hopelessness. In such a state, the young population is driven either towards drugs or religion. Ahmad Tausif, a political science PhD scholar of Kashmir University, put it this way, "The failure of democracy drives people towards religion. In Islam, there is an alternate system of social and political governance which also has the advantage of divine sanction. Hence, when the secular democratic institutions fail to deliver, the people are strongly attracted to the religious injunctions of Sharia law."

Social Media

The social media is one of the strongest pillars and a channel for radicalization. In Kashmir, cinemas and discos were shut down in the 90s due to the pressure of militants and religious extremist organizations. Now, the young population is looking for outlets for the expression of their political views, religious, cultural sentiments, and creative instincts. Social media has occupied that vacuum. In an overarching milieu of conflict, suppression, fear, religious extremism and violence, the young generation tries to find freedom of expression through the social media. In that virtual reality, they have a sense of empowerment and freedom of expression. However, the same social media is acting as a double-edged sword. It has emerged as the most potent weapon for radicalizing the youth. Young school- and college-going students have provoking video and audio clips of militants, extremist religious leaders in their mobiles. They listen to Arabic taranas, and the speeches of Masood Azhar, Hafiz Sayeed and Zakir Naik (based on personal observations). Militant commanders like Zakir Musa, Naved Jutt and Riaz Naiku release their video clips on a regular basis. Their video and audio clips are full of explicit Jihadi extremist content. They are very active on Instagram. Their pictures and videos are a rage among the young population. There are hundreds of WhatsApp groups circulating false, one-sided and extremist messages. During CASO operations, WhatsApp groups are majorly involved in mobilizing people for stone-pelting. These groups also align well with the Islamic concept of Ummat or brotherhood. The extremist organizations have successfully tapped the power of social media to generate a strong sense of religious identity and feeling of oneness with Muslims all over the world. If Rohingyas face atrocities in Myanmar or Muslims in Yemen or the US or other parts of India, then fake or real narratives are generated and spread across the J&K like wildfires on the social media. One can witness the results in the form of strong sympathies for Rohingyas in Kashmir these days because of such propaganda. Extremist organizations and militant groups also spread fake news, disinformation and manipulate young minds. There is an urgent need for the security agencies to focus on Instagram than the other apps.

Role of Mainstream Media, Hindu Extremism and Civil Society Activists

The coverage of Kashmir events in the mainstream Indian national media is also acting as a major spoiler. Kashmiri youth feels that Indian mainstream media portrays all Kashmiris as terrorists and accuses even the mainstream Kashmiri politicians of being Pakistan supporter. The glorification of Major

Gogoi (who used Farukh Daar as a human shield) in the national media generated deep resentment across the Kashmiri society.

The 24/7 TV news channels indulge in bitter debates on communal matters, getting fanatic Muslim and Hindu religious leaders who create a highly polarizing environment. Usually, one hardly takes such journalism seriously, but in Kashmir, people tend to view it as a reflection of the sentiments of mainstream India. Even in the remote villages of Kashmir, people regularly watch mainstream Indian national news channels and debates running on them.

Many Kashmiri politicians and youth leaders believe that religious radicalization in Kashmir is a reaction to Hindu extremism. They say that Hindu-Muslim dynamics in India have an enormous impact on Kashmiri mindset. Therefore, the unfortunate incidents of beef-lynching and communal riots create a feeling of insecurity among Kashmiris. Furthermore, they also see radicalization as a misguided attempt to protect their identity when Kashmiris feel insecure about the talks of tempering with Articles 35A and 370 becoming a dominant narrative in the national political discourse. To an extent, this may be real but religious radicalization has its internal dynamics and it has been going on independently of the happenings in the overall socio-political scenario of India.

However, despite this, one cannot deny the fact that the national media is projecting a highly biased and negative image of Kashmiri people for gaining television rating points. Recently, the new Governor Shri Malik also stated that national media's coverage of Kashmir is very negative. It will be detrimental to our long-term interests in Kashmir.

Similarly, civil society groups are also playing a destructive role in the entire picture. By blowing the sporadic incidents of beef-lynching, communal riots, and Hindu extremism out of proportion, they are creating a false narrative and a highly biased image of Indian establishment and society. A total of 30 crore Muslims are living peacefully in India with all the constitutional rights and privileges. Communal incidents are an aberration, and given the sheer size, population, diversity and the history of social frictions in the country, their numbers have not been alarmingly high. Mostly communal conflicts are localized, arising out of non-religious reasons. However, civil society activists and the opposition political parties have been blowing things out of proportion for political point scoring or out of ideological hatred. There is hardly any rationality behind such narratives. The oft-quoted narratives of the rising intolerance, "emergency-like-conditions," government-being-controlled by fascist and dictatorial forces" are not reflective of the complete picture of the reality. Such narratives smack of intellectually dishonest and sinister motives. However, they are having the worst impact on the young minds of Kashmir, generating false and fictitious fears of a sweeping and violent form of Hindu extremism emerging as a significant threat to minorities. Kashmiris perceive it as a threat to their identity too.

The civil rights activists never talk about human rights violations and atrocities by militants. There are countless stories of atrocities by militants. They indulge in raping the females of the houses where they seek shelter. The victims do not speak out of fear or loss of social prestige. The civil rights activists allegedly on the payrolls of anti-national elements tend to turn a blind eye to such inhuman incidents. Furthermore, they also refrain from discussing the most serious issue of emerging sectarianism and radicalization in Kashmir. Their ideological stance is weakening the state narrative. In severe cases of terrorism like Yakub Memon's death sentence or the matters of genuine social reforms, the malicious propaganda battle engaged in by civil rights activists weakens a democratic state and its ideology from within.

Global Islamism

The religious and geopolitical events in the Islamic world of the ME are also having an impact in fueling radicalization. Global jihadism and growing awareness of geopolitical happenings in Syria, Yemen, Myanmar, Pakistan, and Iran have a significant influence on radicalizing Kashmiri youth. In Kashmir, one witnesses a trend among the youth to study International Relations and Human Rights in higher studies. However, such secular intellectual pursuits may be misleading. It is further learnt that Pakistan-based actors are encouraging the youth to study the subjects mentioned above to enhance their understanding of global Islamic movement. The larger goal is to use the secular knowledge and concepts of HR to defend the extremism and militancy in the name of minority rights, multiculturalism and right to self-determination.

Barring a few exceptions, almost all from the educated lot, including PhD scholars interviewed in the course of field study, endorsed the view that Islam had great relevance in determining the future of Kashmir. Many scholars of political science and sociology openly expressed their desire to introduce Islamic law in Kashmir. The facts on ground testify this. The new generation of militants includes PhD scholars, engineers, and doctors. Some students from upmarket public schools like Green Valley, Srinagar, have also joined militancy. Even in the rural areas, one comes across people empathizing with Palestinians and Rohingyas for their sufferings. They displayed an impressive awareness of the events in the ME. The interactions with the students and scholars in Kashmir revealed that when President Erdogan won the elections in Turkey, there were celebrations in Kashmir. One can find a large number of local individuals contributing to Turkish government's media platform *TRT World*. *TRT World's* extraordinary focus on Kashmir issues and presenting a biased and one-sided narrative is highly disturbing and alarming.

Delhi has failed to present a nuanced understanding of Kashmir. There is no long-term vision and policy. India's response to proxy war and the concomitant challenge of radicalization has at best been ad hoc and piecemeal. Organizations like JeI and Ahle-Hadith were allowed to grow unabated for short-term and narrow political gains.

Prison Radicalization

In Kashmir, the legend goes that the first batch of radicalized local Kashmiri youth came from the local prisons in the 1990s after they were incarcerated with the Mujahiddins sent from Afghan theaters to Kashmir, by Pak-based actors. Even now, prisons are important nodes for indoctrination in the entire web of radicalization. In prisons, young men get opportunities to interact with fellow Jihadis, extremist clerics and hundreds of OGWs. Sources maintain that religious discourses in extremist religious doctrines are imparted by individuals already present with such ideas. Islamic literature is freely available in ample quantity.

Shia Radicalization

In response to global events and fast-spreading Wahhabi network, the Shia radicalization is also on the rise in J&K. One can find several hoardings of the Ayotolah Khamani in Kargil, Leh and the Shia-dominated regions of the valley. Sources have confirmed that the local Shias are visiting Iran for their religious studies and there is also a massive influx of Iranian scholars in Kashmir. Traditionally, Shias have remained away from militancy and helped in strengthening the democratic effort in Kashmir. However, lately, under the influence of foreign-returned scholars, the anti-India sentiment is on the rise among Shias. After Burhan Wani's death, there were seminars in Iranian universities, and he was declared a pious man. In August 2018, there was a demonstration by Shias in a press colony in favor of Article 35A, where they raised the following slogan:

> "Aie Zalimo, Aie Kafiro, Kashmir hamara chod do."

A prominent Shia leader of J&K, Anjuman-e-Shaire Shian, and also the member of separatist Hurriyat Conference expressed serious concerns about the increasing radicalization, Iranian penetration and the rising anti-India feelings among the Shia community.

Gujjars and Pahadis

Kathua rape case, followed by intense communal polarization and hateful media rhetoric, has made the Pahadis and Gujjars vulnerable. They have traditionally been India's great strength. However, there is a strong likelihood of religious extremist organizations capitalizing on their vulnerabilities. If that happens, it can be major security threat because they are deeply entrenched in India's borders with Pakistan and in times of need, they act as assets for our security forces. They have been instrumental in tracking infiltration movements and checking them in time.

CASE STUDIES AND RELEVANT EXAMPLES

In the next section, this chapter will discuss a case study of an ex-Lashkar militant. Having reviewed the broad factors in the matrix of radicalization, understanding an individual's journey of radicalization will help identify the specific trigger points and pathways of radicalizations. Of course, one size does not fit all, but the case study mentioned below will enhance the policymaker's understanding of the process of radicalization and will be beneficial in creating an effective counter-radicalization mechanism.

Zamal Khan (name changed) is a young scholar from Gandarbal district, pursuing post-graduation in Peace and Conflict Studies in a local university. His bearded appearance gives an image of a serious PhD scholar steeped in Marxist political thought. He is a good conservationist and often engages in discussions on identity politics. As a person, he comes out as sincere, polite and a soft-spoken man, though at times one may see nuances of ideological aggression. Now he wants to enroll for a PhD program at Jadavpur University in West Bengal. However, his life is not like that of other scholars. His past is more interesting than his present.

He was raised in a religious middle-class family. In class 11th, he came in touch with Islamic Jamiyat-ul-Talba, the student wing of JeI. There he received an intense exposure to the thought of Maududi, Ibn Taimiya, Syed Qutb and Hasan Banna. He used to attend 'Tarbiyat Ijtemas" (training sessions) where he was taught Islamic political movements, Quran and Hadith along with political Islam of the thinkers mentioned above. Besides, they also used to have long discussions on "Takfeeri." In Ijtemas (discussions) also, Islamic future of Kashmir and its merger with Pakistan were openly advocated. He remained with IJT for two years. His inclination, belief, and passion for religion were strengthened as a result of his association with JeI and socialization with like-minded people at JeI. Later, as a college student in Srinagar, his passion for religion took him to a Salafi madrasa in Central Kashmir. He attended Arabic classes there from 9 am to 5 pm. The focus was on Quran and Hadith. The Maulvis refrained from discussing political Islam. However, they appreciated the teachings of Zakir Naik a lot.

There, he met a fellow student named Taimur Khan (name changed), from South Kashmir. Taimur was in touch with militants and working as an OGW. At the same time, the rape incident of Asia and Nilopher had created severe unrest in Kashmir. People alleged that security personnel were responsible for that. Zamaal, who was neck-deep into Islamism by then, perceived the rape incident as an attack on their Islamic identity by Kafirs. He shared his interest to join militancy with Taimur, who initially feigned ignorance. He avoided Zamaal, giving excuses that he would have to speak to his friend who had connections. After 15 days of discussions, during which Taimur was confirming the credentials and the real intent of Zamaal, he agreed to take him to Sopore. Zamaal was introduced to the District Commander and Chief Operations Officer of LeT. Both were polite and courteous to him. After that, his training started in the forests. He was trained in handling AK47, pistols and hand grenades. Besides, they used to have long discussions on religion. He was introduced to the concepts of Harbi-Kafir (kafir with weapons and in the state of war with Muslims) and Gair-Harbi Kafir (kafirs without weapons).

His commanders argued that kafirs have launched a systematic attack on their Islamic identity in Kashmir and it was their religious duty to fight them.

Zamaal maintained that LeT staunchly believes in Ahle-Hadith and is far more radical and extremist than HM. During his training, he met several porters who came from Pakistan with weapons and money. They used to trace their locations with GPS gadgets. Porters were sent by ISI handlers based in Pakistan. These porters also brought drugs from Pakistan. LeT did not accept drugs because they found raising money through the sale of narcotics un-Islamic, but HM often raises money by selling drugs.

After his training, he was deputed in Srinagar. He lived in a rented room. He got his regular supply of money and weapons. His task was surveillance and recce of the city. He used to roam around the city recording videos of Srinagar, including government buildings, military installations, and other vital buildings. These recordings were regularly sent to Pakistan in USBs (pen drives). He lived there for one and a half years and after that, he, along with his two associates, was assigned a mission to kill a policeman. Three of them successfully conducted the mission, and the policeman died on the spot.

After four days, he was arrested by the police. Zamaal had asked his friend from Central Kashmir to bring money for him and his associates. His friend was arrested on the way to Srinagar by the police, and through him, he was arrested by the police near Laal Chowk. He was interrogated by the police officers. They found him an educated man, so their main focus was on convincing and de-radicalization. They were courteous and polite. They discussed Islam with him, arguing that his way of Islam was not the real Islam. Police officers also gave him literature on correct interpretations of Islam.

He was booked under IPC Section 302 (for murder) and sent to Jammu in 2011. There, he met some other prisoners with Marxist leaning. One of them Gurubachan Singh aka Pradhan Ji, a Sikh prisoner with a M.Sc. in Mathematics, was a staunch Marxist. He gave him literature on Marx, Lenin, and other leftist thinkers. The time spent in Jammu jail wholly transformed Zamaal's mindset. He had already taken a big leap on his path to de-radicalization. From Jammu, he was transferred to Central Jail, Srinagar. There, he enrolled himself in a PG course in Islamic Studies at Kashmir University. He was a regular student and attended classes thrice a week with the police escort. He was set free in 2016 and after his release; he enrolled for another PG in Peace and Conflict Studies. He is soon going to finish his second masters.

After his release, he was contacted twice by LeT OGWs urging him to come back to the organization. However, rather than saying a blunt no, he preferred to ask for time to finish his studies. He is apprehensive about his former colleagues trying again to contact him, in the current upsurge in militancy. He is trying to get out of the state and start a new academic life.

Reflecting upon his life thus far, he said that though he got de-radicalized because of his intense self-study and the right kind of people he met in the jail and returned to normal life, many others could not. He met several HM militants in Srinagar jail. They became active again after their release from the prison. They did not get de-radicalized because they did not have the right secular-intellectual exposure to comparative religions, political philosophy, and International Relations. Those who rejoined complained about adjustment issues after their release. They had nothing to do. Police torture and the trauma had left them unfit for doing anything else. The easiest thing for them was to go back to their previous ecosystem, which they did.

Zamaal opined that for any Muslim in Kashmir, religion is the most crucial factor in his existence as a militant—if not before joining, then indeed after joining the group. Moreover, for the majority, religion is the motivating factor for joining too, according to him.

Other Examples

1) In a casual interaction with class 10th students of a private school in Central Kashmir (Budgam; management board is affiliated to National Conference), when asked about their ambitions, nearly 50 per cent of them said that they wanted to join militancy. They were very vocal and passionate in declaring their unwavering loyalties to Zakir Musa, the new poster boy of Islam in Kashmir. All of them wanted Azadi and an Islamic Kashmir in future. All of them were willing to accept Rohingya Muslim refugees in their state because they were fellow Muslims. However, they were bitterly against the resettlement of Kashmiri Pundits in the valley, who were original inhabitants of the valley and were driven out in 1990.

2) On Id-ul-Adha last year (2018), there was a blast in Manasbal Park in Gandarbal. There were five accused out of which one was a minor. In the interrogation, they stated that they executed the explosion because the park was used for un-Islamic activities like dating by young couples. They were all semi-literate, and in the jail, they spent most of the time reading the Quran. They displayed no remorse over their action and confidently justified it as an act in the service of God.
3) In almost all these interactions with the individuals supporting Azadi, one never came across any one supporting the idea of the secular, democratic republic of Kashmir. Most of them had no clarity about their notion of Azadi. For the majority, the grievances revolved around Articles 35A, 370 of the constitution and Armed Forces Special Powers Act (AFSPA) and autonomy. For some, Azadi meant joining Pakistan and for others Azadi meant Islamic Kashmir. The Hurriyat's notion of Azadi had no futuristic details except for joining Pakistan and a highly Islamized Kashmir. Hence, it can be seen that there is hardly any vision for the Azadi, but there is a near-absolute consensus on the role of Islam in the future of Kashmir.

Survey of South Kashmir

Presently, South Kashmir is a hotbed of militancy. For the purpose of this study, a survey was conducted in a South Kashmir district (Pulwama), covering 50 families whose one of the members had joined militancy. At the very outset, it is clarified that data sheet for the survey has not been added for security reasons. However, the survey is authentic and can be immensely useful for policy planning and implementation.

The survey results revealed that in 46 per cent of the cases, the triggering event was religious radicalization. In 24 per cent of cases, the triggering event was influence of the friends, family, and events; 21 per cent of them joined militancy because of continuous police torture and harassment. For the remaining 9 per cent, the causes were unknown.

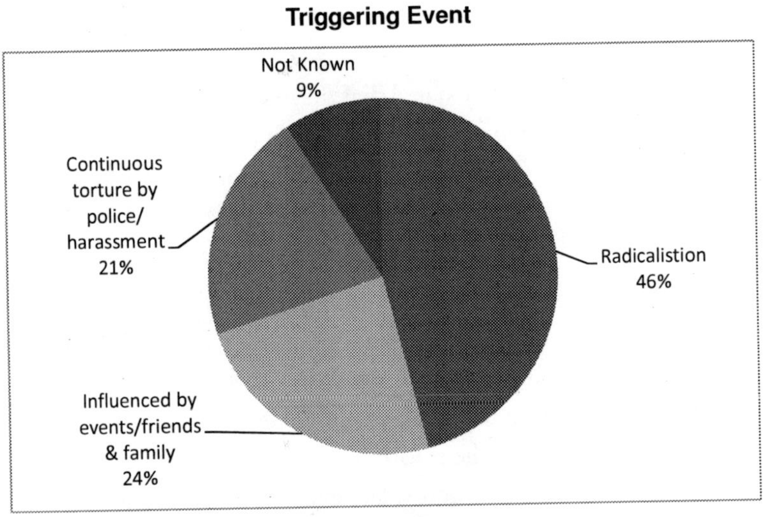

Triggering Event

Radicalistion	46%
Influenced by events/friends & family	24%
Continuous torture by police/harassment	21%
Not Known	9%

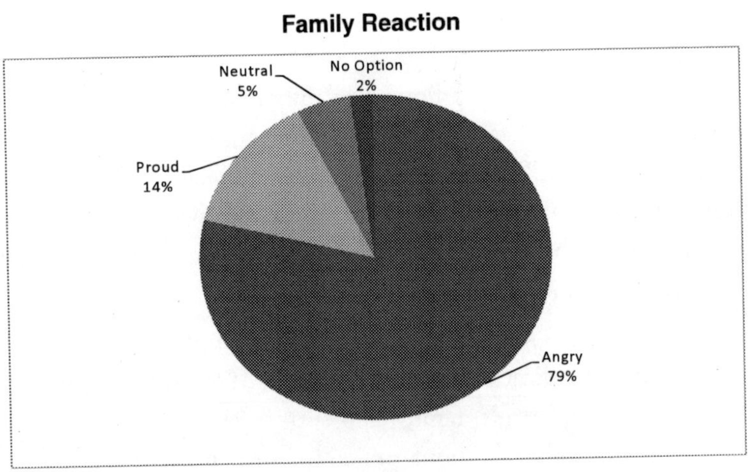

Family Reaction

Angry	79%
Proud	14%
Neutral	5%
No Option	2%

Salient Features of Radicalization in Kashmir

1) In Kashmir, regarding radicalization, there is an attitude of denial. Mainstream politicians call it a situation of hopelessness due to Delhi's high-handedness and the failure of the dialogue process. The separatists and activists accuse that Indian government wants to discredit the movement of Kashmiris by clubbing it with global Islamism and raising the specter of radicalization. A group of Kashmir University scholars, in the course of the survey, suggested that girls are using "burqas out of fashion." The embrace of religious symbols, like skullcaps, beards and above-the-ankle pyjamas, are not seen as even remotely related to radicalization. Instead, these are perceived as a "drift towards spiritualism and religiosity" due to the state of hopelessness, depression, and conflict, in the lack of political solution. Even scholars, academicians, and ordinary civilians shy away from accepting these as indicative of a rising trend towards radicalization. During conversations, they argue that radicalization is not an issue in Kashmir; the root causes are failure of political dialogue and the high-handed approach of Delhi. In some circles of intelligence agencies also, there is an attitude of denial regarding radicalization.
2) The young generation in the grip of radicalization and militancy shows a schizophrenic behavior. There are followers of Zakir Musa who are highly learned, but into alcoholism and prostitution. They take drugs and listen to Arabic taranas (a kind of religious trance music) on smartphones. Young boys and girls are said to have multiple sexual partners, and at the same time, they also talk passionately about Islam. The problem of drug addiction is getting severe. Even young girls have started consuming drugs. The terrorist organizations raise money by selling drugs.

   Here again, there is an attitude of denial among the local population, and it appears a little strange, but one can come across girls wearing Arabic-styled burqas, participating in stone-pelting and having two to three boyfriends at the same time. The situation is very similar to Europe where the young men and women who joined ISIS had little knowledge of Islam. They could barely perform namaz and were drug addicts, petty criminals, orphans, homeless and homosexuals. Olivier Roy's research showed that they were second-generation Muslims migrants who had integration and assimilation issues in the western society. They found their religious identities split. Olivier Roy opined that their fundamental issues were related to identity.

3) Literacy rates are very high, and the young workforce is very talented in Kashmir. Spoken English skills are impressive. As compared to the other states of North India where Universities and colleges have become centers of hooliganism and destructive student politics, reading habits in the colleges of Kashmir adolescent population are impressive. This author witnessed young students in Kashmir University, Pulwama Degree College and Avantipura engaged in intellectual discussions on political thinkers like Marx, Lenin, Francis Fukuyama, and Samuel Huntington. Political science, International Relations, Human Rights studies and Sociology are the most preferred academic disciplines among young generation. Identity and atrocity literature is also very popular. There is a great craze for international relations and fantastic awareness of global geopolitical events. The young men and women are always enthusiastic about constructive political discussions. Women are very active in journalism. The girls are well educated, fashionable and career conscious. One can find them wearing trendy western attires. They watch popular BBC documentaries and Hollywood movies. However, at the same time, they also display a strong inclination towards Islamic fundamentalism. For them, the idea of Islamic Kashmir or an Islamic Political system is like a serious political science issue. These days, there is hardly any craze for Pakistan, but the idea of Islamic Kashmir is very popular. Per capita income and living standards are high. One rarely comes across the kind of poverty which one finds in states like Bihar and Rajasthan.

4) Kashmiriyat is not entirely dead. No doubt, footfalls in Sufi shrines are rapidly declining, but that is not the only or even the most important indicator of Kashmiriyat, which signifies a liberal, tolerant, humane and flexible attitude. It is still very much present. During interviews, one did not come across an attitudinal rigidity among young Kashmiris. They are always willing to engage in discussions. They still reflect deep-rooted cultural values and keen desire for learning modern and scientific education. They are very warm, polite and courteous in casual personal interactions. Kashmiri hospitality is very impressive and one does not come across extreme religious rigidity among the commonplace citizens. Their old traditions and cultural patterns in dining, marriages, dressing and other social events are still intact to a large extent though at the same

time, one also comes across a vigorous phenomenon of Islamization of dressing patterns and other aspects of social and cultural life.

The family system is intact, and women occupy a very prominent and empowered role in the family. Females get huge respect in the society. Molestation and rape incidents are still aberrations. Despite the threats issued by JeI to wear veils and not work in professions like journalism where one has to interact with men, one can find that the general trend among the female folk is to bother least about such threats and explore new and modern avenues of lifestyle and career. The author also came across a large number of artists, poets, musicians, filmmakers, photojournalists, rappers, and fashion enthusiasts.

Unlike Kerala, even the Ahle-Hadith in Kashmir is not like its original Arabic version. It has adapted to the local culture. One can find Ahle-Hadith followers believing in Barelwi practices like Tabiz (amulets). The exposure of lay followers to extreme doctrines of Takfeeri is minimal. Whereas in Kerala Wahhabism has brought a strong wave of Arabization in its wake and created a big cultural rift between Wahhabi followers and the cultural values of India, in Kashmir, there is a still a strong cultural "connect" with Indian values. In the mainstream academic discourse on radicalization, it is found that radicalization dehumanizes the enemy. A radicalized individual gets cut off from his family and friends and lives in a virtual community of like-minded individuals. However, in Kashmir, militants continue their contacts with the family members and friends. In a large number of encounters, it has been observed that militants talk to their family members on the phone before dying.

Kashmiriyat is still intact. Our fixation with the idea of Sufism as the only indicator of Kashmiriyat reflects a weak understanding of the scenario. This narrow approach must be abandoned. Finally, Kashmiriyat in its modern avatar, i.e. aligned with the current times, is India's best bet in Kashmir.

5) It also deserves a mention that years of foreign rule has given Kashmiris a very subtle and refined sense of realism and from that follows a unique ability to adapt and accommodate to the prevailing power equations in society and politics. Also, Kashmiris have a rich history and tradition of producing scholars. They have a very refined aesthetic sense and an intellectual bent of mind. Hence, they do not have a monolithic personality. It is in layers and multifaceted. Thus, the narrative of

radicalization is indeed a serious concern, but not an absolute truth. With dialogue and negotiations and alternative engagement channels, the radicalization matrix or the ecosystem of Islamism can be punctured.

6) Sometimes, analysts wonder that Barelwis/Etaqadis, who represent Hindustani Islam, i.e. the tolerant and accommodative Islam, produce 79 per cent of the militants and constitute a vast majority of stone-pelters. Why so? It is observed that lay Barelwi followers are an emotional lot vis-à-vis Salafis, JeI, and Deobandis. The basis of their belief system is love and reverence for the prophet and their old saints. This is why the emotional faculties of their psyche are very dominant in their behavioral patterns. Their literacy levels and economic condition are poor as compared to the other three. Their knowledge of Islamic teachings and discourses do not fare well vis-à-vis the Saudi-educated and well-paid Islamic scholars of Salafis and JeI. On account of the better organizational structure, funding, political clout, and monetary resources and better knowledge of Islam or the claim to follow the original and unadulterated Islam (in line with the text), the leadership lies with Salafis and JeI (mostly with JeI), be it stone-pelting or militancy or the political movement. Religious sentiments of Barelwis are exploited by intellectual and sophisticated Salafi and JeI leadership for dubious political motives and the vested interests of foreign powers.

   Besides, the growing extremism and fanaticism that one finds among Barelwis these days is a manifestation of the frustration and fear arising out of the grave threat to their identity from puritan Sunni schools, and the Barelwis' inability to do much in the face of losing ground to them, fast. Hence, it is a way of reaction or rather an ugly competition of representing authentic Islam, with extremist Sunni schools.

7) Ordinary Kashmiris often state that the objective of their Tahreek is to protect and nurture Kashmiriyat. However, unfortunately, the Tahreek has taken the heaviest toll on Kashmiriyat only. The young generation's faith in social institutions like marriage, families, elders, and the political institutions like democracy, elections, and government has suffered almost a deathblow. As mentioned above, the social ills like drugs and prostitution are rampant. Youth in the age group of 9 to 28 years believes that the power flows through the barrel of the gun. Today, the biggest threat to Kashmiriyat comes from religious extremism and radicalization, not from security forces, Indian establishment, or the Hindu nationalism.

Policy Recommendations

1) Youth Factor

In any policy-making initiative, the policymakers need to consider the fact that the Islamic radicalization in Kashmir has a very specific component of age. The worst victims are in the age bracket of 16 to 30 years. Furthermore, even 8- to 14-year-old boys are participating in stone-pelting. Police book them in stone-pelting, sometimes they face beatings in the police station, and their parents have to pay bribes to get them released. Their academics get hampered. Such undesired exposure at an early age begins their radicalization, and by the time they are 18 to 19, they are ready to join a militant organization.

On analyzing the radicalization further in the context of the specific age group mentioned above, it comes to light that at its core, it may be a psychological issue, deeply related to the state of depression and hopelessness and a strong desire for an empowered identity.

Hence, the counter-radicalization and de-radicalization policies should have a strong focus on youth in the above-mentioned age group. Youth engagement has to be at multiple levels, in numerous ways and multiple layers.

Boys in the age group of 8 to 16 need better parenting and schooling than policing. Rather than being harsh with them, the emphasis should be on psychological and spiritual techniques of convincing, counseling, re-education, meditation and rehabilitation.

For those who are in the age group of 16 to 30, the alternate engagement channels need to be explored. They could be through sports, there being massive craze for football and cricket. The recent announcement of J&K IPL cricket team has already generated much enthusiasm.

Other channels could be in education, NCC, better employment opportunities in industry, civil society and horticulture. Business groups of India should be encouraged to invest in Kashmir and generate employment. They can also invest in education, cultural and artistic fields, women and child development in CSR activities. There will be massive response to such initiatives. One can find acute joblessness in Kashmir and this has led to idleness. The frustration of youth has one of its primary sources in the nepotism in public service recruitments and poor infrastructure in academic institutions. The youth in Kashmiri is highly talented in diverse disciplines of knowledge.

Besides, their skills in artistic pursuits are impressive. These energies need an outlet. Drama, music and acting institutes can be great channels of engagement.

It needs to be clear that the question here is not of development or poverty eradication, but one of engaging a fertile mind in the right direction and not let the destructive forces prey upon their vulnerabilities and the feelings of resentment that arise in the absence of dignified employment opportunities. Also, it merits attention that in South Kashmir, the rise in per capita incomes led people to invest more in Islamic education and that created space for religious organizations with a political agenda, like JeI. It is not a question of money or poverty. Hence, any initiative that doles out money without productively engaging fertile and politically sensitive young Kashmiri minds could be counter-productive. It is all about psychologically engaging the youth giving them a sense of dignity, empowerment, participation and involvement through employment. Interestingly, in Kashmir, one finds that either the young IPS and IAS officers are heroes of people or the gun-wielding militants. On a deeper analysis, one finds that essentially the quest is for power which the young and restive population is seeking through gun in the conflict-ridden state. Hence, we have to create alternate role models of empowerment. The image of being empowered financially, politically, socially and culturally needs to be worked out for the youth, shifting their dreams from the hopelessness of death and mirage of afterlife to the achievements of this, worldly life.

Furthermore, youth should be given space in the political, social and cultural domain. The youth must be engaged in dialogue. In Kashmir, even when the college students are protesting for everyday issues, several times security forces are sent with guns and lathis. There should not be such occasions. The civil administration should deal with such situations democratically and resolve disputes with dialogue. The youth must be encouraged to join the mainstream politics.

Last but not the least, there is a need for creating new role models for the youth. The new role models can be in the field of sports, films, politics, art, and culture. The youth's perception of empowerment needs a complete transformation—it should move from guns to knowledge, creativity, peace, prosperity and spiritual enlightenment.

2) Counter-Narrative and Alternate Narrative

Radicalization is all about distorting and misinterpreting the religious texts. There is a tendency to quote Quranic verses and the teachings of Ibn Taimiya without discussing the context. For example, according to the Quran, jihad can only be started by the head of the state, and the head has to be elected and endowed with abilities. Militant organizations like HM and LeT have no religious right to wage jihad as they are not a state controlling geographical territory. Secondly, jihad can be waged only to advance the cause of Allah. It can never be used to seek personal revenge and political power.

By that definition, militants like Burhan Wani are not mujahids because they joined militancy to seek personal revenge. The counter-narrative should focus on the inclusive aspects of Islam and the spiritual essence rather the outer ritualistic trappings. Also, counter-narrative can even talk about the silence of Pakistan over the interment of Uighur Muslims in China. Pakistan's claims to defend Islam are hollow and only to advance its strategic interests. The puritan Islamic religious schools with an extremist outlook, feelings of separatism and belief in political Islam can face some resistance from the puritan Islamic religious schools with local roots and traditions of a non-political and inclusive existence. This option may be explored but in the long run, this may not work. The scholars or clergymen belonging to the latter may face pressure from the ground and change their discourse either out of fear or ideological conversion or religious sentiments. Therefore, a systematic and organized counter-narrative is essential to combat the forces of radicalization.

However, in the best-case scenario, such a counter-narrative should come from within the Muslim community/clergy and specifically from within the local Kashmiris, which seems rather difficult to achieve. In that case, the academic scholars (secular) of religious studies and Islamic studies can begin the initiative.

Furthermore, the idea of promoting Sufism to counter Salafi and JeI forces may backfire, leading to greater resistance. It is likely to be perceived as undue interference in religious affairs in a society which already has such illusionary fears about the threat to their identity. Therefore, in the long run, only an alternate narrative can be the best weapon to deal with radicalization. The alternate narrative should celebrate life rather than death. It should worship science rather than dogmas. The alternate narrative has to be secular, democratic, intellectual, scientific, inclusive, tolerant, accommodative, rational and progressive. In the alternate narrative, the place of religion is in the private corners of one's life.

3) Education and Social Service

Academic, social and cultural spaces should not be surrendered to religious organizations with a hidden political and extremist agenda. The state apparatus and secular entities should have a dominant say in shaping and deciding the mainstream social and cultural discourse. If the state and private organizations run schools and colleges far superior in infrastructure and teaching to the educational institutions run by religious organizations, the role of religious entities with dubious motives will get a significant blow.

A curriculum to promote nationalism can be designed and taught. A course module on Kashmiriyat should be taught in every school from 3rd and 4th classes onwards. The curriculum should expose the children to the wisdom of Lalleshwari and Nund Rishi, the eloquence of Kalhana, the chivalry of Lalitaditya Muktapida and artistic achievements of Jehangir. Through education, 1947 and 1990 can be made irrelevant, and with that the separatism also. The roots of identity can be found in the 5,000-year-old history of Kashmir. CBSE curriculum can be made mandatory with sufficient space for Kashmiriyat that includes promotion of local languages. Radicalization through educational institutions should be dealt with in the harshest of the manner because that is ruining a complete generation. National integration initiatives should be systematically executed in the schools. National Anthem recital in morning assembly be made compulsory. However, such initiatives will not be successful if we do not win the hearts and minds of Kashmirirs. They must be commensurate with "healing touch" measures. Lastly DPS can open more schools in Kashmir.

The curriculum should also encourage critical thinking. For this, a separate three- to four-month module can be designed. Only a questioning and a critical mind can combat radicalization.

4) National Integration Policy for Youth

The young students should be awarded fellowships to study in colleges and universities in other parts of India. There should be exchange programs of school and universality students and teachers of Kashmir with those of the other states. The government should also award fellowships to youth for foreign education and exchange programs.

5) Dealing with Religious Organizations with Dubious Motives

There can be a two-track policy for dealing with the religious organization of dubious back ground or track record as discussed below:

a) The religious organizations with clear-cut anti-national, separatist, extremist and exclusivist agenda should either be banned or effectively neutralized over a period of time;
b) Those with purely religious, social and cultural agenda should either be asked to modify or regulate their affairs in such a manner that their activities, beliefs and discourses in no way aid the process of radicalization and disturb the communal harmony.

Furthermore, if due to legal and constitutional hurdles, it is not possible to book them directly under the existing laws, then the law-enforcement agencies can resort to Al Capone strategy, i.e. book them for other offenses such as financial irregularities, provocative speeches, and different possible ways. Targeting the hawala, gulf repatriation, charities and other financing channels of religious organizations is one of the robust ways to control them.

In some policy circles, the approach so far has been to engage such religious extremist organizations. For example, in J&K, a perception prevails that JeI can keep the militancy (violence) in control due to their religious and social clout. This happens due to a lack of understanding of such organizations and their true agenda. Sometimes extremist maulvis are let off or even allowed to deliver arousing speeches for some short-term gains.

It is important to understand that the intellectual and educated leaders of the extremist organizations are cultured and well-mannered in personal interactions. They know how to engage politicians, policymakers and secular academicians reasonably and rationally. However, while so doing, they never compromise on their core agenda. In the long run, they will do the worst damage to India's communal harmony and national security. Hence, the state needs to adopt a zero-tolerance policy for religious organizations with extremist agendas and not cave in to the compulsions of short-term political gains. Furthermore, there is an urgent need of law on radicalization. This has been discussed in detail in the chapter on counter-radicalization policies.

*6) 24*7 Counselling Helpline*

A composite team comprising police officers dealing with counter-terrorism issues, respected Maulvis, spiritual masters, psychologists, community leaders and civil society activists can be set up as the state-level Counseling Center. It should have multiple units in every district. If any case is reported of a person showing signs of radicalization, the team should immediately go to the house and hold counseling sessions with that individual. Counseling sessions can be conducted with stone-pelters, people on the verge of joining militancy and militants facing a jail trial. This body should also help in rehabilitation and reintegration of militants after they finish their jail term. Also, this body should be proactive. They should keep a check on social media posts, identify radicalized individuals, visit individual homes and conduct regular surveys on radicalization. They should also organize public seminars, debates, discussions, and workshops in every district in schools, colleges, and universities. Spiritual organizations like Art of Living and Sadhguru Isha Foundation too could be coopted in this initiative.

7) National Code of Conduct

There is need for a legally binding national code of conduct to protect India's constitutional values. National Code of Conduct should have zero tolerance for any kind of extremism in the name of minority rights or freedom of expression. It should be legally binding for civil society activists, print and electronic media groups, political parties and religious and cultural organizations. National security comes first, and under no circumstances, it can be put under jeopardy to please malicious foreign ideologies and actors behind them and civil rights organizations masquerading as forces of democracy and liberalism.

8) Militancy

In the policy recommendations above, suggested ways to erode the social constituency and legitimacy of militancy, had been mentioned. The idea was to offer new channels of hope, opportunities and engagement to youth. However, there is also a simultaneous need for a stringent punitive approach to deter young and misguided men from joining militancy. The message should be loud and clear that sky is the limit for dialogue within the non-violent zones, and once it moves into the zone of violence and extremist, kinetic action would be the only answer.

There is also a pressing need for an innovative intelligence-based approach to neutralize the militants. The large-scale encounters and the accompanying public stone-pelting makes the militants appear heroic and martyrs in the eyes of the common people. The funerals that follow only further aggravate and intensify the passions. Security forces can have intelligence-based covert operations to break the backbone of militancy. Such operations will have to be multifaceted covering diverse aspects such as terror finance and the supply channels for weapons. Such an approach already seems to be in existence as per a media report. Yet, this is being mentioned here for academic record.

9) Social Media

Terrorist organizations and their over-ground cover, religio-political structures are evolving and becoming more sophisticated in the use of social media. These innovations can be seen in the quality of videos, audio and the written content. For example, visuals are more impactful with music with clear religious imagery in the lyrics. Instagram provides better opportunities for a visual-based engaging interface, so that is being used effectively. The written content is drafted in a very serious manner. Powerful and precise point-wise short paragraphs are being used.

The counter-radicalization apparatus needs to evolve accordingly in using internet and social media, to be able to respond efficiently. There needs to be a well-qualified team of expert researchers to study trends and suggest innovations accordingly. Target group of students in schools and colleges should also be taught to identify fake news. Besides, there also needs to be a heavy traffic of engaging alternate narratives and counter-narratives on social media.

How to Deal with JeI?

The idea behind devoting an exclusive section on JeI is that in the present phase of militancy in South Kashmir, JeI is providing the backbone of militancy. Over the last several decades, JeI has cultivated a strong base in South Kashmir. The biggest challenge in the present phase is the home-grown militancy of South Kashmir where most of the local recruits are joining HM. Hence, the question that needs to be asked is, "How to deal with JI?" That will also provide answers to, "How to deal with militancy?"

There can be two ways of doing this. First is the conventional and bureaucratic approach of engaging and managing JeI. It is the practical and feasible approach given the weak resolve of Indian state, lack of expertise in dealing with such hybrid organizations, the ideological stronghold of Jamaat over the people and its political and social clout. The second way is to neutralize JeI. It is idealistic and a difficult goal.

However, though difficult to achieve, one would like to pitch in favour of the second option because by attempting to neutralize it, the very root of religious radicalization and militancy would be hit hard. If achieved, this route is likely to provide a lasting solution and deserves to be preferred to a "band-aid" approach.

Jamaat: The Furnace of Islamism in Kashmir

Earlier, in this case study (in the earlier sections), the author coined the idea of the ecosystem of Islamism/radicalization in Kashmir. JeI forms the core of that ecosystem. But it must be mentioned that there are other new and upcoming threats which are gradually becoming as threatening as JeI. The present examination, however, will remain confined to JeI's activities only.

Chief of the JeI is called its Amir who presides over the Central Committee comprising 10 to 12 members. Similarly, there are district and tehsil-level organizational set-ups. The members of JeI are called Rakoons. It takes an aspirant four to five years to become a Rakoon. According to a rough estimate, there are 5,000 JI Rakoons in the state of J&K. Then, there are lakhs of supporters, sympathizers and followers. Jamaat is about a lifestyle that strictly follows the principles of the Quran and Sharia. Jamaat theology believes in the idea of political Islam, i.e. a theocratic state.

In Kashmir, JeI forms the bedrock of Jihadi radicalization and terrorism. It constitutes the core of the infrastructure for supporting and sustaining Pakistan's proxy war. JeI cadres in the rural areas organize Ijtemas where they openly advocate violence against India and execute pro-Pakistani agenda. They send letters to individual houses and make personal visits to homes to invite their members to Ijtemas. Their cadres act as OGWs, help terrorist outfits in logistics, movement, sheltering, finance, supply and purchase of weapons, financial assistance to the families of dead militants including finding suitable boys for widows of the militants.

They occupy considerable social space. In rural areas, their role and credibility are boosted because of the corrupt and inefficient public delivery systems. JeI donates money to the needy for marriages and relief expenditures. It has various NGOs running educational and charitable institutions and orphanages. In colleges and schools, the manner of teaching religious curriculum is such that it radicalizes and germinates violent extremism in one's mind.

Trusts are working as front organizations for JeI. The secretary or anyone influential in the management of the trust running educational institutions, charity houses and orphanages generally happens to be an ardent JeI member/ dignitary. These days JeI has particular focus on rehabilitation and settlement of Rohingyas in J&K. Recently, some Wahhabi clerics organized a conference in Indonesia. The event was funded by Pakistan. The conference was on Islamic education and dawah. The delegation of Private School Association of J&K (PSAJK) participated in the event (December 13, 2018, Kashmir Age). PSAJK includes Falah-e-Aam Trust, a sister concern of JeI working in the field of education.

In addition to the above, a large group of Jamaati supporters and sympathizers is present in the civil administration, police, judiciary, banking, political parties, government colleges, schools, and universities. Jamaatis function as HoDs, principals, lower and higher level civil servants, judges and teachers. In the State Secretariat, JeI has effective penetration. JeI supporters within the government set-up play a very crucial role in creating favourable conditions for a smooth execution of JI agenda. They smoothen out the tracks for JeI's subtle and lethal expansion. They shield its members and functionaries against central agencies or the police-initiated investigations.

JeI is a very secretive in nature. In the past, JeI had to face severe state action in 1977-79 and in the 1990s. However, JeI survived these assaults and, over the years, refined its abilities in covert survival strategies. Its front organizations working as educational institutions and charity trusts, though officially not connected, form the real powerhouse of JeI.

Furthermore, due to its all-pervasive social and cultural presence, welfare activities, strong links with terror organizations and powerful foreign and domestic friends, JeI is in the position to exercise social, religious cultural and political pressure in the society. For example, PDP's main support base in South Kashmir is stated to come from JeI. JeI often uses terror and threats to bring people into submission. People are scared of JeI. There is a general feeling that, because of its overwhelming presence and terror tactics, any opposition to JeI may lead to the loss of one's life. The threat is so potent that in the course of field survey, people avoided talking about JeI and its activities even in small groups. There was palpable sense of fear that if their anti-JeI views are known to the omnipresent "spies" of JeI, their lives would be in danger. Simply put, fear appears to be more potent than any genuine love for JeI.

These days, JI is going through an organizational overhaul. The Amir has been changed and there is a new appointee as the head of IJT, i.e. the youth wing of Jamaat. A new secretary general was appointed in December 2018. The new strategy aims to revitalize JeI as an organization. It wants to focus on youngsters, especially doctors, engineers and PhD scholars in colleges and universities. In a bid to woo these young minds, JeI presents political Islam as an ideology in the same category as political ideologies like Marxism and socialism. The idea is to capitalize on religious sentiments and intellectual yearnings of young minds.

Crackdown Strategy on JeI[19]

Having reviewed the structure and nature of JeI operations, it becomes clear that a successful crackdown on JeI is a highly ambitious project. However, this course of action is still considered inescapable and is highly recommended, sooner the better. How often, has one heard the argument that Pakistan controls the militancy in J&K, which is true? Hence, we need to neutralize Pakistani's main instrument of terrorism in Kashmir and that is JeI.

How JeI has built its robust terror infrastructure in the state over the years has already been discussed. The whole project of taking action against JeI has to be carefully planned in a layered approach with a significant component of covert operations. To begin with, the first crackdown must be against JeI cadres infiltrated into the state machinery. This will deprive them of their influence and power which they willfully use to assist the organisation. JeI proxies in the state machinery need to be purged. Their followers in the universities, colleges and schools should be placed under strict monitoring. Teachers and lecturers with JeI background, linkages and ideology must be dealt systematically. Intelligence agencies may have to dig through their voluminous data to examine if sedition cases can be filed against such elements, and then the prosecution should follow.

The next layer should comprise systematic crackdown on JeI's front organizations like schools, colleges, charity organizations, and orphanages. They too could possibly qualify for action under the sedition laws. Careful scrutiny of class room lectures, curriculum, sources of financing, call records and their links with JI Pakistan and other handlers based there can provide very useful clues to lead the investigation to the desired ends.

The third layer of action could be planned through intellectuals to effectively counter JeI activities by launching a virtual propaganda war against them. A large number of people believe that JeI leaders incite ordinary and poor Kashmiris for Jihad, whereas they send their own children to study outside the state and lead comfortable lives. Their involvement in financial and moral corruption, criminal acts and killings must be exposed.

JeI leaders indulging in massive corruption is virtually an open secret. They embezzle money from the funds that came from Pakistan for relief work, assistance to the families of dead militants and for providing legal aid to stone-pelters, etc. However, this cannot be done by government agencies. The ordinary people need to be made aware of the immoral and anti-Islam and anti-national activities of JeI. Intellectual narrative has to come out against the propaganda machine of JeI. For example, in universities and colleges, student groups and research forums could be set up to organize regular discussions/seminars on the role and activities of JeI. Such initiatives will find a great deal of traction in the community. It needs a mention that in the long run, the most effective blow to ideological organizations like JeI can come only from the robust counter-narrative. Violent and stringent crackdown may be needed in immediate future; however, it cannot be a replacement for an intellectual counter.

Kashmir valley has high levels of literacy and the youth population is extraordinarily sensitive to political events. Hence, clubs and forums discussing issues like current affairs, religious extremism, global political trends, and economic trends can be useful channels to question the role of JeI in the society. Such forums and clubs can be created in educational institutions in all the districts, well-supported and protected. Otherwise, they will avoid speaking anything out of fear. Also, the Barelwi maulvis, Ahle-Hadith and nationalist Deobandi maulvis can also be encouraged to expose JI leaders and its supporters for indulging in un-Islamic acts like terrorism and stone-pelting.

The fourth layer of action could include a crackdown on JeI cadres, supporters, and sympathizers. Their maulvis, districts heads, tehsil heads, central committee members and Rakoons should be taken on the radar. The state can use various measures within the existing legal framework to clamp down on activities encouraging sedition, terror financing. NIA has already initiated legal action by launching cases. This has gone down well with the common people, who unfortunately do not yet have the confidence of publicly expressing their appreciation for the actions taken so far. It may be worth examining whether JeI leaders who attend the funerals or the maulvis who conduct the proceedings eulogizing their acts of terror of the dead militants could come within the legal definition of sedition. However, this is a challenging task because of the political and administrative clout that JeI currently enjoys. It is also worth consideration if convicted JeI cadres/leaders spend their jails-terms outside J&K?

The fifth layer can be of officially banning the JeI. As stated earlier, this has already been done by the government of India and needs no further explanation.

While executing the measures mentioned above, the state machinery needs to be discreet and strategic. A layered action plan has been suggested because if action begins with a ban, JeI cadres will go underground and its front organizations will function well. Besides, JeI is used to such actions in the past. It may gain sympathy of the people by playing the victimhood card. Hence, a new strategy was suggested for the crackdown, creating smokescreens and illusions. For example, while clamping down on JeI, if the state takes some strong action against a corrupt official or a politician, the entire social media focus will be on the move and people will hardly bother about the crackdown on JeI.

Furthermore, we also have to keep the old impression intact. Until now, there has been a practice of engaging JeI for controlling violence and agitations. We can continue giving that impression by occasional interactions and discussions with the moderate factions of JeI.

Pros and Cons of the Crackdown

Pros

(a) India will be able to deal a death blow to radicalization and terrorism in the state. Once JeI is made ineffectual, we would have almost defanged terrorism.

(b) This will render the militancy unorganized and powerless. It will be easy to crush an unorganized entity.

(c) It will dry up the resource base, recruits, logistics, finance, and safe shelters. Without the well-oiled protective shell of JeI, it will be extremely difficult for terrorist organizations and Pakistan to keep Kashmir on the boil.

(d) The sense of deep fear of the JeI, mentioned earlier, will go away and people will come out openly against the JeI, its ideology and militancy. The state will be able to identify and cultivate new stakeholders with commitment to peace and association with India.

(e) A crackdown on JeI will also deal a significant blow to militancy resulting in fewer encounters/security operations. As a result, the existing high level of alienation and anger prevailing because of security operations will not find fertile ground. The state's development and governance activities will get recognized, and our credibility will improve.

(f) Once JeI is neutralized, it will be easier for mainstream political parties to revert to a secular and nationalist narrative. They will get rid of the duality of masters.

Cons

(a) Though necessary, it is an extraordinarily ambitious project given the record of resolve and strategic planning of the Indian state. There are numerous instances where JeI sympathizers in the state machinery have hampered the activities of NIA in J&K, in a significant way. Hence, the state needs to have a firm resolve, a well-planned strategy, and robust implementation.

(b) Crackdown on JeI-backed educational institutions and charity organizations might lead to thousands of teachers being rendered unemployed and education of the children getting adversely impacted. In such a situation, the action will become highly unpopular. It has to be ensured that the state action does not put employment of the teachers and education of the students in jeopardy. Therefore, one could think of taking action against hardcore Jamaati teachers and elements in the management, and replace them with other teachers. The administration can also be changed. The religious curriculum and its teaching style can be majorly amended. For example, spiritual aspects of Islam which emphasize peace, Tauhid, and mutual harmony can be taught. At the same time, the state also needs to improve the quality of education. Also, the state has to occupy the social space which JeI has been holding. It cannot be done immediately and will need a sustained effort over a period of time. However, in the immediate future, we can begin with the outreach activities.

(c) In some quarters it is argued that JeI should be engaged with because it can keep violence under control. The law enforcement machinery and intel agencies can use JeI to monitor and control civilian protests and terrorism. However, this is not the case. Such a view reflects a lack of long-term vision and foresight. JeI has taken enough advantage of this perception. They have made only formal gestures to promote peace and help Indian agencies by handing over small baits. Keeping that illusion intact, they have firmly strengthened themselves in the society and nourished a fertile ground for radicalization and terrorism. They have firmly rooted for Pakistan in Kashmir. Hence, such notions may act as hindrance in the plan, and need to be dispensed with, in the larger substantial interests of the state, India and the world community.

(d) JeI has expertise in covert survival tactics and will come out unscathed, if not reinforced from the ban.

(e) Actions against JeI cadres will make them heroes and they will garner public sympathy. However, this can be controlled to a large extent. As mentioned earlier, layered crackdown will be useful in denying them the status of "heroes."

(f) There could be an argument that state action would cause further alienation and resentment amongst the people. This should not matter seriously since the level of alienation, resentment, and anger against the state is already quite high. From here, the sense of alienation can go downwards only. Such a crackdown can never be achieved under a political dispensation.

(g) The project could fall flat and fail if not carried out with a sound strategy and a long-term plan. For example, after the arrest of JeI cadres and supporters, it is essential to ensure that they remain behind bars. If there is nothing to prosecute them for and they come out soon, the crackdown can become counter-productive.

Conclusion

Lately, as evident in various measures related to restructuring, JI is trying to revive and revitalize its structures at the district and sub-district levels. The prevailing view is that over the last two years (2016-18), these structures had more or less vanished. The cadres are there but the organization is missing. As a result, JeI is functioning only covertly. The Pak-based handlers and JeI leadership are afraid that the militancy in the state will eventually slip out of their control in the face of the ongoing relentless campaign of the security forces. As of now, in the matters of recruitment, logistics, and operations, the control of Syed Salahuddin and ISI handlers is not very strong and the hiring is happening most under peer-group initiative. Pakistan will never want the militancy to go out of its control. Therefore, it would prefer to keep foreign terrorists more active and in control of things.

Recent developments also indicate that the mood on the other side is to bring the militancy down and back under their control. Not only this, there are strong indications that Pak-based actors are making vigorous efforts to influence the political dynamic of the upcoming assembly elections in J&K. The idea is to let the democratic politics revive and keep the levers of power in the valley for the reasons, more than obvious.

The movement in Kashmir is going leaderless and directionless. The youth, high on drugs and a false sense of gun-heroism, is finding a sense of redemption and legitimacy in religion. Radicalization and desire for Jihad have become powerful sentiments. The young recruits after joining a militant group feel that they are more Islamic than even the Hurriyat leaders. A leaderless, directionless and disorganized state of militancy may strengthen the role of religious extremism in the short term, resulting in more recruitments, encounters, and emotionally charged funerals. But in the long run, such disorganized and directionless movement will lose steam and will be difficult to resurrect.

On the militancy front, the assessment is that after the imposition of the Governor's rule (June 2019), situation has improved in the sense that the security forces are in greater control. To a large extent, credit for this goes to the successful neutralizing of high-value militants and equally also to the pro-people approach of the first "political" governor of the state. Incidents of stone-pelting and new recruitment of militants have come down. However, the present "silence" should not lull the authorities into a false sense of complacency. It is important to mention that in the current winter season, an element of fatigue and seasonal decline in the cross-border infiltration would have also contributed to a comparative lull.

There is still a strong need for a genuine political outreach and effective crackdown on the radicalization infrastructure in the state. If this does not happen soon, there is a strong likelihood of upsurge in home-grown militancy. Furthermore, with the Kashmiri militant organizations like HM losing significance and momentum, they are likely to be replaced by ISIS-like organizations such as AGUH with the strong belief in the establishment of

Islamic caliphate. The situation can be disturbing if they get support from transnational terrorist organizations which are likely to strengthen in Afghanistan after the American withdrawal from Afghanistan.

Lastly, in Kashmir, India's best insurance against radical terror is Kashmiriyat, which is currently facing the most significant threat from the forces of religious extremism. Kashmiriyat needs to be protected and promoted.

Any policy to address the challenge of radicalization must reflect a sound understanding of the ecosystem of Islamism as discussed at length in this chapter. The strategy has to be holistic and multidimensional. If the strategy is piecemeal and addresses only one or two constituents of the ecosystem, it is bound to fail because an attack on one or two components will generate reactions and compensation from the other parts. The intra- Islamism ecosystem' harmony (different components support each other) has matured over the last three decades and is a tough challenge for its best defense against the counter-radicalization regime. Lastly, even if we are considering a modest aim to manage the problems of Kashmir, it will be easier to do so in the Kashmir minus JeI than the Kashmir with JeI.

Baklava Inroads: Turkish Moves to Woo Indian Muslims

The last part of this chapter, as mentioned in the subtitle, relates to a rather recent phenomenon of Turkish interest in India's radicalization scenario. Mr. Recep Tayyip Erdogan has been President of Turkey since 2014 and before that he was the Prime Minister since 2003, with an uninterrupted rule of 16 years and counting. He has emerged as the most recent and sophisticated player after the Saudi-funded Wahhabism[20] and Pak-sponsored chaotic jihadism. Erdogan's inroads among Indian Muslims are least discussed in the Indian media and strategic circles. There is also near-total absence of any literature in the public domain. However, in the course of field research for data collection, one came across informed interlocutors who revealed alarming outreach activities by Erdogan among the Indian Muslims.

Abdullah Bozkart, in his article[21] for the online media portal, "Turkish Minute," wrote that Erdogan is making vigorous efforts to woo Indian Muslims. Turkish embassy and consulates are laying the groundwork for this. Diplomats and consular officials are reportedly approaching prominent Muslim clerics, businesspeople, community leaders, Muslim politicians, and bureaucrats. He further mentioned that extremist Islamic clerics are acting as the main conduits for establishing a support base for Erdogan among Indian Muslims. Sheikh Salman Nadwi, a controversial cleric who earlier issued statements supporting Baghdadi but later withdraw it after a backlash, is one of them. Nadwi, previously, had written a letter to Saudi rulers, promising to raise an army of 500,000 Muslims[22] in India which could be deployed for Jihad anywhere. Such a man holds high importance for Erdogan who is no less imaginative in supporting proxies in Syria.

The Indian strategic experts view Erdogan's initiatives as merely aimed at undermining the influence of Gulen movement (faith-based Islamic education movement) and rule out the possibility of any larger political ambitions. However, their understanding of Erdogan's real motives appears flawed.

Sources inform that Erdogan's real ambitions are to revive the institution of the caliphate by 2023[23] to claim political and spiritual leadership of the Islamic world. This may sound like a conspiracy theory to those who are not well-versed with the history of ME. The popular perception of the Saudi-Iranian rivalry being the fulcrum of geopolitics in ME hides the history of Ottoman-Wahhabi/Saud rivalry. It was the Ottoman Turks who demolished the first Wahhabi Empire.[24] The treaty of Serves (1920) ended the caliphate, and Kemalist Turkey became a westernized secular democracy. However, as it happens with countries with rich civilizational history and political glories of the past, be it Iran, China, Russia or Turkey, the desire for political resurrection hardly dies. Also, they emerge most unexpectedly, when the opportune moment arises. Erdogan's recent authoritarian maneuvering in the domestic affairs and his manipulative and aggressive strategic posture in Middle Eastern politics may lend more substance to the romantic idea of a revival of the caliphate.[25]

#Erdogan: #Turkey is the only country that can lead the #Muslim world (Headline in a pro-government newspaper, *Yeni Safak*, 15 October 2018)[26].

The caliphate project appears more like furthering of Erdogan's ambitions of seizing the political leadership of the Muslim world. Given the glorious past of Ottoman caliphate, even if he can acquire the position of Caliph in name, again, it will strengthen his claims and enhance his status. Suddenly, he becomes a spiritual power center also for millions of Muslims spread across the world, giving a strong moral and religious legitimacy to his claims for the leadership of Muslim world, backed by his robust diplomatic maneuvering. As compared to Saudi Arabia, which is increasingly being seen as a US outpost in the ME, Erdogan is likely to have greater credibility in popular perception.

"His caliphate" will be more like a symbolic spiritual authority with strong political undertones exerting powerful influence on Muslim minds not only in the ME but even beyond.

Unlike Saudi leadership, Erdogan will not be obsessed with sectarian Shia-Sunni rivalries. It appears that he has a broader vision to lead the entire Islamic world and not bleed his resources and squander away his authority in fighting Shia states. Erdogan is already engaging Iran and Qatar, Saudi foes, with a liberal form of Salafism. Some of the deliberations in South Asia Strategic Research Center (GASAM, in Turkish), a think-tank, suggest that he has significant plans to alter the geography of the Middle East by reviving the old Ottoman Empire. In the GASAM deliberations, it is often argued that the former Ottoman Empire never suffered from internal feuds and Muslims were not weak against the foreign forces in the old Empire, so the current artificial boundaries need to be revised. The dreams of altering the geography of ME may sound a bit far-fetched but it has a substantial element of truth. Such nefarious designs are capable of wreaking havoc on the world peace.

As compared to Saudi Arabia's monarchy, despite the upsurge of populism, authoritarianism, and religion under Erdogan, Turkey's institutions of state are far stronger and stable. Democracy is mature and robust though there are serious questions raised about authoritarian manner in which the opposition is being crushed. Yet, Erdogan's claim for the leadership of the Islamic world will be stronger, and in response, one should expect a far more aggressive challenge from Saudi Arabia, in Middle Eastern affairs.

Though a bit premature, a question being already whispered is how will Erdogan-centered global Islam play out vis-à-vis the global Islamism based on violent jihad perpetrated by trans-national terrorist organizations, either acting on their own or as proxies of the states. It is difficult to say much about it at this stage. The dynamics of the interplay will depend on the clout exercised by the respective narratives and the actors involved and those having vested interests. Added to this is also the fact that Erdogan is no "saint" and his enthusiasm and deft at using proxy-jihadi groups need little elaboration. Turkey's dubious links with IS have been under debate for quite some time now. Dutch General Intelligence and Security Service (AVID) has claimed that IS is using Turkey as a strategic base to reorganize threats to Europe. The AVID report also claims that for a long time, Turkey was "a spring board for an unprecedented number of foreign fighters who travelled to Syria from all over the world"[27]

GASAM was established by Ali Sahin, a Pakistani Islamist, now serving as the deputy minister for European Affairs in Erdogan's cabinet. He functions as the leading platform to propagate Erdogan's thoughts on the revival of Caliphate, among the South Asian Muslims. GASAM organizes conferences, inviting Islamic clerics, Muslim politicians and community leaders from South Asia, to create an intellectual and religious narrative on the importance and necessity of the revival of the Turkish Caliphate. Ali Sahin is playing a pivotal role, by developing innovative projects with YTB (Presidency for Turks Abroad and Related Communities) specifically for South Asian Muslims, to export AKP's Islamist ideology to Indian Muslims.[28]

In April 2016, GASAM had organized in Istanbul, a conference on the caliphate movement in India. AKP Deputy Zehra Taskesenlioglu and PM's Chief Advisor Omar Korkamaz participated in it. Interestingly, Nadwi's son Yunus, who is studying in Turkey, is a regular panelist in the conferences organized by GASAM. Yunus is also functioning as the liaison man between Erdogan's Islamist coterie and Indian clerics, facilitating visits and propaganda work by Turkish Islamists among the Indian Muslims. With his help, controversial Islamist clerics like Arsalan and Sardar Demirel (Pak-educated Islamist) have visited India several times. Arsalan is a member of International Union of Islamic Scholars, a Muslim Brotherhood linked organization led by pro-Erdogan Imam Qaradawi, who had earlier advocated suicide bombings and armed jihad in Syria. Demirel, staunchly anti-western Islamist, visited Kolkata in 2016[29] to participate in a protest march against the government's idea of a Uniform Civil Code (reform measure to bring Muslim divorce laws in line with secular laws of India).

Another controversial Wahhabi preacher Zakir Naik, notorious for inspiring the Dhaka terror attack in July 2016, and currently facing an arrest warrant in India, has also been received warmly in Turkey several times. He reportedly enjoys cordial relations with extremist Islamist clerics like Yildiz and delivered a speech at TUGWA (Islamist group run by Erdogan's son Bilal) in 2017. Turkey is also funding NGOs and front organizations for outreach among Indian Muslims which are likely to be used in future on the lines of Erdogan's initiatives with the Turkish diaspora in Germany and other EU countries.

During informal interactions, several Turkish businesspeople and dissidents in India who have been carefully observing the outreach activities of Erdogan among Indian Muslims have confirmed the facts mentioned by Bozkart in his article. Some of them were Gulenists, and they even feared assassination attempts on them and the monitoring of their movements in India. Confirmed sources maintain that in conferences organized by GASAM, Kashmir issue is frequently raised, equating it with the Palestinian situation. The most recent high-profile meeting known as World Muslim Minority Summit was held in April 2018, in Istanbul. According to informed sources, another was being planned for November (6th-9th) 2018. Several Muslim clerics from Lucknow, Hyderabad, Bhopal, and Kerala have participated in such conferences.

Furthermore, as mentioned earlier, *TRT World* has published many exaggerated and one-sided stories on Kashmir. Additionally, Erdogan administration is also making intense use of social media to reach out to Indian Muslims. These videos are available in circulation in Kashmir. They carry high-quality propaganda material prepared by professionals as part of a strategic communication programme with long-range objectives. Many such videos are becoming viral among Indian Muslims.

According to knowledgeable sources, the Turkish AKP regime is also using Turkish Cooperation and Development Agency, or TIKA, and the official Yunus Emre Institute to reach out to the Muslim youth in India, through student exchange and cultural activities. Also, Erdogan's machinery has also been communicating on a regular basis with prominent madrasas of India. Someone who visited a Salafiya mosque in Varanasi found that they were having regular communication with Turkish Islamists.

Erdogan's victory in recent elections led to huge celebrations from Kerala to Kashmir.[30] One can witness a warm reception for Erdogan's initiatives among the Indian Muslims, and in all likelihood, the response will be encouraging in the future. It may be emphasized that Turkish initiatives suggest a broader political aim such as the revival of the caliphate than any short-term goals to counter Gulenists in India because they, in any case, have a very insignificant presence in India. If Caliphate is the ambition, wooing Indian Muslims makes perfect sense, because support from the world's third largest Muslim population (India) will not only strengthen Erdogan's claim to caliphate psychologically and politically but also provide a robust religious legitimacy.

In the ME, Erdogan's claims for caliphate will face tremendous resistance, but in India, there is a reasonable possibility of the Muslim community enthusiastically supporting the revival of Turkish Caliphate for various reasons.

Firstly, the two prominent Islamic schools in India, i.e. Deobandi and Barelwi schools, like Turkey, follow Hanafi Sunni Islam, with a vast majority of Muslims being Hanafi in India. Erdogan's idea of political Islam will have a strong resonance in India rather than the Wahhabi version of political Islam because Wahhabism will face resistance from local Hanafi schools. Secondly, there is a substantial history of reverence for Ottoman caliphate. After the revolt of 1857, to escape British persecution, several Indian clerics took refuge in the Ottoman territory. In 1919, Gandhi Ji launched Khilafat movement against dismemberment of Caliphate by the British, with massive support of Indian Muslims.[31] Thirdly, the culture and temperament of Indian Muslims are such that the brutal and extremist methods of ISIS caliphate or Saudi-styled extremist Wahabism will not have much traction, as already proven by the fact that in spite of world's third largest Muslim population, merely 112 Indians traveled abroad to join ISIS. Fourthly, in the current scenario, the Hindu nationalist footprint is getting stronger in India, the Muslims are already feeling threatened. In such a situation, the idea of the revival of caliphate may be perceived as a source of identity and will find a good market in India.

With his global political ambitions and proximity to Islamist groups like the Muslim brotherhood, Erdogan is gradually being perceived as a symbol of Islamic radicalization. India, therefore, needs to take cognition of the Turkish outreach among its Muslims to strengthen the forces of radicalization in India. Else, Baklava may taste bitter to Indian authorities in the long run.

NOTES

1 Dar, Muzammil Ahad, "Falai Aam Trust: Providing Education for All," *Greater Kashmir*, December 4, 2015, https://www.greaterkashmir.com/news/opinion/falai-aam-trust-providing-education-for-all/

2 Mir, Tariq, "Kashmir: From Sufi to Salafi," Pulitzer Center, November 5, 2012, https://pulitzercenter.org/reporting/kashmir-sufi-salafi

3 Singh, Arti, "Here's How Schools of Faith, Mobiles Are Radicalising Kashmir," *Times of India*, July 19, 2017, https://timesofindia.indiatimes.com/india/how-mosques-and-mobiles-are-radicalising-kashmir/articleshow/59507200.cms

4 Mir, op. cit

5 Singh, op. cit

6 ibid

7 Singh, Tikoo Arti, "Here's how schools of faith, mobiles are radicalizing Kashmir," *Times of India*, July 8, 2017, Accessed: September 16, 2018 https://timesofindia.indiatimes.com/india/how-mosques-and-mobiles-are-radicalising-kashmir/articleshow/59507200.cms

8 Dehlvi, Ghulam Rasool, "Salafism in Kashmir: Why is Media Silent on the Salafi-Wahabi

Preachers in the Valley?," *First Post,* September 17, 2018, https://www.firstpost.com/india/salafism-in-kashmir-why-is-media-silent-on-salafi-wahhabi-preachers-in-the-valley-3034022.html

9 Singh, Tikoo Arti, "Here's how schools of faith, mobiles are radicalizing Kashmir," *Times of India,* July 8, 2017, Accessed: September 16, 2018 https://timesofindia.indiatimes.com/india/how-mosques-and-mobiles-are-radicalising-kashmir/articleshow/59507200.cms

10 Mir, op. cit

11 ibid

12 Hyderi, Majed, "Division Among Muslim Radicals Spurs Fear of Civil War in Kashmir," *Asia Times,* September 10, 2018, https://www.asiatimes.com/2018/09/article/fears-rise-of-civil-war-in-kashmir-despite-divisions-among-muslims/

13 ibid

14 *Zee News,* "Desh Hit: Fatwa Against People Who Paid Tribute to Atal Bihari Vajpayee in J&K," September 7, 2018, https://zeenews.india.com/video/india/deshhit-fatwa-against-people-who-paid-tribute-to-atal-bihari-vajpayee-in-jk-2139378.html

15 Raina, Muzaffar, "Masked Youths Grab Mirwaiz Pulpit, Briefly," *The Telegraph,* December 30, 2018, https://www.telegraphindia.com/india/masked-youths-grab-mirwaiz-pulpit-briefly/cid/1680337

16 Pakistan Defense, "Letter by Scholar Mannan Wani on Why He Chose to Pick up Gun," July 16, 2018, https://defence.pk/pdf/threads/letter-by-scholar-mannan-wani-on-why-he-chose-to-pick-up-gun.568030/

17 "Hizbul distances itself from Musa's statement threatening to behead Hurriyat leaders," *Hindustan Times,* May 13, 2017, Accessed: July 17, 2018 https://www.hindustantimes.com/india-news/hizbul-distances-itself-from-musa-s-statement-threatening-to-behead-hurriyat-leaders/story-pjDLyUixCGqYgujWt8KOnM.html

18 Hyderi, Majid, "Division among Muslim radicals spurs fear of civil war in Kashmir," *Asia Times* September 10, 2018, Accessed: October 10, 2018 https://www.asiatimes.com/2018/09/article/fears-rise-of-civil-war-in-kashmir-despite-divisions-among-muslims/

19 This piece was written in December 2018, the day a new JeI general secretary was appointed. It is indeed a matter of satisfaction that the government has already acted on these lines and announced ban on JeI J&K on Feb 28, 2019; Kumar G, Aravinth, "Government Imposes Ban on Jamaat-e-Islami Jammu And Kashmir," NDTV, March 1, 2019, https://www.ndtv.com/india-news/government-imposes-ban-on-jamaat-e-islami-jammu-and-kashmir-2000910

20 Pandya, Abhinav, "Does Saudi-funded Muslim radicalization threaten India?," *Haaretz,* April 16, 2018, Accessed: March 3, 2019 https://www.haaretz.com/middle-east-news/does-saudi-funded-muslim-radicalization-threaten-india-1.6008341

21 Bozkart, Abdullah, "Erdogan's dangerous game of wooing Indian Muslims," *Times Headline,* August 18, 2017, Accessed: March 3, 2019 https://www.timesheadline.com/opinion/erdogans-dangerous-game-wooing-indian-muslims-7173.html

22 ibid

23 Vatandas, Aydogan, "Erdogan's ambition for the caliphate and the failure of Turkish democracy," *Consortium News,* June 25, 2018, Accessed: March 4, 2019 https://consortiumnews.com/2018/06/25/erdogans-ambition-for-the-caliphate-and-the-failure-of-turkish-democracy/

24 Crooke, Alstair, "You can't understand ISIS, if you don't know the history of wahhabism in Saudi Arabia," *Huffington Post,* August 27, 2014, Accessed: March 3, 2019 https://www.huffpost.com/entry/isis-wahhabism-saudi-arabia_b_5717157

25 Pandya, Abhinav, "Caliph Erdogan? Why Turkey's President is quietly courting Indian Muslims," *Haaretz*, December 17, 2018, Accessed: March 3, 2019 https://www.haaretz.com/middle-east-news/.premium-is-turkey-s-erdogan-quietly-courting-indian-muslims-to-crown-him-caliph-1.6786101

26 ibid

27 "ISIS using Turkey as a strategic base," *Ahval,* November 6, 2018, Accessed: March 3, 2019 https://ahvalnews.com/isis/isis-using-turkey-strategic-base-dutch-intelligence-report

28 Bozkart, Abdullah,op.cit

29 ibid

30 Chakravarty, Ipsita, "Turkish President Recep Tayyip Erdogan has many cheerleaders among Muslims in the sub-continent," *The Scroll,* June 27, 2018, Accessed: March 3, 2019 https://scroll.in/article/884243/turkish-president-recip-tayyip-erdogan-has-many-cheerleaders-among-muslims-in-the-subcontinent

31 "Khilafat Movement—Indian Muslim Movement," Encyclopaedia Britannica, https://www.britannica.com/event/Khilafat-movement

5

COUNTERING RADICALIZATION: STRATEGY AND MEASURES

To organize and execute a terrorist attack, the terror groups need recruits, supporters, funds, weapons, ability to travel unimpeded, other kinds of logistical and material support and the reach to the vulnerable targets. Hence, an effective counter-terrorism strategy needs to be multifaceted involving a wide range of policies and measures. In a multi-faceted counter-terrorism strategy, counter-radicalization and de-radicalization should form pillars of the overall strategy because radicalization prepares the ideological, social and cultural base for the use of terror as a weapon by a terrorist organization. All the above-mentioned requirements in executing a terrorist attack need a fertile ground and that is prepared by radicalizing a society.

The measures to address conditions conducive to terrorism are one of the three main pillars of the UN Global Counter-Terrorism Strategy[1] (Chapter 2, Preventing Terrorism, Key Concepts). Radicalized socio-cultural set-up ensures ready supply of recruits for all the tasks involved in the execution of a terror attack. Hence, radicalization is one of the most basic conditions that is conducive to the spread of terrorism. The UN Security Council Resolution 1373 (2001; Chapter 2)[2] also imposes legally binding obligations on all states to suppress the recruitment of the members of terrorist groups.

Terrorist radicalization is a process whereby a person accepts the legitimacy of terrorist violence as the right and the justified course of action for achieving the desired objective. Ultimately, this may lead a person, but not necessarily, to indulge in or support an act of terrorism. Terrorist radicalization happens in a variety of circumstances in different ways and at different speeds. There are different permutations and combinations of an enabling environment with the personal circumstances and the psychology of a given man or woman. The

Organization for Security and Co-operation in Europe's (OSCE) working paper[3] on the community-police approach to address radicalization states, "There is no single profile of a terrorist, no clear-cut pathway towards terrorism. Possible drivers of terrorist radicalization are varied and complex and combine in a unique way in each case." Geographical, political, demographic, social and cultural contexts are major determining factors in the process of radicalization. For example, the speed, intensity and the rigor of radicalization in Pakistan will be very different from that in Indonesia and India because of the differences in the political, cultural and social set-up.

Terrorist radicalization is an ongoing and evolving process of interaction between several individuals and external influences like terrorist propagandists and recruiters, religious preachers, larger developments in society and the actions of public authorities. A charismatic recruiter may be a "pull factor," pulling an individual down the path of radicalization whereas the lack of satisfying employment, experience of trauma, search for identity and experience of bureaucratic arrogance, violence, torture and humiliation at the hands of state agents may be "push factors." The UN and OSCE lists of conditions conducive to terrorism include "prolonged unresolved conflicts, dehumanization of victims of terrorism in all its forms and manifestations, lack of rule of law, violations of human rights, ethnic, national and religious discrimination and lack of good governance."

Besides, structural factors like socio-economic and political conditions like deprivation, human rights violation, poverty and the lack of education are myriad psychological, ideological and interpersonal factors which go a long way in explaining the radicalization. Psychological and cognitive factors, such as one's self-image, a sense of identity and belonging, expectations, beliefs and attitudes, trauma and negative feelings of displacement, can have a major impact on how a person responds to external stimuli. For example, Prof. Olivier Roy found in his research that in France, second-generation Muslims of migrants from Morocco and Algeria joined jihadi terrorism because they could not integrate well into the French society. They faced discrimination in employment and education. The state of joblessness, failed relationships pushed them towards drugs, alcoholism and other forms of substance abuse. In such a state of vulnerability, they were desperately searching for an identity, meaning, a purpose and an anchorage. Jihad gave them a purpose and a meaning of life.

The spread of, and exposure to, ideas and narratives that legitimize terrorism and cultivate its appeal are critical pull factors. Many terrorists/ violent extremists skillfully tailor and disseminate their message in such a manner that will reach and appeal the particular individual or group targeted for radicalization and recruitment. There are different approaches that can be used to legitimize and enhance the appeal of terrorism, including the following:

1) The rationale that the ends justify the means, arguing that violence is an essential necessity in the pursuit of imperative social, ideological, political or other goals and that there is no alternative;
2) Demeaning intended victims on the basis of intolerance, hate, and denial of universal human dignity;
3) Projecting terrorism as something exciting, alternative or antiestablishment; and
4) Building on the charisma and/or perceived legitimacy of terrorists and, in particular, their leaders.

Social interactions, interpersonal relationships, and group dynamics act as the major pull factors, except in instances of self-initiated radicalization. People are drawn to Violent Extremism and Radicalization Leading to Terrorism (VERLT) through their personal acquaintances—peers and relatives. In many cases, they are sought out by terrorist recruiters. Terrorist recruiters identify, prey on and nurture vulnerable men and women, gain a control on them by providing material and/or psychological support, and misuse their trust to manipulate them or indoctrinate them into becoming involved with terrorism. Sometimes, the social milieu makes the task of such recruiters very easy. For example, in a society like Palestine, there appears a social acceptance and an unstated consensus of terrorism as a weapon and a strategy. Similarly, in Kashmir also, one can witness an increasing acceptance of violent extremism as a way of protest and the pathway to glory, martyrdom and heaven (jannat). It can be seen in the form of a large number of local militants joining terrorist organizations. Lately, the hitherto unheard of, practice of local youth volunteering for Fidayeen attacks is also gaining ground due to intense religious radicalization, as witnessed in the case of Pulwama Fidayeen attack which led to the death of 40 CRPF personnel. In such a milieu, the terrorist propagandists have an easy access to recruits. In Pakistan, fanatic schools of Islam like Deobandism and Wahhabism have become so deeply entrenched that it is very easy to recruit the cadres for a terrorist organization, including suicide bombers. On top of it, the "proxy war" with India makes terrorism the most lucrative business and an appealing career fetching pecuniary benefits and social prestige.

The detailed discussion above on the concept of radicalization facilitates a better understanding of and the rationale behind the different measures suggested in the following section. However, in the analysis above radicalization has been discussed as a general concept. The purpose of this essay is to explore the right set of counter-radicalization strategies for addressing the challenge of Islamic extremism in India.

The ideology of Jihad will continue to torment the humanity for at least another decade or even more. Fundamentalist Islamic ideologies are at a cross with the Westphalian international order whose basic entity is a nation-state. The treaty of Serves (1919) dismantled the Islamic idea of the political system in the Middle East and since then Jihadism in one form or the other has strived to go back to the political system of the caliphate, with the caliphate existent in 7th-century Arabia as the most authentic and pure ideal. Major world powers have failed to act in a concerted manner in the Middle East, so the jihad will continue to spread. And, then there is a template. Jihadis from Afghanistan spread across the globe and now Jihadis from Syria will do the same in different parts of the world.

India will continue to face Jihad because it is backed by Pakistan where jihadi groups are gradually becoming part of the state just like the Hamas and Hezbollah in the Middle East. Furthermore, India is facing a refugee influx from Bangladesh where Jihadism was emerging as a prominent force. In addition, there is an intense wave of Wahhabi radicalization and the local extremist Islamic schools sweeping across the country.

Under the above-mentioned existing and evolving narratives, based on the discussions in the previous chapters, a set of recommendations that could be considered for implementation are described next to address the challenge of radicalization in India.

1) Counter-Radicalization: Step 1

Correct Diagnosis

The first step should be to diagnose the problem correctly. It is often argued that if radicalization does not lead to violence, it is not dangerous. This is a faulty assumption. It needs to be recognized that the ideologies like Wahhabism,

Deobandism (Pakistani version), and Salafism are potentially dangerous with their notions like Takfiri and Jihadism. The roots of the problem lie in these ideologies. These groups may be peaceful in their activities but the ideology and the message they propagate are violent. For example, Deobandis believe that the first loyalty of a Muslim is towards Islam, not any nation-state. In the second and third chapters and in one of his previous essays, "Post–ISIS: The Future of Global Jihad,"[4] the pernicious effects of such exclusivist ideologies thriving on exclusivist framework were critically analysed. Reference is invited to the two above-mentioned essays to learn more about the ideological aspects of Islamic extremism in detail. It is worth mentioning that a seemingly "peaceful" publication like the Urdu weekly *Nai Duniya* is publishing an Urdu book "Aur Talvaar Toot Gayi" (And the Sword Broke) by Nasim Rizwi,[5] which cultivates jihadi extremism among Indian Muslims. Urdu dailies such as *Roznama Sangam* of Patna and *Roznama Sahafat* and *Rozanama Inqilaab* of Delhi ran articles eulogizing Ghazwa-e-Badr, Prophet Muhammad's first battle against infidels.[6] Hafiz Sayeed's Lashkar is a social service and charity organization in public domain but the ideology which it subscribes to is the reactor of terrorism. Similarly, it was seen in the recent ban on Jamaat-e-Islami (JI) in Kashmir (after the Pulwama Fidayeen attack), by Indian government, that many mainstream political parties of Jammu and Kashmir and the media organizations were defending JI on the grounds of its charity and welfare work, conveniently sidelining the hatred and venom, it is injecting in young minds.

It has to be admitted that the justification of Islamic extremism and terrorism emanates from the concept of Jihad and other justifications illustrated in the Quran. The conducive conditions like humiliation, unemployment, corruption, and bad governance, the violation of human rights, injustice and deprivation exist in some form or the other, everywhere. They provide the fertile ground to jihad propagandists and recruiters enabling them to push individuals into the fold of terrorism. But in course of time, the material and secular grievances take the backseat and the violent ideology of jihad takes moves upfront. For example, in Kashmir the radical ideologies of Jihad and political Islam propagated by Wahhabis and JI are the main mobilizer, unifier and inspirer for violence, rather than the earlier notions such as the lack of the right to self-determination. In the case of Palestine also, the secular motivations are shrinking, leaving the space to be occupied by the religious doctrine of jihad.

Further, if political violence emanates from purely secular reasons then it has spatial and temporal limits. Christians from India will not go to fight for Irish Republican Army or Hindus from north India never went to fight alongside LTTE, though the later included a lot of Hindus. But if Iran funds Hizbollah and Hamas, there has to be a religious reason for that. Initially, the jihadi ideology is a unifier, a mobilizer providing justification, psycho-spiritual and moral strength for violence but in course of time, it becomes the most powerful motivating factor. The ideology in itself is also powerful enough to radicalize. For example, perpetrators of 9/11 and Gulshan area attack in Bangladesh were all educated individuals from upper middle class families. And, ISIS has made the Jihad religious in its absolute sense (refer to the essay "Post-ISIS: The Future of Global Jihad" and "What ISIS Really Wants?" by Graeme Wood).

Therefore, it hardly makes sense to call it violent extremism. Unless we take the problem head-on first, by shedding off the cloak of political correctness, and second, by addressing it as jihadi extremism, i.e. its most original and authentic form, we cannot arrive at an effective strategy to combat terrorism at its roots, i.e. the ideology.

2) Counter-Radicalization: Step 2

Building a Counter-Narrative

In the Indian security establishment, political, academic and socio-cultural circles, there is a strong belief that Indian Muslims are different from the rest of the world and they have enough resilience to foreign extremist ideologies which they have developed over the past 10 centuries of multi-cultural living experience. However, the afore-mentioned belief currently appears more like wishful thinking. No doubt, India's Islam and its Muslim community have some unique features of resilience originating from the years of co-existence with Hindus, the evolution of Sufi spiritualism on the lines of the Vedantic concept of the unity of being. There are strong reasons for the radicalization of Indian Muslims for various reasons. Firstly, along with the pleasant aspects of communal harmony and the flourishing of the common Hindu-Muslim culture, there is a parallel history of Islamic extremism, bigotry, conversions, and persecutions of non-Muslims in India. I have already outlined the extremist ideas of Sheikh Ahmad Sirhindi, persecutions of Hindus and Sikhs during Aurangzeb's reign, "theory of distance" of the Shah Walliullah Dehalvi, development of Wahhabism in India and the long British struggle against it, communal politics of Muslim League, partition riots and the series of communal riots in the post-partition India. Secondly, the recent upsurge of Hindu nationalism has provided enough fuel for nurturing the perception of Islam in danger in the minds of Muslims in India. Thirdly, the Muslim community in India was relatively isolated from the global trends in the Islamic world earlier, and whenever the contact with the larger Islamic movements took place, it did have its impact on Indian Muslims. Today, the scenario is starkly different. Due to advancements in internet and communication technologies and various other reasons outlined earlier in this paper, the contact of the Indian Muslim community with the global Islamic trends has become firm and widely pervasive. The global geopolitical developments, like US interventions in Middle East and Afghanistan and the oil-prosperity of the gulf, have contributed to the process of radicalization of Muslims even in the Muslim majority countries. An ostrich-like attitude about Indian Muslims and their resilience does not appear to be a rational approach. Fourthly and very importantly, radicalization in its essence is a sentiment which has a robust demographic angle. It is a problem which is mostly a problem of the youth (barring exceptions). Young minds between the ages of 16 to 30 are the most susceptible to radicalization. Ideologies ultimately end up being the channels or rather vehicles for radicalization. However, the religious doctrines tend to have a much stronger, comprehensive and lasting influence over the young minds.

Interestingly, India has one of the youngest population profile in the developing world. By 2020, the median age in India will be just 28, compared to 37 in China and the US, 45 in Western Europe, and 49 in Japan. There are various other factors like lack of jobs, poor education, corruption, polarized and communal politics, psychological and identity-related crises issues of the youth. All the factors mentioned above make India a likely spot for radicalization.

Ideally, right after the independence, the intelligence agencies and the broader security set-up in India should have devoted intellectual and financial resources on mapping the threat of Islamic extremism to India because, when Islamic extremism was not a threat to the world community, it presented a significant threat to India so much so that, in the views of some, it even led to the partition of India. However, our agencies have possibly lacked a futuristic approach in mapping emerging threats and generating sound intelligence analysis of such risks. In response, India should have created a counter-narrative to Islamic extremism from the very outset. Perhaps, this did not happen as the political bosses always determined the agenda, and they lacked sufficient vision and awareness on the project of building a counter-narrative. Instead, political opportunism dominated and after the Babri Mosque demolition, they instead stooped low into the phenomenon of "competitive secularism" and gave in to Islamic extremism for the selfish interests of vote-bank politics. The result was seen in the form of terror-preachers and hate-mongers like Zakir Naik roaming around the country with the tacit acceptance of the state for almost a decade, with their extremist and hateful speeches nourishing an intellectual breeding ground for jihadi terrorists. Any question on clerics like Zakir Naik came to be considered as an attack on the secular spirit of the Indian nation. However, lately, especially after the emergence of the ISIS phenomenon, awareness for building a counter-narrative to extremist Islam has been majorly felt because it was the remnants of the counter-narrative (developed in the medieval era), represented by traditional-moderate Indian Islam, that prevented India from becoming a hotbed of ISIS or AQ ideologies.

First and foremost, it needs to be mentioned that the general feeling among the Indian strategic circles is that the counter-narrative should come from within the community. This appears quite reasonable because the issue is highly sensitive and there are strong chances of its politicization leading to communal polarization if it comes from outside the community. The counter-narrative has to be comprehensive, i.e. religious, social, cultural, political and economic. Furthermore, it has to be systematic, organized and institutionalized. The state can explore the option of supporting and facilitating such initiatives in a non-partisan manner.

Furthermore, the use of technology, internet, and social media must be leveraged in the best possible way to reach out to a maximum number of people. The Civil Society, media, educational institutions and the private sector should also be actively involved in this initiative. Lastly, it needs to be customized and tailored to the conditions and needs prevalent in India. PM Modi made a great beginning with presiding over a Sufi conference[7] in Delhi. The presence of the Prime Minister of India was highly symbolic of what narrative the state wants to project. The counter-narrative will also lend support, confidence and strong psychological strength to those Muslims who are putting up a great fight against extremist ideologies in the midst of highly adverse circumstances marked by the fast-spreading appeal of global jihad.

In the religious domain, the counter-narrative can be developed through a proper spiritual and contextual interpretation of the Quran. A nuanced reading of the text itself will furnish a robust defense against extremism.

First of all, it needs to be mentioned that Jihadism has spread widely across the world among the Muslim communities of diverse sects. It is so because it forms the essential element of the theology of consensus which builds the edifice of the religious beliefs and practices of the various Muslim sects (consensus theology is common to all denominations and sub-sects of Islam). This is the reason why Jihadis are not moved when clerics claim that Islam is a religion of peace and plurality and issue fatwas against terrorism. Merely issuing fatwas against terrorism will not serve the purpose. There is a strong need to crack down on the stagnation that has engulfed the Islamic theology, through logical reason and proper, spiritual and contextual interpretation of the text, as stated above. Sultan Shaheen, an expert voice on the reformation in Islamic theology and the editor of "The New Age Islam" has suggested that there is a strong need to reexamine the consensus theology of Islam and make it relevant to the needs of the globalized world of 21st century. In his view, the alternative theology must focus on peace, respect for diversity, plurality, human rights, gender justice, and inclusion.

The consensus theology believes in the universality, divinity, and infallibility of the Quran. All its verses are accepted as Allah's command to its devotees and these are interpreted in a literal sense, disregarding the fact that many of the verses of Quran were meant for the then obtaining context and are no longer relevant now. For example, the war verses of the Quran dictate that Muslims should always fight the Kuffar and be on the offensive against non-Muslims. They must stay away from non-Muslims and they have to bring them to the fold of Islam either by force or persuasion.

The alternate theology must state that these verses were meant for those specific conditions of war which prevailed in the seventh-century Arabia. Those injunctions were intended for the period when Islam was facing an existential threat and struggling for its survival. Today, Islam has become a global religion. It no more faces any threat to its survival, and hence, the war verses are not crucial in a literal sense. They are important only as an account of the early days of Islam when it faced an existential threat. Furthermore, in the original war verses also, it is mentioned that those polytheists who respected the treaty with the Prophet, ruler of Madinah, were not to be harmed. However, the literalists straightway read the verse 5 of the ninth Surah (Ayat-i-Saif) and conclude that all infidels/non-Muslims have to be killed.

In addition, in Madinah, Prophet Muhammad (PBUH) released "Misakh-e-Madina" (the Covenant/charter of Madina) in which he declared that all those, i.e. Muslims and non-Muslims, who lived in Madina were the part of his Ummaat. His Ummaat included Jews and non-Muslims too. There were eight Jewish tribes that were part of the prophet's Ummaah. The charter formed the basis of the multi-religious Islamic state in Madina. The religious beliefs of all the tribes, including the non-Muslims, were respected and it was declared that during the negotiations and conflicts with the foreign states, all the tribes, irrespective of their religion, were to be present. The document should form the basis of Islam in the 21st century, and it established the most original principles of coexistence with non-Muslims, for Muslims. Maulana Hasrat Ahmad Madni, head of the Jamiyat Ulema-e-Hind (Deobandi Organization) opposed Jinnah's demand for a separate country for Muslims on religious grounds, by citing Misakh-e-Madina.

There is a consensus among all the Muslim sects that Hadith (sayings of the Prophet) are akin to the Quran which was of the nature of divine revelation. The Hadith were collected 300 years after the death of the Prophet. Furthermore, the presence of political motives cannot be denied behind granting Hadtih a near-equal status to Quran. In the 48th year of Prophet's demise, his entire family was killed and political power and leadership in Islam were taken over by the enemies of Islam who had fought against the Prophet their whole life and accepted Islam only after the Prophet won Mecca. To subvert Islam from within, the enemies of Islam raised the institutions of Hadith, Sunnah, and Ulema as equal in status to the Quran. Ulemas were accorded the status of the heirs of the Prophet. Hadith and Sunnah contain many injunctions and actions which were performed by Prophet as a human being (as he said) and were relevant to the time and society he lived in, but not to the current times. The new alternate theology has to bring the focus back on the Quran. Hadith and Sunnah fall under the purview of the debate and can be modified or adapted to the current context through the Islamic practice of Ijtihad (deductive/inductive reasoning). The new alternate theology has to dislodge Ulema and Hadith from their existing position of eminence. These institutions developed under the despotic, tyrannical and dynastic rule of Khalifas who designed the institutions mentioned above to seek scriptural justifications of their unjust and politically motivated actions. The Ulema (religious scholars) were also pressurized to undermine Quran which essentially guided Muslims to the spiritual path of salvation and strengthen the legitimacy of Hadith which suited their political interests.

Thirdly, Sharia laws were also mostly derived from pre-Islamic Arabic societies, but they are accorded a divine status in the consensus theology. The new alternate theology needs to debunk the myth of the divinity of Sharia laws and shift the focus back to the Quran.

Fourthly, the new theology of peace should state that the Meccan verses of the Quran constitute the foundation and the edifice of Quran and the later Medina verses of sword cannot abrogate them.

Fifthly, another essential element of the consensus theology that the Muslims should migrate from Darul-Harb (house of war) to Darul-Islam (house of Islam) should also be rejected. Such an idea has no relevance in modern times. On a closer look, one finds that Muslims living in democratic and multicultural societies have better rights and greater freedom to profess and practice their religious beliefs.

As regards political Islam, according to a prominent Salafi cleric I interviewed, the entire idea of political Islam is baseless and anti-Islamic. It is so because according to Quran, Jihad is always done to serve the cause of Allah, not for seeking personal revenge or for acquisition of political power, money, women and land. However, political Islam has clearly defined objectives of achieving political power, and Islam is only the channel being used to do that.

The counter-narrative building exercise is a specialized task. It cannot be left to generalist bureaucrats. In India's case, one comes across many instances of uninformed, crude and casual attempts at such a task. One such strategy that is based on assumptions and an insufficient understanding of Muslims in India is to support and encourage Barelvi/Sufi Islam as a counter to extremist Islamic ideologies. This may not be the most appropriate approach. First of all, it needs to be clear that even the Sufi/Barelvi sects believe in the theology of consensus outlined above. The Sufi/Barelwi factions also have their versions of highly extremist ideology and attitude. Besides, they also suffer from dogmatism, orthodoxy and a conservative approach. The young generation of

Muslims is losing faith in Sufi/Barelvi systems because they have come to be occupied by corrupt clerics. There are lots of superstitious practices, black magic, and ritualism in Sufi/Barelvi systems in India which have deprived the Islam of its original simplicity. The Sufism is losing its "ruhaniyat" (spiritualism). Besides, the Imams of Sufi/Barelvi systems in the hinterlands of India are not well-educated in Islamic teachings. The new generation is not interested in mysticism and spiritualism. Their communication strategy is very primitive. The foreign ideologies like Wahhabism have strong financial backing, use modern and highly advanced communication methods, and run well-furnished schools which teach modern sciences and Islam both. In Kashmir, recently, some attempts have been made to promote Sufi/Etaqadis as a counterweight against Salafism and political Islam, but they have not borne fruits and hardly got any traction with common masses.

Another approach can be to explore Islamic systems that are midway between the ritualistic literalism of Wahhabism and the mysticism of Sufi Islam in India. There are such systems historically and culturally rooted in India and can offer a balance, satisfying the yearnings of the new generation for a more deterministic and literalist Islam. However, efforts to promote such schools should also ensure that such schools be sanitized of extremism and obscurantism and any thoughts, beliefs and systems that threaten the security and communal harmony of India. Furthermore, in the ultimate sense, it should also be realized that there is no alternative to the promotion of rationality, scientific temperament, spiritual outlook, and logic.

The evolution of state and legal systems during the Muslim rule in India can also offer insights for building a counter-narrative. "Al Hidayah" was the most influential Islamic jurisprudence text constituting the foundation of the Hanafi system in India. The text was written by Burhan al-Din al-Farghani al-Marghinani in the 13th century. It explicitly mentioned that culture and custom are essential in determining the jurisprudence. The text implied that the temporal laws would have precedence over Shariat. The book became the bible of the state system in India, and it was the base of the Anglo-Muhammad law, later.

Right from the early Sultanate period of India's medieval history, there was a clash between the clergy and the king. The clergy favored a rigid and orthodox interpretation and implementation of Sharia whereas the king/state favored a liberal or sensible implementation which accommodated the interests of the vast subject population of Hindus also. In the Mughal era, whenever there was a clash between the Sharia and the state law, the state law prevailed. The Mughal rulers were inclined towards enlightened despotism rather than a Sharia-based theocracy. Akbar abolished Jizyah in 1564, banned forcible conversions of war-prisoners to Islam. He allowed religious freedom to non-Muslims. His numerous interactions with non-Muslim scholars shaped his religious views. He invited Brahmin scholars like Devi and Purushottam. The Jain scholars Hari Vijay Suri, Vijaysen Suri, and Jin Chandra Suri visited him. He also had discussions with the Parsi religious authority Dastur Mehar Ji Rana and Jesuit Fathers Montserat and Acabiva. He celebrated Hindu festivals and banned the killing of animals on certain days. In Badayuni's historical account, Akbar is severely criticized for his liberal religious attitude. Badayuni also alleges that he banned Haj and keeping of beard by Muslims. However, Badayuni's allegations appear a little exaggerated.

Akbar combined the religious and political authority in the office of the emperor. In 1979, at the suggestion of Shaikh Mubarak, his spiritual counsel, he released an "Infallibility Decree" (Mazhar) which bestowed him with the status of final arbiter in both religious and political matters. He was declared the Imam-e-Adil. The Sunni nobility and the orthodox segments of clergy led by Shaikh Abdun Nabi raised a banner of rebellion and tried to project Mirza Hakim (Akbar's half-brother and ruler of Kabul) as the Mughal emperor. However, with the support of Iranians, the vast majority of Sunnis and Rajputs, Akbar was able to crush the Ulemas. Later, Abul Fazl's divine theory of kingship, which recognized the king as the shadow of the God, completely undermined the influence of the clergy.

Akbar's doctrine of Sulh-i-Kul was to ensure harmony and peace between different religious communities that inhabited in his empire. Sulh-i-Kul incorporated the philosophical insights of Islam, Jainism, Hinduism, Buddhism, and Christianity. Furthermore, it was also aimed to cultivate a cult of following among his nobles and commanders and strengthen his position vis-à-vis the Ulema.

The Indian Muslims were never attracted to the grandeur of the Caliphate in Baghdad. The focal point in South Asia was the Mughal emperor. Babur was the first to declare himself, the emperor and severed ties with the Caliphate.

Also, the idea of Wahdat-ul-Wajud (unity of being) found greater acceptance in India because it resonated with the Vedantic concept of Brahman, which had been propounded in India centuries earlier. In the realm of culture, Sufi and Bhakti movements flourished. The Sufi poetry of Amir Khusro, Jaaysi and others has numerous references to Hindu imagery like "panghat" and "vileen." Muslim saints like Raskhan worshipped Krishna. Later, in the post-Mughal era also, the different regional Muslim kingdoms exercised tolerance in the matters of religion. Over the centuries of co-existence, a composite Hindu-Muslim culture had evolved.

After the revolt of 1857, Muslims faced severe British persecution and to escape that, many clerics fled to West Asia and Ottoman regions and their interface with the Caliphate began, and with that, the effects of the geo-political developments in the larger Islamic world of the Indian Muslims.

In the domain of international relations, the counter-narrative should also discuss the geopolitics of Jihad, the economy of Jihad and the strategic value of it for the political stakeholders in international politics. The counter-narrative should shatter the sheen of religion and divinity around Jihad. The counter-narrative can elaborate on how the religious institutions/preachers and even the so-called secular institutions like army, intelligence agencies, global powers, arms dealers and non-profit organizations politicians and the large bureaucracies might want to sustain the conflict for their pecuniary, monetary and existential benefits. For example, in Pakistan, army sounds alarm bells of threat from India and nurtures hyper-nationalist sentiments on Kashmir with the purpose of getting a huge share of state resources and budget. If it stops doing that, the futility of allocating huge budget to army gets exposed. Also, in this exercise, it uses religious concepts of Jihad to the hilt.[8]

Furthermore, the duplicity of states sponsoring Jihadi extremism should be brought to light. For example, Pakistan's hypocritical behavior is evident in the fact that it expresses fake concerns for Muslims in Kashmir whereas it maintains silence over the gross human rights violations and mass internment of Muslims in China. In Pakistan, the electorate has repeatedly rejected the religious parties in elections whereas for Kashmir it wants a primitive system of political Islam.

Stories of drug money being used to finance major militant organizations must be narrated to emphasize the anti-Islamic nature of modern Jihad. For example, in Kashmir, terrorist organizations and activities are funded by drug money. Taliban was funded by the opium trade. The Namaz-i-Janaza in Kashmir is used for the recruitment of terrorists and for making political speeches, which are un-Islamic because Namaz-i-Janaza is a religious occasion meant for silent prayers.

The counter-narrative should also focus on real issues like corruption, development, illiteracy and poor governance against the false and utopian notions of Jihad. Recently, in Jammu and Kashmir, Governor Shri Satya Pal Malik's crackdown on corruption and focus on governance issues has shifted the public debate from Jihad, separatism, and militancy to developmental issues.

The state narrative should also be strong. In the absence of a robust, inclusive, tolerant, honest and genuinely secular state narrative, the religious extremism flourishes in the society. The compulsions of democratic politics should under no circumstances be allowed to brook any appeasement to extremist ideologies and threaten the national security.

3) Shattering the Myth of Victimhood

Terrorist organizations like Al Qaeda thrive on the narrative of "Islam in danger." Strategically, this narrative is projected across the Muslim societies. Media, social media, and the academia must challenge this narrative tooth and nail. They must highlight the persecutions of Christians in Nigeria and Sudan, persecution and forced conversions of Hindus, Christians, Ahmadiyyas, and Shias in Pakistan. Indian history is full of stories of persecutions of non-Muslims during the rule of Muslim emperors or because of the activities of Islamic extremists. The message that needs to be projected is that persecution because of one's religious identity is not uncommon. It is not something confined to Muslims only. Even non-Muslims are facing that in predominantly Muslim societies. However, it deserves a mention that Islamic doctrines that regard non-Muslims as "dhimmis" and religiously sanction to levy the discriminatory Jizyah tax from them are against humanity, democracy and equality. This doctrine could easily be used as a shield by terrorist organizations to justify persecution of non-Muslims. Nevertheless, the message will inevitably have its appeal with rational and sensible minds. The alternate narrative should also bring forth that Muslims have remained in powerful political and economic positions and are serving in powerful administrative positions in India which is Darul-aman (land of peace) and Darul-Muhayada (land of compromise and agreement) where the constitution guarantees equal political, religious and economic rights and opportunities to Muslims. Dawoodi Bohra Muslims have a predominant presence in the economy of Mumbai and Chiliya Muslims are an economically powerful Muslim group in Gujarat.

4) Communication Strategy

Finally, it comes to the right communication strategy to make the project of building an effective counter-narrative, a successful one. The counter narrative should have an assertive and overwhelming presence in society and politics. The target audience should discuss the themes propagated by the counter-narrative and question the established narratives on Jihad taught by the extremist clergy and terrorist organizations. For example, terrorist organizations have an overwhelming social presence particularly in South Kashmir. Through social media and a network of Madrasas, they have successfully communicated their narrative and gained effective penetration in the society. However, the Indian narrative is missing on social and print media. Internationally, the "TRT World[9]" portal of Turkey publishes more material than India and its videos and other online contents are highly professional. Its videos are immensely popular in the Kashmir valley and international academia, in spreading disinformation. India needs to rope in fresh talent of experts in strategic communication and employ their skills to create a robust communication infrastructure for the dissemination of the counter-narrative.

5) Learning From Singapore

Singapore is also, like India, is a multicultural, multiracial, multi-religious and multi-ethnic society. Singapore's efforts in counter-terrorism[10] have been quite successful especially in building social resilience against terrorism. It can be a good model for devising our counter-terrorism strategy. The idea is to build a safety net in the peacetime through building trust, relations, and confidence between the different communities. Inter-Faith Dialogue Circles can be created in each district and Harmony circles can be constituted in schools, workplaces and in local organizations. At the national level, a National Resilience/Harmony Council can be created to guide the activities of the above-mentioned bodies. Community engagement forums at sub-district levels can be very effective in enhancing the psychological and social resilience of communities against terrorism.

A proactive approach is needed in the outreach activities with migrant Indian workers who work in the Middle East. For working with the radicalized detainees, Religious Rehabilitation Councils including moderate Islamic scholars can be constituted. They can provide the counter to the religious arguments of the radicalized detainees. These moderate scholars can be an instrumental force in organizing psychological and information operations in the overall counter-terrorism strategy.

In addition to building social resilience through above-mentioned measures, National Integration Policy also needs to be reinvigorated. It can be done by free education, medical help and other forms of development aid to all BPL families irrespective of caste and religion. Such a policy will reduce the caste- and religion-based frictions, and extremist ideologies will not have a leeway in leveraging India's social fault lines to their advantage.

6) Education

India is home to world's fastest and largest growing adolescent population with 35% (358 million) of its population being in the 10-24 age group.[11] The youth of India, which is respectably addressed as its demographic dividend, can be a great asset if its strength is harnessed in a constructive manner. And, if there is no program, vision and course of action to transform India's youth into assets, it has all the potential to become our greatest liability. While we talk of radicalization, the youth has to be the primary focus of our strategy as it has been observed that it is the young generation which is coming under the sway of extremist ideologies and is being injected with the venom of hatred. Hence, we need the right kind of interventions through education to make the youth imbibe a healthy mindset. The objective is to cultivate scientific temper, critical reasoning and the spirit of inquiry among the youth. For this, the starting point should be the schools. The teaching in western and Indian philosophy, social and political philosophy, classics and comparative religions can be immensely helpful in nurturing an aware and a rational mind. Along with this, the students must be encouraged to do yoga/meditation, physical exercises and sports which will equip them with sound physical and mental health and confidence.

7) Counter-Radicalization Law

A stringent and effective legal apparatus is needed to check radicalization. While discussing the legal instruments in counter-terrorism, there arise the issues of curtailment of civil liberties like freedom of expression. However, it must be borne in mind that counter-terrorism is like a war effort. We are fighting a global war against terrorism. And, unlike conventional wars, this war is very unusual. The enemy is elusive, civilians are used as shields, ethical codes are distraught and the rules are hazy. The strategy, methods and the modus operandi of terrorism are widespread and multi-dimensional including bioterror, cyber-attacks, information and psychological operations, insurgencies, lone-wolf attacks etc. So we have to be extra careful, attentive and sensitive in cognition, identification of the enemy and the reflex response mechanism. All this requires an understanding of fight against terrorism as a war effort against terrorism. In wartime, civil liberties do not necessarily have a free run. They can be and must be restricted if the need arises for the sake of national security. If there has to be a trade-off between national security and civil liberties/human rights, the state authorities have to strike a judicious balance between the two.

Hence, extremist Islamic ideologies need to be examined and analyzed beyond the conventional framework of freedom of expression, minority rights and freedom of religion. It has been observed and even advocated in some intellectual and public policy circles that if violence is not accompanying an ideology, it can be co-opted even with its extremism. An effective counter-terrorism strategy must begin with zero tolerance to any kind of extremism.

In this backdrop, extremist preachers such as Zakir Naik must not be tolerated at all, just because they command the obedience of a large Muslim population. We have to get our basics right—zero tolerance means zero tolerance. Deobandi madrasa or a Wahhabi cleric may not be teaching anything overtly anti-national. However, the very notion that a true Muslim has his or her primary loyalty towards Ummah first and then others is in itself divisive and exclusivist in nature with all the potential to unleash a terrorist violence.

Strong legal measures need to be put in place to check the preaching and spread of such ideologies. The glorification of Jihad in peaceful ways by Islamic scholars and editors must be made a criminal offense. The law enforcement machinery and intelligence agencies must enjoy legal protection in the execution of their duties. Sting operations like those by FBI must be used and they should be admissible as evidence in the courts. Legal measures to crack down on financing of the radicalization activities can also be very helpful. It is easier to book extremist organizations under money-laundering and financial irregularities as in most of the cases, the funding is through hawala and other illegal channels. Poor auditing and non-compliance in proper book-keeping can also be a useful tool to control radicalization activities. Furthermore, the curriculum taught in schools and colleges run by extremist organizations like Jamaat-e-Islami (Kashmir) and their trusts like Falah-e-aam should be scrutinized. If the content promotes hatred, violence and anti-national sentiments, then the management boards and other authorities should be booked under the charges of sedition. Besides, the overt and covert links of extremist organizations with terrorist organizations can also be examined in depth and after investigations the key stakeholders can be prosecuted.

8) Effective Oversight and Accountability

To prevent radicalization, counter-terrorism policies need effective oversight and accountability mechanisms involving executive, legislative and impartial, and independent judiciary. They should also include civilian oversight by media, NGO, and the general public. In the absence of an effective accountability mechanism, there may be gross human rights violations which may in turn facilitate the process of radicalization and extremism leading to terrorist violence by providing a fertile ground to the terrorist outfits engaged in radicalization. UN bodies like Counter-Terrorism Committee and Counter-Terrorism Implementation Task Force have developed an array of best practices which can be immensely helpful in developing a sound legal architecture to tackle radicalization that is compliant with international human rights laws. The law enforcement machinery in different states must be given training in such best practices through workshops, seminars, crash-courses and short-term and long-term training sessions.

9) Regulating Madrasas

The world of Madrasas is like a dark world which has so far stayed immune to state and general societal surveillance. These are used as channels through which extremist ideologies are disseminated. The propagandists of extremist's ideologies spread their religious message at the congregations in the madrasas and mosques. So far they have remained sanctimonious because in general parlance, they are treated as religious symbols and are sentimental issues for the entire community. However, it is time now that the dark and murky world behind the nurseries of terror must be penetrated. The Madrasas must be derecognized as schools. All children of 6-14 years must attend normal schools and religious education should be allowed only after one reaches the age of 18. As regards religious education, the emphasis must be on the core philosophical message and not on the ritualistic and scriptural aspects as they have the potential to breed dogma, exclusivism, superstition and a narrow-minded approach. Science and Math must be taught to students in madrasas.

Jessica Sterns in her study of Madrasas[12] found that children studying in madrasas face sexual abuse. After such traumatic experiences, the children face low self-esteem and post-traumatic stress disorder (PTSD) which makes them vulnerable to extremist propaganda. Therefore, there has to be openness in the activities of madrasas and such activities of sexual abuse must be tracked, reported and the culprits brought to justice at the earliest. All the madrasas, mosques, khanqaas and dargahs must be registered as NGOs. Funding sources, channels, disbursement of funds and the use of money must be strictly scrutinized. They all must furnish the quarterly report of their finances, activities, visitors, and outreach to the government. The foreign funding of madrasas must be curbed effectively.

10) Role of Media, Academia and Public Intellectuals

It has been observed that there are clusters of journalists, intellectuals, and politicians who favour and propagate a highly one-sided view of socio-political happenings in the country. They do it for vested political and economic interests or ideological hatred or rather an ideological blindness. For example, rumors of "saffron terrorism" were doing rounds in India. Later, systematic investigations found such theories as baseless and lacking evidence. Such conspiracy theories serve no good except narrow and short-term political objectives. But in the society, such theories fuel the fire of radicalizing Hindus and Muslims alike. Furthermore, one comes across several academic campuses with tons of research papers raising the specter of Hindu fanaticism, often making illogical comparisons of Hindu nationalist parties with Nazi Germany. Incidents like Babri mosque demolition and the Godhra riots are portrayed as if the doomsday has arrived for India's religious minorities at the hands of Hindu nationalists. Furthermore, Dalit and minority issues are blown out of proportion, without a nuanced understanding of the evolution of India's social institutions, religious traditions, and cultural moors. The coverage of communal incidents is also one-sided. For example, while reporting on the Malda riots of 2015, some of the media outlets were deliberately not reporting the emergence of Malda as a hub of Jihadi activities and the role of Jihadi ideology in such disturbances. On the other hand, the role of Hindu organizations was portrayed in an exaggerated and distorted manner.

Such an approach is a double-whammy. It injects fear and insecurity in the minds of the minorities, legitimizing and strengthening the narrative of "Islam in danger" on which the terrorist organizations mostly thrive and spread, aiding the process of radicalizing. In addition, Hindu nationalist organizations feel that they have been misrepresented and the overall media and the academic set-up are nurturing hatred against them. In turn, they get alienated and antagonized, and in order to woo the common people to their side, propagate the duplicity and biased attitude of media/academia/political groups (the "politico-intellectual complex" of India) pursuing appeasement politics at the cost of national security.

There is also a tendency to come with an apologetic defense of dreaded terrorists. Such attitude was seen in the case of Afzal Guru and Yakub Memon, both proven terrorists awaiting death sentence. A prominent historian compared a Hindu nationalist organization with ISIS. Conspiracy theories alleging a prominent Hindu nationalist organization of orchestrating the 26/11 terrorist attack in Mumbai were patronized by the politicians of national stature, for petty electoral gains. Even the ISI-funded stone-pelting/civil unrest, terrorist movement and the separatist leaders in Kashmir also get the shield of such an apologetic defense by the self-proclaimed left-liberal intellectuals.

Such intellectual dishonesty and spin-doctoring at the least shield the slow process of radicalization and at the most, bolsters the process of radicalization. Therefore, the intellectuals, historians, and journalists need to introspect their role in this war on terror and act wisely, listening to their inner conscience, to protect the lives of those innocent civilians who meet with brutal deaths in terrorist attacks. They should be honest, impartial and objective. It must be kept in mind that such tendencies make the media the biggest weapon in the hands of terrorists.

11) The Domain of Intelligence

An effective and smart intelligence and counter-intelligence apparatus is again a bedrock of a sound counter-radicalization strategy. Unfortunately, in India, most of the state intelligence agencies (CID Zonal Offices) are in a dysfunctional state. They are understaffed, lack sufficiently skilled personnel and weak in infrastructure. The officers lack motivation and passion. CID postings are traditionally regarded as punishment postings. They lack sufficient knowledge of terrorism-related issues like geopolitics of terrorism, terror financing, radicalization and theoretical structure of extremist ideologies. Even senior police officers have very limited understanding of terms like Barelwi and Deobandi. At the district level, one finds very low levels of awareness on rituals, dress patterns and theocratic systems of extremist ideologies.

In Kashmir, lower level intelligence officers get posted for a period of 2-3 years. By the time they acquaint themselves with the local cultural and social dynamics, they are transferred to other places. There is also a strong need to create an effective structure for better coordination between different intelligence agencies with a view to strengthen effort against radicalization and terrorism. Also, the mentality of "use and throw" (with respect to the "assets") needs to be got rid of. Our agencies need to be professional in such matters. If they do not keep the trust of their assets, then they will lose credibility in the long run.

We need what is described as Revolution in Intelligence Affairs (RIA). Regular training, workshops, and seminars on terrorism issues must be conducted for field-level and senior intelligence officers. Such workshops and training modules must aim to carve a sharp and incisive intelligence brain that is sensitive and alert to the social-cultural, economic and political developments related to terrorism.

In every district, a counter-radicalization cell should be constituted as part of the counter-terror apparatus. Officers and staffers of the counter-radicalization cell must be experts in tracking online recruitment. They should be trained in online infiltration and exfiltration in closed online jihadi groups and portals. Furthermore, they should have keen eye on local developments. For example, recently, in a small place like Udaipur (Rajasthan), the local Muslims agitated in the favor of accepting Rohingyas as refugees. This development should have raised a few eyebrows in the intelligence world as Udaipur is relatively peaceful place where the local Muslims are least bothered about global Islamic issues. The agencies should investigate if there is any underground activity of terrorism propagandists/recruiters and agents cultivating the mindset of hatred. The activities of madrasas, visits of religious scholars and preachers also must be tracked and carefully studied. If in small villages, lavish mosques are coming up, then inquiries must be done to find out the funding sources. It should all form part of a proactive approach but not too intrusive as to hurt the community.

In addition to the intelligence set-up, the district- and sub-district–level police and administrative officers should be given a basic-level exposure to terrorism issues such as the theoretical knowledge of the extremist ideologies, identification of propagandists through their dress patterns, belief systems, rituals, behavioral attitudes and lifestyle.

12) Community-Policing Approach to Prevent Terrorism and Countering VERLT

Terrorism and violent extremism pose serious threat to community security, and not just state security. Local communities have emerged as the focal points in counter-terrorism policies. Community-oriented approaches are based on involvement, support and the trust of men and women from the local communities in the formulation, implementation, and evaluation of counter-terrorism policies to enhance their effectiveness.

OSCE[13] defines Community Policing or police-public partnerships "as a philosophy and organizational strategy that promotes a partnership-based, collaborative effort between the police and the community to more effectively and efficiently identify, prevent and solve problems of crime, the fear of crime, issues of physical safety and security, social disorder and neighborhood decay in order to improve everyone's quality of life."

Community policing can be very useful in countering Violent Extremism and Radicalization That Lead to Terrorism (VERLT), but its limitations should also be realized. They emanate from the fact that the police have a key role in criminal justice response to VERLT but their role in proactive crime prevention initiatives is highly restrictive as that involves several social, economic and political factors. It can, however, benefit terrorism prevention in the following ways:

a) Anchoring police into respect for human rights and the rule of law: Community policing, if implemented in compliance with international human rights norms, can be very beneficial in building public trust in police. For this, community police officers must get specialized training in human rights issues;
b) Improving public perceptions of the counterterrorism effort, and the interaction with the police;

c) Improving communication with the police on counter-terrorism and thereby raising general awareness among the public of the threats from extremism;

d) Improving public vigilance and resilience;

e) Enhancing policemen's understanding of communities to better engage and cooperate with them: Community police officers should be posted for the long-enough period to build trust and confidence with the public. Once the community members build trust-based relations with individual officers, it is easier to track the activities of the extremists and terrorist elements in the community;

f) Helping in timely identification and referral of critical situations;

g) Improving the quality and quantity of intelligence: It has to be ensured that community policing does not become a front for running a covert espionage operation against a particular community.

While implementing community-policing programs, the state agencies must ensure against over-reliance on community police officers for intelligence gathering as specialized counter-terrorism officers and intelligence officers have different skill-sets. The motive of community policing is to build trust to facilitate effective implementation of overall counter-terrorism policies and prevent radicalization. However, there should be regular interaction between the counter-terrorism officers and community police officers. Furthermore, particular communities should not be stigmatized and the community policing should not intensify the frictions within the community.

Most importantly, it must be kept in mind that international norms of UN and OSCE have been documented and formulated for a general guideline and to provide an overarching framework. While putting them in practice in India, they must be chiseled to suit India's domestic socio-political conditions. For example, in Jammu and Kashmir and in the Naxal-affected areas, it may be very challenging to use community-policing approach. The terrorist cadres have a good base among the local communities. And, they often act as spies for terrorist organizations. They also provide cover to terrorists' activities and their movements. One has to be very guarded and cautious while using community policing as it may threaten the life of our armed forces personnel.

13) Dealing with Online Recruitment and Virtual Jihad

In 2002, Osama bin Laden wrote to Mullah Omar,[14] "It is obvious that the media war in this century is one of the strongest methods; in fact, its ratio may reach 90% of the total preparation for the battles." Supporting this view, Ayman al-Zawahiri opined in 2005, "More than half of this battle is taking place in the battlefield of the media. We are in a media battle in a race for the hearts and minds of our Umma." The virtual jihad or online jihad has gained prominence and credibility. It has emerged as a strong alternative for those who cannot go to the field to fight the real jihad. Besides, it also facilitates and strengthens the real jihad by intense radicalization drive. The online jihad prepares fertile ground for the real jihad. The deft use of social media and online presence by ISIS cost the humanity of hundreds of innocent civilians dying.

Smart and efficient mechanism to counter online radicalization is a quintessential part of a counter-radicalization program. In each district, there must a cyber-wing in the de-radicalization cell. It should have trained cyber-security experts and social media experts. They should also have exposure to the youth psychology, their emotional and intellectual concerns, and aspirations. They should track their social media profile and updates, and identify at-risk individuals. The members of the cyber tram should also be skilled in infiltrating and subverting the online closed-radicalization groups.

Tackling online radicalization is a must as it is the most potent medium for youth radicalization. Issues of privacy, sovereignty and its elusive nature make it a very sensitive area needing a specialized and highly sophisticated approach.

14) Building Social Harmony

The counter-radicalization strategy should also focus on building social harmony between different communities. The activities of extremist groups create a sense of fear in the minority community. Such activities include volatile speeches, provocative statements by prominent political and religious leaders, violence including killings and murders over beef-eating and love-jihad. Such activities provide a much-needed spark for communal riots. Such activities lend credibility to notions like "Islam in danger" from the increasing Hindu extremism.

15) De-glamourizing Terrorism

It is said rather derisively that terrorism is an inspiring field only for youngsters who have no good alternatives. The lack of economic opportunities, underdeveloped state institutions, bad law and order situation, poor development administration and educational backwardness creates a vacuum in which terrorism emerges as a "lucrative" career option. It brings monetary benefits in the form of large salary package and in some societies even a social status as a freedom fighter. For the youth, it holds a special charm as it offers a thrilling life full of adventure.

In Kashmir, terrorists like Burhaan Wani and Sabzar Bhatt often uploaded their pictures with latest guns and gadgets with pride of someone achieving a prized status. Such a lifestyle has an appeal with the youth. Many of the foreign fighters who joined ISIS were lured by the adventure, glamour of militaristic life, sense of fulfillment and purpose (fighting for a divine cause) and sex slaves. Money too was an attraction.

Such glamorization is unreal, unsustainable and in the end, self-destructive. There is urgent need to deglamorize terrorism. The most effective way to do this would be presenting a counter-narrative by unleashing opportunities through economic growth and political dialogue, and by making social life exciting and vibrant. Often the fact that several groups and individuals have strong economic stakes in terrorism is overlooked. Radicalization drives are organized to furnish a ready supply of recruits for terrorist war fronts across the globe.

By unleashing economic growth and creating employment opportunities, glamour around terrorism will end. New positions in the corporate sector, development sector and administration will carry, in the Indian context, much greater social prestige, administrative authority, job satisfaction and of course, a good salary. There still are many Kashmiri youth nurturing the dream of joining IAS/IPS to make Kashmir a better place. They do not have abiding faith in the ideology of gun and jihad. They strongly believe in the democratic ethos of India.

Even though the situations are widely different, even in Afghanistan, the American investment in development has started bearing some, though limited, results. Now, the Afghan youth is studying in American and Indian universities and getting attracted to lucrative careers in development sector, consulting, management, government and international organizations like UN and ASEAN.

However, it would be a totally misplaced assumption that economic developments, job creation and such other similar measures would completely wipe out the scourge of radicalization and terrorism. Alongside, the economic opportunities, gates must be opened for political dialogue. Civil liberties must be improved and cultural activities like music, poetry recitals must be promoted. Vibrant campus life full of diverse activities and exchange programs should be developed. Communications channels must be created. These and many other related steps will certainly contribute to reducing grievances and with that, the appeal for radicalization which emanates from social and political injustice. And, with economic growth, scientific education, the influence of backward and rigid extremist ideologies will also reduce.

The economically developed Muslim groups like Dawoodi Bohras and Chiliyas have stayed away from extremism and terrorism. In India, one hardly ever comes across Bohra-Hindu riots! Though Bohras are very religious and particular in observing their customs, they have smoothly mingled with rest of the communities as their interaction with other non-Muslim communities is dominated by economic factors rather than the religious ones.

16) Coordinated South Asian Effort

The menace of radicalization and terrorism in India cannot be addressed without comprehending it as a South Asian phenomenon. The ISI and its proxy terrorist organizations like Lashkar and Jaish based in West Punjab (Pakistan) act as the principal drivers of radicalization in India. Similarly, to a limited extent though, jihadi outfits based in Bangladesh also have an impact on the situation in India. Money for financing terrorism and radicalization is often funneled through some of the neighbouring countries. Some recent reports also hint at the presence of ISI recruiters in Myanmar among the Rohingyas. Vigorous Salafi radicalization and Tableeghi activities amongst the Rohingya Muslims of Myanmar have been going on for decades.

Hence, counter-radicalization policy should aim at a coordinated South Asian effort to address the challenges of radicalization. Even Al Qaeda created Al Qaeda in Indian Subcontinent (AQIS) which shows that they see the entire region as a well-connected hunting ground. Hence, our approach needs to have a South Asian focus.

In this essay, the counter-radicalization strategies have been discussed at length. The analysis has been based on international best practices with suitable modifications and improvisations needed to suit the local conditions obtaining in India. Any discussion on radicalization will however remain incomplete without a serious look at and discussion on the de-radicalization measures. De-radicalization has a different target group and it needs a specialized approach. It will be discussed in the next chapter.

NOTES

1 "Preventing Terrorism and Countering Violent Extremism and Radicalization that Lead to Terrorism: Community Policing Approach," Organization for Security and Cooperation in Europe, Feb 2014, Accessed October 29, 2018

2 ibid

3 ibid

4 Pandya, Abhinav, "Post-ISIS-Future of Global Jihad," Vivekananda International Foundation, November 28, 2017, Accessed October 29, 2018, https://www.vifindia.org/article/2017/november/28/post-isis-future-of-global-jihad

5 Ahmad, Tufail, "We are losing Kashmir-Ten way to counter Radicalization in India," *First Post*, September 9, 2016, Accessed October 29, 2018, https://www.firstpost.com/india/we-are-losing-kashmir-to-islam-ten-ways-to-counter-radicalisation-in-india-2997302.html

6 ibid

7 "Full text of PM Modi's Speech at World Sufi Forum," *NDTV*, March 17, 2016, Accessed October 30, 2018, https://www.ndtv.com/india-news/full-text-of-pm-narendra-modis-speech-at-world-sufi-forum-1288303

8 Pandya, Abhinav, "A Realistic Understanding of Pakistan," Vivekananda International Foundation, September 12, 2016. Accessed November 10, 2018, https://www.vifindia.org/article/2016/september/12/a-realistic-understanding-of-pakistan

9 https://www.trtworld.com/video/social-videos/the-kashmir-conflict-in-under-4-minutes/5a40bd0841736a1f528ad8ce

10 Gavin Chua Hearn Yuit, "Singapore's Approach to Counter-Terrorism," *CTC Sentinel*, December 2009, Accessed October 30, 2018, https://ctc.usma.edu/singapores-approach-to-counterterrorism/

11 Thukral, Ganguly Enakshi, "Understanding Adolescence in India," *NDTV*, January 28, 2016, Accessed October 30, 2018, https://everylifecounts.ndtv.com/understanding-adolescence-in-india-616

12 Stern, Jessica, "Mind Over Martyr," *Foreign Affairs*, October 30, 2018, Accessed October 30, 2018, https://www.foreignaffairs.com/articles/saudi-arabia/2009-12-21/mind-over-martyr.

13 "Preventing Terrorism and Countering Violent Extremism," op. cit

14 Akil, Awan, "The Virtual Jihad," *CTC Sentinel*, May 2010, Accessed October 30, 2018, https://ctc.usma.edu/the-virtual-jihad-an-increasingly-legitimate-form-of-warfare/

6

Developing a De-radicalization Program for India

Addressing the challenges of radicalization needs a nuanced approach based on a sound understanding of the diverse aspects of radicalization. One such aspect which cannot be ignored in the overall counter-terrorism strategy is the measures to de-radicalize the jihadi detainees to ensure that they do not return to the fold of jihadi ideology and their old terrorist organizations, once they are released on completion of their prison sentences. In this chapter, it is proposed to discuss the concept of de-radicalization and the models that have already been tested across the world to explore the possibilities of developing an effective de-radicalization program in India.

The efforts in countering radicalization have a broader focus. The idea is to prevent the individuals from radicalizing and joining a terrorist organization. The aim is to prevent the movement from growing by cutting the supply of fresh recruits, i.e. the foot-soldiers of jihad including the suicide bombers. In addition, it should cut at the ideological roots of extremism, thereby eroding the social, political, and cultural and geographical support system of any terrorist organization.

However, de-radicalization has a narrow focus. The target groups are hardcore and softcore jihadis who are already radicalized. Mostly, it includes jihadi detainees in prisons in India and abroad and if the focus is not too narrow, it can also include those individuals who have already radicalized and are trying to join a terrorist organization. Or those who are already in the process of joining a terrorist organization but have not yet indulged in any terrorist violence.

Thus, in counter-radicalization (prevent the disease), the target is those who are at the risk of radicalization or are in the initial or even advanced stages of the process of radicalization, but have not graduated yet. In contrast, in de-radicalization (cure the disease), the target is those individuals who are at the risk of committing an act of terrorist violence or have already committed such acts.

Before delving deeper into the different facets of de-radicalization programs, it deserves a special mention that the current times are very crucial for the overall counter-radicalization and de-radicalization efforts for various reasons. The counter-terrorism efforts have significantly eroded Al Qaeda's strength in its strongholds like Afghanistan, Iraq, Yemen and Saudi Arabia, and places where it was trying to grow such as the Indian sub-continent. As far as the other major group ISIS is concerned, it is generally agreed that this organization is almost finished in terms of its territorial possessions. Internal frictions and differences make it highly unlikely for IS and Al Qaeda to unite in the near future. But, it is worth mentioning that the territorial reverses of ISIS are not accompanied by a proportionate decrease in its ability to inspire the lone-wolf jihadis. Ideology seems to have come up as a very strong motivating factor in terrorism. Therefore, now is the moment to take radicalization head on.

Fortunately, very few Muslims from India (76) traveled to the Middle East to join ISIS. And, they too went from states like Kerala and Andhra Pradesh where the foreign extremist ideologies had already made heavy inroads. In North India and other parts, the extremist Takfiri ideology and jihadism does not have a stronghold. This is one of the most important reasons why Al Qaeda has not yet succeeded in India.

As regards the challenges posed by radicalization, its pernicious spread and the forces involved have already been highlighted in the previous chapters. Hence, in terms of priorities, India needs a greater focus on countering radicalization rather than on de-radicalization as there is always a tradeoff between the policy decisions including allocation of resources to counter-radicalization or de-radicalization. However, we still need to evolve our own de-radicalization program for even the small number of radicalized individuals. The number is increasing fast, and in future, one might need a strong de-radicalization program. Secondly, we need to invest in the de-radicalization programs because many times in terrorism-related cases, the investigative agencies do not have the evidence that is admissible in the court of law. Hence, the agencies are not able to get long prison sentences for the convicts. And, the individuals are released after some time. In the absence of an effective de-radicalization programme, most of them return to their previous terrorist organizations and indulge in terrorist violence. For example, Abdallah al-Ajmi,[1] who was repatriated to Kuwait in 2005 from the US, was acquitted of terrorism charges in Kuwait. Subsequently, he carried out a suicide attack in Mosul which killed 13 Iraqis. Effective de-radicalization programs are useful in making such individuals less dangerous for the society. If Abdallah al-Ajmi had received such rehabilitation and reintegration program, he might not have done what he did. To put it simply, if we don't want to spend money on de-radicalization later, then we better spend more on counter-radicalization today.

For this essay, an attempt has been made to study the de-radicalization programs of Saudi Arabia, Indonesia and UK to explore the possibilities of replicating some of the best practices developed in these countries in their de-radicalization programs. But it is important to remember the crucial differences in the conditions and challenges encountered by the above-mentioned countries and those obtaining in India. For example, the Saudi de-radicalization program was designed primarily for the returnees from the Guantanamo prison camps. A majority of them were members of Al Qaeda and a range of other transnational Jihadi terrorist organizations. The degree and the intensity of their radicalization were very high and the role of jihadi/takfiri ideology as a motivating factor was significant. Besides ideology, there were other factors like the collapse of the state in Iraq, resentment against US intervention in the Middle East, rage against western values and the perception of their own governments as aligned with the US. Hence, their program was designed keeping in mind the factors mentioned above. In the UK and other European countries like the Netherlands and France, the jihadi extremists mainly consisted of the second-generation young Muslims who could not integrate well into the European society. They faced "perceived" discrimination in social life and employment. They were not happy with the soft Islam practiced by their parents, and for many of them, Jihad was a "cool" thing to do just like one finds the "Rap" cool.[2] Then, there were other reasons like frustration because of drugs, broken relationships etc. They fell prey to radicalization not primarily because of religious reasons but because of psychological reasons, in a quest to search meanings of life.

In Indonesia, the detainees under the de-radicalization program were mostly those members of Jemmah Islamiyah who had disagreed with the central leadership after the Osama Bin's 1998 fatwa that sanctioned the murder of civilians in jihad. Though they believed in the idea and the duty of Jihad, but questioned the need, morale and the rationale, to kill civilians. The de-radicalization program was focusing on those who had already dissociated themselves from Jihadi outfits.

In India, one does not come across a huge chunk of individuals joining transnational terrorist networks like Al Qaeda and ISIS. The spread and reach of Wahhabi extremism is not very strong yet. The local Islamic belief systems like Barelwi and Sufi systems are putting up a strong challenge to extremist ideologies. Secondly, Muslims have lived in India for more than a millennium, so there is no such integration problem as one witnesses in Europe, though in a larger sense some voices do argue that even after more than 1000 years of stay in India, Muslims have not integrated well enough. Hence, while structuring a de-radicalization program, these differences will have to be factored in. As Jessica Sterns observed (in "Mind Over Martyrs"), any rehabilitation program must be based on a clear understanding of what drives people to terrorism. In India also, we need a systematic research on the interplay of various radicalizing factors before arriving at a consensus de-radicalization and counter-radicalization program.

De-radicalization versus Disengagement

De-radicalization primarily implies a complete shift in a person's beliefs, sympathies, attitudes, values, and faith in a particular ideology. In the context of this essay, it means changing a person's belief in the ideology of jihad and Takfir. Disengagement, however, aims at changing a person's behavior. In this case, it could mean weaning away a person's mind from the acts of violence and other illegal activities. Andrew Silke,[3] giving examples of "Dissociati" and "Insertion" world's best disengagement programs of Italy and Spain, opines that disengagement is realistic and achievable while the de-radicalization is exceedingly difficult. He informs[4] that modern-day de-radicalization programs begin on the premise that the individual still has a firm faith in the terrorist ideology and is committed to his/her cause. The modern programs of Saudi Arabia, Indonesia, and UK aim to convince the individual that these beliefs are flawed and mistaken. And, once they confess to their crimes and are convinced of the futility of their belief, they are supposed to be de-radicalized.

But the question arises whether that is even possible? The claims of success vary. As regards Saudi program, it is stated that it has met an astounding success. The Saudis claimed a reoffending rate of less than 3% and the Indonesians claimed less than 1%.[5] Though Saudi government has not disclosed the list of those who completed their program as of 2009, there were 11 graduates[6] who made it again to the country's most-wanted list of terrorists.

The claimed effectiveness of these programs must be treated with caution. Firstly, no systematic evaluations have taken place. Secondly, re-offending by terrorist prisoners is very low, to begin with (less than 5%).[7] In England and Wales, between 2001 and 2008, there were 196 convictions for terrorism-related offences and most of them were associated with Al Qaeda. They were all given minor prison sentences and later released in 2009. Till 2011, none of them had been rearrested for terrorism-related activities. When this can happen in the absence of a de-radicalization program, it is not surprising if the countries running rehabilitation programs claim to have achieved success.

Recent research[8] indicates that many prisoners do not completely shed their belief in the ideology. They continue their sympathies with the organizations and its activities but they get disengaged from the violence. It has also been observed that many members of a terrorist organization eventually abandon violence without going through a de-radicalization program quite like an individual leaving a volunteer military program after serving for a couple of years. But like the volunteer military cadre, the terrorists retain the sympathy and pride for what their organization does.

In cases of radicalization driven solely by ideological indoctrination, de-radicalization is extremely difficult, almost impossible. Suppose a person is fighting for civil liberties or against a particular law, then his belief in the ideology of violence can be shaken if he is convinced that the desired ends are achievable through non-violence because in this case violence is purely a methodology. It is tactical. But a person indulging in terrorism out of a sense of religious duty is not easy to be de-convinced. He or she does not desire anything in this world. His desires are other-worldly which will be fulfilled only through fulfillment of his religious duty. If in his interpretation of the holy text, he wants to bring sharia through 7th-century methods of war, one can't change his mindset because his motivations are very different. The European programs focus a lot on dialogue and counseling with moderate Imams to change the mindset of the jihadi terrorists but it appears futile to waste resources on changing someone who has already fixated his mind on the creed of death. Last but not the least, prison corruption also hampers the success of the de-radicalization programs[9] like it happened in Indonesia.

Therefore, it is recommended that there should be reasonable allocation of resources on disengagement rather than de-radicalization. Disengagement programs can work effectively and successfully with financial benefits like housing, employment, and family. Having said this, it may also be mentioned that the role of dialogue cannot be dismissed. Therefore, India would need a program which is a judicious and a realistic mix of de-radicalization and disengagement. After all, India is the land of strong Sufi traditions and the enlightened mystics of Vedanta who have a history of melting hearts and minds. If Sri Sri Ravishankar can bring FARC and the government of Colombia for a truce, then why can't we utilize our spiritual capital in de-radicalization? And, bear in mind that we are not doing it for the first time. Around 2200 years back, Buddha made a saint out of the dreaded dacoit Angulimaal!! More recently, the efforts of Sri Sri Ravishankar and his team in Jammu and Kashmir have resulted in the formation of a political party, Jammu and Kashmir Awami Forum, which is firm in its belief in Indian constitution. It is the first fully nationalist political party in the militancy-hit Kashmir region. Interestingly, it is a party led and formed by common people who are frustrated with the opportunism of political dynasts in the state and the three decades of militancy. Many of them have lost family members either as victims of terrorist violence or as those who joined terror outfits and were killed in encounters with security forces.

De-radicalization Model for India

The following principles can serve as the strong philosophical foundation for India's de-radicalization program:

1) De-radicalization program in India should incorporate the best practices from the experience of other countries but the program should be contextualized, i.e. it should be India specific. It should be suited to the needs and requirements of our society.
2) Focus should be on dialogue with religious clerics. In this context, some countries prefer to engage moderate Imams whereas the others like Indonesia work on the idea that the "radicalized" will only respond to "radicals." This is so because a highly radicalized mind is too strong

to change with soft reasoning or moderate approach. Kirsten E. Schulze,[10] quotes Police General Ansyaad, head of Indonesia's counter-terrorism desk in the Ministry for Political, Security and Legal Affairs, who in her article for Combating Terrorism Center's journal *The Sentinel* observed, "In the mind of radicals, all Ulama have already failed because they failed to establish the Islamic state. Their credibility with militants is zero. What is needed, therefore, is a reformed radical mind with different views...to talk to other radicals." Moderate imams can be helpful in the counter-radicalization but in de-radicalization, they don't have much hope. Majid Nawaz, a former jihadi has turned into a reformer and when individuals like him speak against jihad, it carries a unique appeal. A jihadi can relate to him as they share a similar history.

3) The de-radicalization program should be premised on the belief that with kindness and "soft-power" (money and in-kind aid), one can liquidate the individual's motivations for jihad and change his perceptions, such as his community is facing an existential threat and so forth.
4) For an average Indian mind, there is a special reverence for a religious scholar across the spectrum. Religious identity cum authority holds a very special status and sanctity to that person. So in India, Islamic scholars and holy men can be more successful than engagement through radicals. Sufi mystics and preachers with following across the religious spectrum could be roped in along with Islamic scholars/ preachers and the radicals on a case-by-case basis.
5) De-radicalization program should focus on psychological counseling. Most of the terrorists experience the conditions of war. Many individuals turned to terrorism after intense radicalization process in madrasas where they often face sexual abuse. They also face brutal torture in prisons. All these experiences are traumatic and often lead to post-traumatic stress disorder (PTSD). Hence, psychological counseling and spiritual healing can be immensely helpful in de-radicalization programs.
6) Extended outreach to families, friends, and relatives can also be highly effective in de-radicalization. Both Saudi and Indonesian programs rely heavily on this. In India, it could be very effective because the institution of family is still very strong in India.

7) Additionally, art therapy, vocational training, sports and religious re-education should also form components of the de-radicalization program.
8) In rehabilitation and reintegration, the detainees should be assisted in finding employment, family and a wife after release. Job training and career elements can be very effective in the cases of Jihadis with past criminal records, i.e. those whose religious motivations were not very strong.
9) Fear and humiliation also lead individuals to jihad. Classes in restoration of self-esteem can also be very helpful.
10) The ideal approach can have a focus on the motivations of individual offenders. It can have three components: prison-based services and rehabilitation programs, assistance to help released prisoners in integrating into society and the post-release services. In the post-release services, the involvement of the community is essential to reduce the rates of recidivism.

Structure of Program

After typically being found guilty of charges, they can be sentenced to one or two years depending on the intensity of the crime. After serving the sentence, they should undergo intense psychological counseling and religious dialogue convincing them of the futility of their belief in takfiri and jihad. After that, if they confess their guilt and condone for what they have done in the past, they can be sent to a confined custody to a rehabilitation/care center. In the care center, they can be given comfortable environment including sports and recreation through television, music and limited internet access. Additionally, they should be given art therapy, psychological and spiritual healing. They can leave the center for short periods to visit their families and even their families should be allowed to visit them. The bereaved families of other jihadis who are either dead or under detention should also be allowed to meet them so that they realize what their families have to go through because of their actions. Financial assistance should be given to them and their wives, e.g. in the form of school fees for their children, to feed and clothe their family members. Prisoners should be allowed to attend weddings of relatives. Authorities can help facilitate the marriage of the detainees also. The families should be provided with travel expenses and accommodation when they visit the detainees in the rehabilitation centers. Police and their reformation guides can also participate in their weddings, and engage them in religious discussions and religious and cultural activities like praying and breaking Ramzaan fast.

Upon release, they should be given identity cards, start-up money and help in finding jobs. These activities build trust and help them in reintegrating into the society. However, it must be ensured that the entire effort does not get reduced to buying peace at the cost of justice. The idea of monetary help is to help them reintegrate and live a better life once they are released, but the most important part is to make sure that they genuinely abandon violence. Otherwise, it will simply be capitulating to terrorism to buy peace, which in the long run will have disastrous effects on the morale of the society and law enforcement agencies.

Limitations

The experience of de-radicalization programs in different countries also brings forth several limitations. Firstly, "radicals" talking to a reformed radical is a good principle, but in practice the radicals who work with police, soon lose their credibility with their subjects who might see them as traitors. For example, Majid Nawaz, an ex-jihadi from UK who now vehemently speaks against jihadi extremism, is seen as a right-wing bigot even by the moderate Muslims.

Secondly, prison corruption and the prison system could be detrimental to the success of the program. For example, in Indonesia, prison corruption is allegedly undermining their de-radicalization program. Hardcore Jihadist prisoners infect the other prisoners in integrated jails and moderate jihadis in the segmented jail with their extremist views and are able to radicalize them. Due to lax enforcement of regulations, they can get access to mobile phones, laptops, and the internet, and then use the jails for planning terrorist operations outside. And they can also use technology to distribute jihadi reading material to spread their extremist views. In India too, non-enforcement of rules in the prisons can be an extremely difficult challenge to overcome.

Thirdly, in the absence of a systematic and well-funded government rehabilitation program, upon release of the prisoners, most of them are left without any anchorage. The released jihadis are poor and deficient in skills, leaving them with few options but to go back to the terrorist organization.

However, in spite of the above-mentioned limitations, de-radicalization is an effort worth making. First of all, the overall record of success of countries like Saudi Arabia, Indonesia, and UK has been high. Secondly, while structuring the program and implementation, due care can be taken to ensure that the above-mentioned limitations do not hamper the success of the program.

To conclude, even if the success rate is low, the security personnel will get an in-depth understanding of a terrorist's mind and motivations. The networks which the program personnel will build will be immensely helpful in improving the quality and quantity of the intelligence. The success, even if low, will be a strong weapon to expose the inhumane, irreligious and unethical nature of the belief in jihadi extremism. And, last but not the least, even the meagre success will be a great psychological and moral victory against the ideology of jihadi extremism.

All being said, while structuring a de-radicalization program, the nuances are extremely important. For example, let us discuss the nuances with respect to a de-radicalization program in Kashmir and Kerala. In South Kashmir, along with religious radicalization, socialization with militants is the most important reason for joining militant organizations. The subtext of socialization has a strong religious element as well as a shared sense of victimhood. However, if socialization with militants had not been there, the levels of recruitment would have been much lower. In effect, it means that the self-radicalization of religious nature (through social media or by getting inspired by a preacher/ recruiter resulting in lone-wolf attacks) or madrasa radicalization is not in the forefront. It is there, but not in a dominant position. Most of the militants of South Kashmir are derisively called "facebook mujahids" who chose gun to seek glory and glamour. The religiously inspired militants and the dedicated cadre of the older generation Jihadis often have contempt for them on the grounds that they hardly have any knowledge of religion. Such "facebook mujahids" are joining Hizbul Mujahiddin. They also have grievances related to unemployment, resentment against politicians, police atrocities and denial of justice by state authorities. Hence, the de-radicalization program for them has to be different from that of highly radicalized militants and terrorists. Such "facebook mujahids" can be brought back to mainstream, if there is an engaging dialogue process and employment avenues. If there is a promising de-radicalization program, many of them will be motivated to surrender and surrenders will demotivate new aspirants. However, the de-radicalization program in terms of counseling content, duration and rigor, for religiously indoctrinated and hard extremist would-be fidayeens of Jaish-e-Muhammad and committed terrorists of LeT has to be very different than that for the Hizbul Mujahiddin militants. Furthermore, the treatment of over-ground workers (OGWs) has to be milder and addressed separately in de-radicalization centers.

The fighters who joined ISIS from Kerala and those who are inclined towards Zakir Musa's caliphate doctrine are hardcore religious extremists. Any promise of employment or dialogue will serve no utility in such cases. They have chosen jihad, hatred and violence purely out of religious indoctrination. The de-radicalization program for them will be very intense. To mentally break such committed and hardcore elements is a challenging task. It may not be possible to achieve that with purely soft techniques and counseling. There may arise a need to explore methods for psychologically shattering such highly radicalized minds. Once their strongly guarded world of extremist belief system and hatred shatters, there emerges a possibility of disseminating new ideas in their minds. It is also advisable to keep them under strict monitoring and surveillance for a much longer duration.

Exploring the Possibility of Developing the Islamic Radicalization Index

On the basis of the research work done for this study and the review of New York Police Department's study of Islamic radicalization, it is proposed to examine the concept of Islamic Radicalization Index for India. Though the concept in itself is still a debatable subject and needs an independent research project to develop it into a sophisticated tool for policy analysis, there is a need to have a basic exposure to its objectives and examine the feasibility. It needs to be explicitly mentioned at the very outset that the concept of Islamic Radicalization Index is not an attempt at defaming or profiling, with racial bias against a particular religious community, and curtailing human rights and civil liberties. The objective of the tool is to "drain the ocean of the bad fishes" so that the entire community is not blamed or stigmatized for the actions of a fringe group. Moreover, since this study is about Islamic radicalization, the tool should be so designed that it specifically measures Islamic radicalization. Similar tools can be developed for measuring other types of radicalization experienced in the society at large.

Britain's counter-radicalization strategy, "Prevent" issued a set of guidelines in 2015 to identify the signs of extremism. In many academic and policy circles, it is alleged that the British "Prevent" strategy failed in preventing Muslim youths from getting radicalized and traveling to Syria to join IS.[11] However, the failure of "Prevent" strategy should not be the reason to doubt the utility of the Islamic Radicalization Index for India. First of all, whether "Prevent" failed or succeeded is still a debatable issue. There is no unanimity on the subject. Secondly, the reasons for its alleged failure can be found in the way the strategy was devised and implemented. AZ Muhammad of Gatestone Institute believes that the strategy was so politically correct that it never addressed the problem of extremism in Islamic texts heads-on. An attitude of diffidence and escapism on such a serious issue because of its sensitive nature was a major stumbling block in the success of "Prevent."[12] Besides, the guidelines mentioned in the strategy were vague. For example, "absenteeism," "crying" and "unhealthy use of the Internet" were listed as some of the behaviors of extremism that may be "a cause for concern."[13] The other criteria to indicate students' likelihood to be drawn towards terrorism included[14]

- A desire for excitement and adventure;
- A desire for political or moral change;
- Family or friends' involvement in extremism;
- Being at a transitional time of life.

All the criteria mentioned above may not be very precise in terms of being quantified. While using such criteria, there are strong chances of misreporting. Furthermore, in Britain, it was expected of university professors and academicians to identify the indicators of extremism which is again a misconceived idea as academicians cannot be expected to become counter-terrorism experts.[15] In Britain, the Muslim community has not integrated well into the society which led to the tendency of viewing "Prevent" as discriminatory and racist.

In India's case, the conditions are very different. First of all, the integration of the Muslims into Indian society is robust. The coexistence of 1000 years has already cemented the communal bond and given rise to a syncretic culture. In such a backdrop, the proposed radicalization index is likely to have higher levels of acceptability among the Muslim community because of their faith in communal harmony and robust integration in the Indian society. Secondly, the index proposed includes a set of concrete indicators over which there appears to be a general consensus. Thirdly, the index is not prescriptive in nature. It is merely suggestive. It stands rooted in the idea that radicalization is a challenge and there is a need to quantify it to understand and address the problem. The index is also premised on the idea that there can be a set of common patterns and experiences about radicalization around the world. In addition, the index is flexible and open to the idea of customizing the index to the local cultural, political and the social context.

The Islamic Radicalization Index can be a robust and a specialized tool in a country like India where Islamic radicalization is a highly sensitive issue, and often the concerns of human rights, individual liberty and freedom of religion are overriding, making it extremely difficult to restrict and legally liquidate the radicalization infrastructure.

First and foremost, the concept gives recognition to the challenge of radicalization as a special and serious concern, in a formal and academic sense, giving it a strong line of defense against activists and politically motivated sabotage.

Second, in a country like India, policing and intelligence infrastructure is insufficient in personnel, surveillance, technical know-how, skills and equipment. In such a scenario, the concept of Islamic Radicalization Index is much needed and can be developed into a highly effective policy tool to track and curb radicalization activities.

Third, such an initiative will be very helpful in keeping track of financing channels, recruitment activities and logistics-infrastructure for terrorist organizations. It will generate an immense storehouse of intellectual resources and data in advance, to preempt, predict and prevent a terrorist attack.

Fourth, it will also weaken and restrict the efforts and resources of terrorist organizations in planning and executing terrorist attacks. In addition, it will help in generating goodwill, removing trust -deficit and prevailing misconceptions about Muslim community in society.

Fifth, Islamic Radicalization Index will not only help reduce the threat of terrorism, but also erase the specter of communal riots which is equally pernicious and threatening in India's case. Through Islamic Radicalization Index, the agencies can keep a watch on the movement and activities of the extremist religious preachers and the agent provocateurs, to prevent the loss of human life in communal riots.

The index will measure radicalization in a specified area which could be a district, state or the entire country. While developing the index, it will have to be customized to the specific needs of India. The objective is to develop a standard tool for mapping and measuring radicalization in India. However, there are diversities in the Muslim societies of different regions in India. Besides, seemingly normal indicators may have more serious implications in different states and special cases such as the migrant Muslim populations. For example, baseline situation in Kerala is much more serious as compared to Rajasthan because of the presence of the extremist Islamic organizations for last three to four decades. Radicalization in community of Bangladeshi refugees has to be taken much more seriously from the security point of view. Hence, I recommend the use of the tool along with a detailed area-wise situation/ assessment reports which capture the local dynamics and furnish evidence-based predictions. This index is intended to be an empirical tool. It will make an intensive use of GIS systems, and will measure radicalization on the basis of set of specified indicators. The relative weightage given to indicators will be different depending upon their intensity and strength as causal factors for terrorist attacks and communal riots. In the category of terrorist attacks, the indicators which contribute directly to the execution of a terrorist attack will be taken more seriously than those which help in creating a congenial environment for providing logistics and nurturing the ideological framework for terrorism. In the second category of indicators, the index will examine factors like effectiveness of state, poor governance, economic grievances, religious discrimination, Hindu radicalization, drug addiction and psychological ailments among the youth and educational status.

Week-long workshops will have to be organized for police, intelligence officers and civil servants to equip them with the basic understanding of radicalization issues and the Islamic Radicalization Index. For detailed analysis and employment of the tool, a team of expert intelligence analysts, terror-finance experts, statisticians, social scientists and psychologists will be required.

The index will examine the following indicators:

As one radicalizes, typical signatures include[16]

1) Alienation from one's former life and affiliation with like-minded individuals;
2) Creating or joining a group of like-minded individuals in a desire to strengthen one's dedication to Islamism/Jihadism (one may join groups like Jamaat-e-Islami, Jamiyat Ahle-Hadith, Jamaat-Tulba, students' wing of Jamaati-e-Islami in Kashmir; in Kerala, Salafi communes are active);

3) Rigid and hateful attitude against Shias and non-Wahabbi Muslims;
4) Giving up cigarettes, drinking, gambling and modern western-styled clothes;
5) Start wearing traditional Islamic clothing, growing a beard;
6) Getting involved in social activism and community issues;
7) Radical posts on Facebook and other social media outlets

Other indicators are:

1) Frequency of the visit of foreign and domestic Salafi/Wahhabi clerics and other extremist religious preachers in an area and the number of their followers in that area;
2) Frequency of the visit of foreign and domestic-extremist Islamic leaders and those extremist preachers who advocate political Islam and dogmatic Sharia laws over the constitution and their following in the area in question;
3) Number of Salafi mosques coming up in the area, their architecture;
4) Rise in the number of people working in the gulf countries, from the area in question;
5) Rise in the number of hawala transactions and remittances;
6) Flow of the money collected in donations on religious occasions;
7) Changes in cultural patterns and lifestyle, like sudden resistance to intermingling with non-Muslims, developments of attitudes against the rituals, practices and beliefs of non-Muslims;
8) Frequency of communal riots in the area;
9) Social media posts on Facebook, Twitter and Instagram and the content on WhatsApp groups;
10) Developing feelings of sympathy for the condition of Rohingyas, Palestinians and other international issues involving Muslims, and their manifestations in the form of charged protest marches, strikes and registering their protests with official authorities;
11) Non-compliance with those school norms and rules that are perceived to be anti-Islamic by Muslim students studying in secular schools (in Udaipur, the author came across instances of Muslim students and their parents making strong demands in a missionary school to allow their children to keep beards and offer prayers during classes);
12) Withdrawal of Muslim children from secular schools and their admission in modern Islamic schools (imparting religious education

with the modern education);

13) Number of Madrasas and Islamic schools and colleges emerging in the area in question;
14) Rise of Islamic religious, cultural and political groups or rise in the number of individual affiliations to such groups already existing at regional, national or international level;
15) Number of students going to prominent centers of Islamic learning in India and West Asian countries;
16) Reactions to the international events in the Islamic world, for example, election of Erdogan as the Turkish president, killing of Osama Bin Laden, American intervention in Syria or Libya;
17) Incidents of sectarian rivalries such as between Barelwis and Deobandis or between Barelwis and Salafis or between the Deobandis and Salafis;
18) Rise in the number of Muslim immigrants in the area and the number of their residential hubs;
19) Moral or ideological support for terrorist organizations and terrorist leaders like Osama Bin Laden, Ayman Al-Zawahiri, Baghdadi and Zakir Musa;
20) Incidents of the involvement of local individuals, organizations or clerics in logistics—facilitating, financing, movement, planning, recruitment and execution of a terrorist attack;
21) Number of Islamic charities and NGOs and their activities.

Secondary Indicators

1) Credibility of and faith in State institutions in the popular perception, i.e. alienation levels
2) Governance and public grievances;
3) Law-enforcement machinery and their attitude towards Muslims in general and behavior with terror suspects and incidents of torture, discrimination on religious grounds , in particular;
4) Economic status (per-capita income, quality of life);
5) Educational status (literacy rates, drop-out rates etc.);
6) Employment status (self-employment or government services/private jobs);
7) Status of the composite Hindu-Muslim cultural practices;
8) Status of Hindu extremism—number and activities of Hindu extremist groups.

Islamic radicalization is a phenomenon that involves human individuals, societies, religious and political organizations as its subjects. The idea of a purely quantitative approach to such a phenomenon may have major limitations in its utility for policy formulation. Hence, Islamic Radicalization Index, like other statistical tools, is bound to have its own limitations too, and may not provide the perfectly accurate picture of radicalization trends. For example, adopting Islamic dressing may be a manifestation of religiosity, spirituality, orthodox attitude or it may be an early symptom of radicalization, depending upon the individuals and the socio-cultural context. However, the indicators are powerful enough to provide a near-total picture of radicalization. While developing it into an empirical tool, the margin of error needs to be minimized. Furthermore, complemented with a sound qualitative/theoretical analysis capturing those aspects which the index may not be able to capture with its quantitative approach, the index may prove to be an effective tool to measure and map the challenges of radicalization.

NOTES

1 Stern, Jessica, "Mind Over Martyr," *Foreign Affairs*, October 30, 2018, Accessed October 30, 2018, https://www.foreignaffairs.com/articles/saudi-arabia/2009-12-21/mind-over-martyr
2 ibid
3 Silke, Andrew, "Disengagement or De-radicalization: A Look at the Prison Programs for De-Radicalization," *CTC Sentinel*, January 2011, Accessed October 30, 2018, https://ctc.usma.edu/disengagement-or-deradicalization-a-look-at-prison-programs-for-jailed-terrorists/
4 ibid
5 ibid
6 Stern, op. cit
7 Silke, op. cit
8 ibid
9 Schulze, Kirsten E., "Indonesia's Approach to Jihadist Deradicalization," July 2008, Accessed October 30, 2018, https://ctc.usma.edu/indonesias-approach-to-jihadist-deradicalization/
10 ibid
11 Gardner, Frank, "Prevent Strategy: Is it Failing to Stop Radicalization?," *BBC News*, March 6, 2015, Accessed October 31, 2018, https://www.bbc.com/news/uk-31756755
12 Muhammad, AZ, "Why Britain's Deradicalization Programs are Failing?," June 30, 2018, Gatestone Institute, Accessed October 31, 2018, https://www.gatestoneinstitute.org/12575/britain-deradicalization-programs
13 Awan, Imran, "Why UK's Prevent Program Doesn't Work?," *Al Jazeera*, April 16, 2018, Accessed October 31, 2018, https://www.aljazeera.com/indepth/opinion/uk-prevent-programme-doesn-work-180411114522226.html

14 ibid

15 ibid

16 Bhatt, Arvin & Silber, Mitchell D., "Radicalization in the West: The Homegrown Threat," New York Police Department, 2007, Accessed October 30, 2018, https://sethgodin.typepad. com/seths_blog/files/NYPD_Report-Radicalization_in_the_West.pdf

INDEX